W9-BLF-713

GRANDPARENTING
TODAY

GRANDPARENTING
TODAY

Making the most of your
grandparenting skills with
grandchildren of all ages

**CONSULTING EDITOR
ELEANOR BERMAN**

INTRODUCTION BY CLAIRE RAYNER

Reader's Digest

The Reader's Digest Association, Inc
Pleasantville, New York • Montreal

Contents

A Reader's Digest Book
Conceived, edited, and designed by
Marshall Editions
170 Piccadilly
London W1V 9DD

Copyright © 1997 Marshall Editions Developments Limited

Library of Congress Cataloging in Publication Data

Grandparenting today : making the most of your
grandparenting skills with grandchildren of all ages /
Eleanor Berman, consultant.
    p.   cm.
  Includes index.
  ISBN 0-89577-954-4
  1. Grandparenting. 2. Grandparent and child. I.
Reader's Digest Association.
HQ759.9.G725   1997
306.874'5—dc21   97-14157

PROJECT EDITOR Anne Yelland
ART EDITOR Frances de Rees
PICTURE EDITOR Su Alexander
DTP EDITOR Mary Pickles
COPY EDITORS Jolika Feszt, Maggi McCormick
MANAGING EDITOR Lindsay McTeague
PRODUCTION EDITOR Emma Dixon
EDITORIAL DIRECTOR Sophie Collins
ART DIRECTOR Sean Keogh
PRODUCTION Nikki Ingram

CONTRIBUTORS Sue Hubberstey (Chapters 4, 7, and 8),
Janice Parrock (Chapters 2, 6, 7, and 9),
June Thompson (Chapter 3), Caroline Taggart
(Chapter 1), Anne Yelland (Chapter 5)

The pronouns he and she, used in alternate chapters, refer to
both sexes, unless a topic applies only to a boy or girl.

Introduction

It was a very surreal moment—2:00AM, a warm June night, the sky ominously dark. The telephone rang and I reached for it, still half-asleep, irritated not for the first time that I'd agreed to have the phone on my side of the bed. And then, even before I picked up the receiver, realizing what the call was about, I woke up very thoroughly indeed.

The moment that you actually *know* you're a grandparent for the first time, that your baby has a baby of his own, is like—well, it's almost indescribable. It was the strangest jolt I'd ever experienced, quite different from the moment I became a parent.

I heard my son's voice burbling in my ear: "It's all right. They're both fine—he's a great big guy, a real boy, with the blackest hair you ever saw, and totally perfect." And I managed to stammer something of my relief and delight. Then I handed the phone to my husband and lay there trying to get my head together.

Of course I'd known it was going to happen, but there is a great gulf between pregnancy and birth. The change from an anonymous bump to a visible, breathing, separate person is of monumental significance to everyone in a family.

Why? After all, isn't a grandparent the epitome of the backseat driver? You've had and reared your babies; your job is done. From now on you're just an onlooker, a supernumerary. Aren't you?

Well no, you're not. First of all there is the profound effect this child has on your perception of yourself. You've been bumbling along happily enough as an average sort of adult; much the same person you've been all through your shared life with your partner, but suddenly you're jacked into Elder status. It's as though when you went to bed you were a comfortable thirty-something and

THE NATURAL WORLD
It's all too easy for us to become blind to the wonders of the world around us, but fortunately children retain their sense of wonder for many years. We often forget how much pleasure young children get from having grown-ups take the time to talk to them, share their knowledge of the world, and play with them.

when you woke up, you discovered burglars had come in the night and stolen 30 years of your life away. You see yourself in the pattern of family—even dynastic—structure as never before.

So there is that to come to terms with. And lots of other things too.

Like, how do I behave with this small new person? How do I behave with his parents so that I don't irritate or upset them as I remember being upset by my children's grandparents? How are children reared today? What sort of toys, food, clothes do they have? Or is it all the same as it always was, and will my wisdom and experience be welcome and valuable? Or must I just bite my tongue all the time from now on?

Questions like these and many more besides are answered in this very book

SIMPLE PLEASURES
Very young children get enormous pleasure from the simplest toys and games. A grandparent who is never too busy to blow bubbles, sing a song, or catch a ball can be one of the most important people in a child's world.

LESS OF A CHORE
Because children have boundless enthusiasm for whatever they are doing, they treat tasks that we grown-ups often label "chores" as play, and regard them as fun, interesting, and exciting. Gardeners rarely need to ask for "help" from their grandchildren.

you are holding. I can tell you that as the weeks grew into months after our own small Simon's birth, and he became first a personality, then a person with decided ideas and opinions of his own, I learned more and more about the special relationship between grandparent and grandchild and the generation in between.

I learned to accept that I was now one of four in relation to this child and not just one of a couple (the other grandparents are quite as important as you are, after all). I learned to take on board totally different ideas about the necessary routine for a baby's life, and to discover that new ideas may be just as good as the old ones, and sometimes better. I relearned the skills of buying

toys and clothes, and of orchestrating family meals that included a vociferous person in a highchair. I rediscovered the delight of finding half-chewed apples or soggy cookies in my stationery drawer, and having a suddenly weary toddler fall asleep in my lap.

I hope other grandchildren will arrive to surround our table on special occasions. There will almost certainly be pains and problems, fears and failures, worries of all sorts. But I'll have this book at hand to help me sort them out. If I need to know the newest jargon in the baby and childcare world, if I need to get my head clear on matters ranging from day care to adolescent angst, here is the resource that I am confident will aid me.

SPECIAL DAYS AND HOLIDAYS
Grandchildren reawaken half-forgotten memories of special times—exploring a babbling brook, going to the zoo, eating ice cream cones at a fair. But they also reintroduce delight at more-ordinary pleasures, like picnics and long walks.

SKILL AND PATIENCE
Sometimes grandchildren seem to mature overnight. One minute, there's a young schoolboy who can't sit still; the next, a child with the patience to master chess.

LOVING FRIENDSHIP
As a grandchild grows into adulthood, love and trust mature and deepen, and a strong relationship will become one of great respect and companionship.

Whether you've bought this book for yourself, or it's been presented to you by one of your children as a preview of what's to come, you're in good hands. Welcome to the world of the grandparent. It's an amazing, exciting, deeply satisfying experience. Enjoy it to the full.

Claire Rayner

—Claire Rayner

CHAPTER ONE

Your Newborn Grandchild

Becoming a grandparent for the first time is a uniquely personal experience. Just as no one could prepare you for how you would feel when

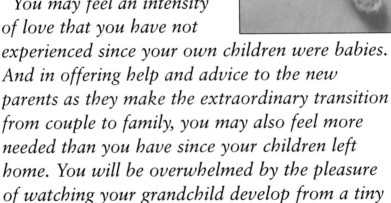

you held your first child in your arms, so reactions to becoming a grandparent vary. But the perception that it will make you feel old before your time is simply not true. It is more likely to mark the beginning of a rejuvenating and deeply rewarding time in your life.

You may feel an intensity of love that you have not experienced since your own children were babies. And in offering help and advice to the new parents as they make the extraordinary transition from couple to family, you may also feel more needed than you have since your children left home. You will be overwhelmed by the pleasure of watching your grandchild develop from a tiny

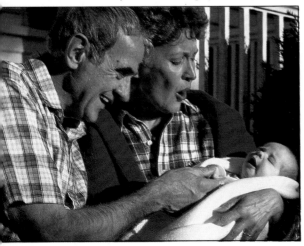

helpless baby into a unique human being in whom you see echoes of yourself and your children. Like many other grandparents, you will have a privileged place in the baby's life for many years to come.

Your role as a grandparent

What sort of grandparent do you want to be?

The grandparent you want to be, or are able to be, depends on a number of things: where you live, your relationship with the new parents, your financial circumstances and theirs, and your state of health. If you live close to your child and his or her partner, you may see your new grandchild almost every day; if you live farther away or perhaps do not have a close relationship with your child or his or her partner, your visits may not be as frequent.

Grandparenting is immensely rewarding. You are able to be relaxed with your grandchildren in a way that parents cannot always be, since you do not have the day-to-day duties of childrearing. Grandparents, who never seem too busy and who may be more approachable than parents on some subjects, can play an important role in a child's life. The prospect of a new baby is an opportunity to repair any rifts that might exist in the family. Sharing a grandchild may bring you closer to the other set of grandparents too.

You will blend better into the new family if you discuss important matters with the parents-to-be before the birth. They will be grappling with many issues at this time: how to cope in general, whether to breastfeed or bottlefeed, should the mother go back to work after the baby is born, what to do about child care. If you find that you have serious differences with your child, try to talk them through now, so that they don't become problems later.

Particularly if this is their first baby, the parents-to-be are probably feeling apprehensive about the responsibility they are about to take on. Don't undermine their confidence if their way is different from yours. If you are generally supportive and accommodating, they will seek your advice when they are in real doubt about what to do.

Discuss cultural or religious differences ahead of the birth if at all possible. Your son or daughter is not necessarily rejecting your beliefs in following his or her partner's wishes, but rather acknowledging how important those wishes are to them both. If such matters are discussed in principle, it will be easier for everyone to understand and accept the decisions that are made.

Child-care arrangements

If the mother plans to go back to work, the parents may ask you to look after the baby on a regular basis. This is of course a great compliment. They would not entrust their child to anyone in whom they did not have absolute faith. Think carefully, though, about what it would entail.

You may have to spend a lot of time in the baby's home, as babies are happiest in familiar surroundings, or adapt your own home to accommodate the baby and all the things you need to care for him. Will your other commitments allow you to do this? Do you have the energy and the patience to respond to the needs of a newborn? Will your enthusiasm last beyond the first few weeks, or will you get bored? What will happen if the new parents have a second child, or if another of your own children has a baby and needs your help too?

If you are happy with the prospect, this should be a period of great joy and fulfillment. If the idea does not appeal to you, it is better to say so now so that the parents can make other arrangements early, instead of feeling you have let them down later. (Realistically, you should think about committing yourself for at least a year, an average period of employment for a nanny.)

Respecting rules

If you are not going to be closely involved on a daily basis, you will want to visit your grandchild and have him visit you. Although nobody can be entirely consistent about parenting or grandparenting, the new parents will have ground rules that you should follow. If they ask you not to bring a new toy or put a coin in your grandchild's piggybank each time you visit, don't. Respecting the parents' wishes from the start will make things easier later, when differing views about candy and television watching come to the fore.

One unbreakable rule is that you should never smoke or allow anyone else to smoke near a baby or small child. Smoking

In ideal circumstances, becoming a mother is an acknowledgment by your daughter of her regard for your parenting skills. Grandchildren bring families closer together, even when conflicts may have loosened the bonds over the years.

dramatically increases the risk of crib death (or SIDS, Sudden Infant Death Syndrome) and can cause asthma and other lasting problems. If you or your partner smoke and your house is always smoky, you may find the new parents reluctant to bring their baby to visit you. If you can't quit, make sure that at least one comfortable room in the house is as smoke-free as possible.

Single parents

If your daughter is about to become a single mother, you may find it difficult to accept the situation. Calm discussion is the best approach; your daughter may deliberately have chosen to become pregnant, or found herself pregnant and decided to bring up the baby alone. Whatever the reason, a baby needs to be loved and cherished—whether he has one parent or two or whether he was planned or not.

Ask her to talk to you about the situation and try to understand that she is serious about motherhood and the baby, however unconventional you may feel her approach is. She is embarking on a difficult and potentially lonely road and will welcome your support and love if you can give it without passing judgment (see also p. 33).

In at the start

Helping to bring your grandchild into the world

Most mothers-to-be have someone in the delivery room to give them practical support during labor and delivery. This helper is usually the baby's father, but there are many circumstances in which this is not the case. If a man is particularly squeamish, the couple may decide it is better for him not to be there; inflexible work schedules and unpredictable births may prevent the father from being there; and a woman intending to raise her child alone may not want or need a male presence. It is possible, in any of these situations, that your daughter might ask you for help. (Equally, she may choose her sister or a friend, so don't be offended.)

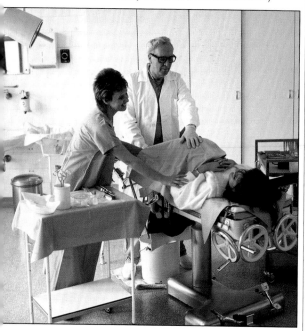

Mothers-to-be usually have the opportunity to visit a delivery room in advance of the birth. If you are to be your daughter's birth partner, go along too. It is important that you know what the various pieces of equipment are used for, as well as the mother-to-be's wishes regarding such subjects as continuous fetal monitoring and the use of a drip to speed labor.

If you are to be a birth partner, attend prenatal classes with your daughter so that you can brush up on what will be expected of you. As a birth partner, you will comfort the mother-to-be, helping her to relax in the early stages of labor. At other times you will encourage her to breathe as she was taught to do and advise her when she needs to push. If the labor is long, she may lose her concentration and you will need to remind her about what she should be doing.

The first decision your daughter may make is where to have her baby. You can help here—especially if she is working and you are not—by phoning or visiting suitable hospitals, talking to the staff, and finding out if their philosophies dovetail with what your daughter wants. If she thinks she would like a home birth, she may face opposition from health-care professionals. Some health-care providers believe that all first babies should be born in a hospital, but they are more open-minded about home births if a woman has already had one complication-free delivery. It is, however, your daughter's right to have her baby at home if she wishes. Be as supportive as possible if she has difficulty in getting her way about this, but make sure she listens to the professionals too—if complications are likely, she would be safer in a hospital.

Your daughter may formulate a birth plan, detailing her wishes and hopes for the birth. Birth plans generally include such information as whether a woman wishes to be given painkillers, how strongly she feels about avoiding an episiotomy or Cesarean section, and if she wants her baby put to her breast immediately after the birth. If she wants a natural birth, she will try to avoid drugs in order to feel in touch with what her body is telling her to do. Women who opt for painkillers generally receive Demerol, which is injected intravenously. If this is done early enough in labor, its effects on the baby are minimized. Others choose to have an epidural anesthetic, which numbs the lower torso.

You should participate in these discussions early on. When the time comes, you are going to be the intermediary between your daughter and the medical staff caring for her. You must be prepared to honor her wishes (think in advance about how you will cope with seeing someone you love in pain), but you should be clear on whether there is scope for an on-the-spot change of mind if things get more painful than your daughter imagined. She

may not be able to make the decision when the time comes, and you may have to do it for her. Obviously, if there are serious complications with the birth, listen to the medical staff: they are likely to recommend painkillers if the labor is unexpectedly difficult, or if they think that she is becoming overtired, or if labor is progressing too quickly and needs to be slowed down. But if everything is proceeding normally, the medical staff should respect the mother-to-be's wishes.

There may also be discussion about the position in which she wants to give birth. The term "active birth" means that the mother may stand, sit, squat, or even walk around, and generally take an active part in the process of giving birth. All these positions have their merits—squatting or kneeling is best for positioning the pelvic organs for the birth; standing up may be better for the baby's oxygen supply; being propped up on a bed may be more restful during a long labor and makes it easier for doctors and midwives to help. The main things are that the mother-to-be should remain comfortable and her baby safe.

After the birth you may find that the baby is whisked away for tests or because he needs oxygen or special care. But unless something is seriously wrong, he should be returned to his mother soon. The new mother will be too tired to argue about anything at this stage, so it is up to you to make sure she is satisfied with what is going on. This is an important time for mother and baby, and they should not be apart unless there is good reason.

A HERITAGE CHEST

If his parents do not do so, there are all sorts of mementos of your grandchild that you might like to preserve. You don't need a special container—a cardboard box will do—but if you can afford something more worthy of the name heritage chest so much the better.

Among the things you might like to collect are:
• His hospital identification tags
• His first lock of hair
• His first bootees or other "first size" clothes
• His first tooth
• A newspaper for the day he was born
• A set of the coins that were in circulation in the year he was born (available in presentation packs).

You can continue to add to this over the years, keeping discarded toys, early attempts at drawing and writing, school reports, and photographs. Most of us become more nostalgic as we grow older, and there will come a day when he is grateful that you kept all this "junk," a unique record of his childhood.

Understanding the jargon

Keeping up-to-date with birth and child-care practices

In 1946 the first edition of Dr. Benjamin Spock's *Baby and Child Care* caused a furor for its controversial suggestion that parents should respond to their babies' needs when they are expressed, rather than keep the infants on a rigid timetable. This seems extraordinary today, when so many doctors and well-qualified people echo this sensible and caring advice in books, magazine articles, television programs, and parenting classes.

Prominent among today's child-care writers are Dr. T. Berry Brazelton, Arlene Eisenberg, Heidi E. Murkoff, and Sandee E. Hathaway (authors of *What To Expect When You're Expecting*), and William and Martha Sears. Although they differ in their emphasis, all are unanimous in encouraging a new mother to follow her instincts, find her own rhythm, and do what seems best for her and her baby.

At the same time, a more flexible attitude toward labor and birth has evolved: mothers-to-be are encouraged to have more say in how they deal with pregnancy and birth and to consider their hopes and wishes for the birth. Your daughter or daughter-in-law is likely to read books and attend classes and enter her pregnancy and labor with these philosophies uppermost in her mind. If you want to keep up with her, read these books too, so that you understand her thinking on various issues. (If you are to be her birth partner, see pp. 14–15.)

Prenatal care

Since you had your own children, prenatal care and childbirth practices have changed. Prenatal testing, for example, is now usual. The most common tests are:

• An initial blood test, which determines blood group, rhesus factor, iron levels, and immunity to certain diseases, notably rubella (German measles). Many couples check these factors before they conceive.
• An ultrasound scan to confirm that the baby is the appropriate size for his gestational age. It may also help to identify such problems as spina bifida or heart defects. In late pregnancy, ultrasound may be used to check the position and condition of the placenta and the baby, alerting medical staff to the possibility that a Cesarean section might be necessary.
• Blood tests for genetic disorders. Some disorders are most common among

Prenatal classes often follow the philosophy of a particular childbirth educator: in Lamaze classes, for example, couples learn exercises to help prepare the body for labor and birth. If you are going to be the birth partner, you should attend these classes, too.

Feeding a baby when he is hungry—rather than leaving him to scream until a feeding is due—makes the whole experience calm and as rewarding for you as it is for your grandchild.

particular ethnic groups, so testing is usually recommended only to those deemed at risk. They include: sickle cell anemia (1 in 10 blacks is a carrier; 1 in 625 affected); cystic fibrosis (1 in 25 white people of northern European origin is a carrier; 1 in 2,500 affected); thalassemia (1 in 25 people of Mediterranean origin is a carrier; 1 in 2,500 affected); and Tay–Sachs disease (1 in 30 Ashkenazi Jews is a carrier; 1 in 3,600 affected).

• Tests for chromosomal disorders, especially Down syndrome. This is more prevalent in older mothers, so tests are usually offered to women over 35. Tests include chorionic villus sampling (CVS) and amniocentesis.

• Tests for neural tube defects, such as spina bifida. The most common test is the alpha-fetoprotein (AFP).

You may or may not know whether your family has opted for a particular test or been told the outcome. Having a test, getting the result, and acting on it can be emotionally draining. In these situations, take your cue from your son or daughter—if he or she wants you to know, they will tell you—and offer all the support you can.

Sometimes called parenting or childbirth classes, prenatal classes prepare the mother-to-be for labor and birth and include advice on such subjects as exercise during pregnancy, massage, relaxation, pain relief in labor, and breastfeeding. All stress the importance of mothers-to-be feeling in control of their labor and of the role of the whole family in childbirth.

Immunization

Vaccinations have eliminated many childhood diseases that were once prevalent. The major vaccinations for babies occur in four stages, at 2, 4, 6, and 15 months, and consist of the "quad vaccine" against diphtheria, tetanus, whooping cough, and HIB (*hemophilus influenzae* type B). HIB protects against a number of illnesses, notably meningitis. Polio vaccine is given at 2, 4, and 6 months; hepatitis B at 1, 2, and 6 to 18 months; and MMR (measles, mumps, and rubella) at 12 to 15 months. It is recommended to vaccinate against chicken pox when the baby is 15 months or older.

Support groups

You may have felt isolated when you had your baby or you may have been living with or near your family, or been friendly enough with neighbors to have company and advice from women who had children of their own. Today many new mothers lack this informal network, and more organized support groups have developed. There are lists of useful organizations at the end of every child-care book and in your local library. If your daughter or daughter-in-law has problems, there is somebody at the end of a telephone line who can give advice on breastfeeding problems, crying or colicky babies, and who can support and help her if she feels isolated, has had a multiple birth, is a single parent, or has a baby with special needs. Many associations have local chapters, where parents of babies of similar ages (or with similar problems) can meet.

Basic baby facts

What you may have forgotten about tiny babies' wants and needs

It is all too easy to forget how small and vulnerable new babies are, especially if the last tiny baby you held was your own and if, as for many parents, the first few weeks with your baby passed in a blur.

Babies' looks and skills

Some babies are born bald; others have a full head of dark hair, which will probably fall out and be replaced by something lighter. If he does not have much hair, the pulse on the top of his head will be clearly visible under the fontanelle, one of several soft places on the head where the bones of the skull have not yet fused together. Such soft places are normal and close during the first couple of years of his life. The baby's head may have been pushed slightly out of shape if he had a difficult birth, but this will correct itself after a few months. Most newborns have deep blue eyes, which often change color as the children grow older.

The baby's body may be covered with a fine "fur," which drops out during the first few months. His skin will be highly sensitive. Avoid toiletries for the first six weeks, and after that use only specially formulated baby products. Clean his diaper area gently with moistened cotton, and dry all the folds of the skin to prevent irritation.

The genitals of newborn babies of either sex may seem disproportionately large and swollen. This will subside after a few days.

Newborns are helpless. They can suck, cry, and eliminate waste, but you have to do pretty much everything else for them. Their needs are basic. If your grandchild is crying, he is probably hungry, uncomfortable (and in need of a clean diaper), bored and wanting attention, or—possibly—sick or getting sick.

Your grandchild can focus on objects up to about 10 inches (25 cm) away and can mimic gestures and lip movement. Stick your tongue out at him several times, and he will do the same back to you. He will also have a strong gripping reflex; even the tiniest baby can grasp and hold on to your

The muscles in a newborn's neck are weak, so you must always support the baby's head with a hand or arm when you are holding or carrying him. By the time he is two or three months old, he will have more head control, but you should still support his head until he is about six months old and holding his head upright all the time.

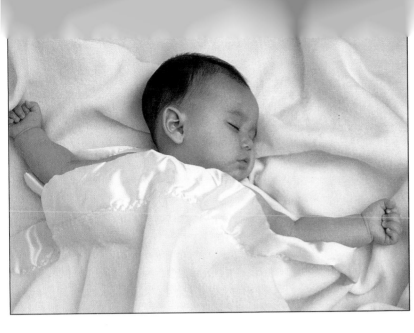

Overheating can be dangerous and is thought to be one of the contributory factors in crib death. If the room where the baby is sleeping is well heated, don't overload him with bedclothes. Two or three layers of light covers are better than one heavy one.

finger. He will lose this ability after about three months and will have to relearn how to hold things.

Most babies sleep when they are not being handled or fed (unless they are colicky, when they can cry a lot). But by three months your grandchild will be alert, fascinated by jewelry or anything bright, and by his own fingers. He will smile for the first time when he is six to eight weeks old.

Newborn babies cannot regulate their temperature by sweating or shivering, so it is vital to make sure they are neither too hot nor too cold. Use blankets rather than a quilt so that you can remove or add layers if necessary. Undress the baby only in a warm room. A lot of heat is lost through the head, so make sure he is wearing a hat in cold weather. Remember, too, that since he is not getting the exercise of walking uphill or pushing the carriage, he may not be as warm as you are. Cuddling is a good way to transfer some of your body heat to him.

How to handle a newborn

Newborns are fragile, but there is no need to be afraid of this vulnerability. Pick him up gently but with confidence, and always support his head. When you put him down to sleep, lay him on his side or back. Then check that he is comfortable; he cannot move himself out of an awkward position.

Tiny babies respond to a soothing tone of voice. They will be startled by a loud noise but will not normally be disturbed by noises or conversation, so once they are

asleep, there is no need to whisper or tiptoe around them. A baby may find a continuous background hum soothing. If he can't sleep, try turning the radio on low or ask someone to vacuum in another room.

Babies hate having things pulled over their head, and some dislike being dressed and undressed. Buy clothes with wide necklines or front fastenings, and change the baby's clothes no more than necessary.

Babies' health

It is normal for a baby to lose up to 10 percent of his birth weight in the first few days, but he should be back to birth weight when he is 10 days old. In the first three months, a baby grows 2–3 inches (5–7.5 cm) and gains just over 4 pounds (2 kg).

Babies' immune systems are not fully developed, so your grandchild has little resistance to infection. Make sure everything he touches is clean. Some pediatricians believe that it is sufficient to wash bottles in a dishwasher that uses hot water and hot air for drying; others still advocate sterilization. All babies regurgitate some milk after almost every feeding. Put a clean towel over your shoulder before burping him. Be prepared for a lot of diaper changing: a baby may need to have his diaper changed as often as 10 times a day. But be alert: vomiting and/or diarrhea can quickly lead to dehydration. Contact the doctor if the baby has watery, green, or smelly stools, pus or blood in his stools, or if his temperature exceeds 100°F (38°C).

Gifts for the baby

Choosing clothes and equipment for the first weeks and months

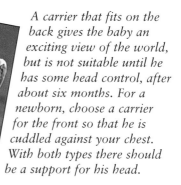

When you hear that you are to become a grandparent, it is an understandable reaction to rush out and buy something—either for the baby or for the nursery. But it's wise to resist the urge until later in the pregnancy, when you have had a chance to talk through choices with the parents-to-be and perhaps the other grandparents. Always consult the parents before you buy anything substantial or expensive for a baby. He needs only one carriage, one crib, and one car seat, so make sure that no one else is planning to buy the same thing and that the parents are happy with your choice.

If you can, take the prospective parents shopping with you, be honest about your price range, and buy what they want. Nothing will alienate them faster than if you spend a lot of money on something they do not want and are then hurt if they don't use it. Make sure it's practical too—don't buy a large chest of drawers for a small bedroom, or a heavy carriage that must be carried up and down stairs.

Transportation

Some carriages are structured so that the top lifts off the wheels, and the chassis folds up for easy storage in a small space or the trunk of a car. Some have a wire basket underneath, which is

A carrier that fits on the back gives the baby an exciting view of the world, but is not suitable until he has some head control, after about six months. For a newborn, choose a carrier for the front so that he is cuddled against your chest. With both types there should be a support for his head.

useful for shopping or for carrying a diaper bag. High carriages with large wheels give a smoother ride, although babies are not too bothered about this as long as the mattress is comfortable. Smaller carriages are lighter to push and easier to maneuver. A young baby must be able to lie flat—strollers come later.

Babies and young children must be firmly strapped in when traveling by car. A rear-facing car seat is mandatory for newborns.

Newborns can be carried on an adult's chest in a sling, which leaves the adult's hands free but gives the baby warmth and closeness. You can use these carriers for short trips outdoors—if you walk with one for too long, you and the baby can become too hot—and indoors, when your warmth and proximity may help soothe a baby who is fractious.

A carriage for city streets must be lightweight, easy to maneuver and should protect the baby from extreme conditions, from cold winds to blazing sun. A single chassis in which the baby can first lie flat and that can then be converted to a stroller is more practical than a traditional carriage, although the latter lasts longer and can be handed down in the family.

Somewhere to sleep

Bassinets or cradles are soft and warm for a newborn baby, as well as convenient for his parents. The baby will be asleep a lot of the time, so it makes sense to be able to carry him in his bed. A cradle can sit on the floor or on a steady table so that the parents can keep an eye on the baby and he can have company while they do other things. A basket or cradle with a hood gives extra protection from the weather if you take him outside in it. If there are pets in the house—cats in particular can be jealous of new arrivals—buy a light, loose-meshed net to lie over the cradle (with the hood down) to keep inquisitive paws out.

Your grandchild will soon grow out of his cradle and need a full-size crib. Make sure the slats are close together (no more than 2 inches/ 5 cm apart) so that his head can't get stuck between them. The sides should drop down so that it is easy to lift the baby out. He will sleep in a

A bassinet is small enough for a new baby to feel secure: many seem "lost" in a full-size crib. Baskets are also easy to carry from room to room. Most babies need a crib from about six months. If you are buying second-hand, check the distance between the slats—safety standards are tighter now than they once were. Choose sheets and light blankets, with a heavier blanket for extra warmth in winter.

From his earliest days a baby can focus on a mobile hung about 8–10 inches (20–25 cm) above his face. If it is asymmetrical, keep him interested by changing it around every few days. When buying a mobile, hold it above your head and look up at it to get the view the baby will see. Some look wonderful from the side, but are uninteresting from below!

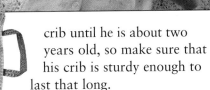

crib until he is about two years old, so make sure that his crib is sturdy enough to last that long.

Bedding is important. It should include an innerspring mattress protected by a waterproof sheet, cotton sheets, and a cotton cellular blanket. Make sure all these are made of flameproof materials and that the mattress fits the crib snugly, with no spaces at the sides or corners where a baby could catch a hand or leg. Choose materials that can be put in the washing machine and, preferably, in the dryer too. Don't buy a comforter for a newborn baby; he needs layered bedding, so that it is easy to remove or add a layer if he gets too hot or cold. Avoid pillows, since they reduce the baby's ability to lose heat if he becomes too hot (a possible factor in sudden infant death syndrome). Special infant sleeping bags may be convenient if the baby kicks off his bedclothes in the night, but make sure they allow plenty of room for him to move his feet and are loose around the neck and wrists.

▶

Gifts for the baby

Other equipment

Around the house, you can put a baby who is beginning to take an interest in his surroundings in an infant seat, which allows him to be slightly propped up, see what is going on, and have company while adults are getting on with their work. Some of these seats are of molded plastic and adjustable—the younger the baby, the nearer to horizontal he should lie. Others are of canvas, which gives him the additional fun of some gentle bouncing.

Many parents choose vinyl or wood flooring for the baby's room because it is easier to keep clean, in which case a nonslip rug might be a cozy addition. A baby monitor, with a speaker for the baby's room and a receiver that allows his breathing to be heard in other parts of the house, can be reassuring for new parents and alerts them as soon as he is awake.

Storage space in the baby's room is essential. If storage is not built-in, a chest of drawers or set of stacking wire storage baskets will be helpful. Soft towels, a changing mat (with straps and a solid bottom), a bathtub, and another nonslip mat to go on the floor next to it are also practical gifts. Changing tables are not useful for very long, so check whether this is one of the parents' priorities.

Other basics include bottles and a bottle warmer if the baby is to be bottle-fed; a diaper bag; and wipe-clean holdalls for all the other miscellaneous things that accompany a small baby whenever he goes anywhere. Diaper bags or nursery organizer bags can hang at the end of the crib to hold toiletries and other essentials. If you are adept with a sewing machine, you can make one of these yourself. A baby gate will become essential the moment the baby is mobile if his house (or yours) has stairs.

A car seat is a must; many designed for newborns have carrying handles that make it easy to move the baby from the car to the mall or back home even if he is asleep. Choose clothes that have wide necks or snaps or buttons at the shoulder, and that have easy access to a diaper (below) to make dressing and changing easier.

Clothes

Opt for layered clothing, so that it is easy to take something off if the baby gets too hot. Choose natural fibers for garments that will be next to his skin, but since he will dribble all over even his nicest clothes, they need to be machine-washable and colorfast.

Babies grow out of clothes quickly, so don't buy too much of any one size. In particular, don't buy a lot of first-size clothing—supposed to fit babies up to three months—until he is born and you know that he is not an 11-pound (5-kg) record breaker who will be into larger sizes in a week. If in doubt about the size, buy big: loose-fitting clothes are comfortable, and he will soon grow into them. Undershirts and sweaters that do not have side or front fastenings should have wide necks or snaps on the shoulder so that they can be pulled over the head easily. Check whether the parents have any color preference. Most don't choose pink for girls and blue for boys anymore.

If you plan to knit or sew clothes for the newborn, bear in mind his likely size and the time of year when the garments will be

CUTTING COSTS

A baby does not need everything around him to be new. If you are on a tight budget, you may be able to find a nearly new crib or carriage advertised for sale in the local paper. As long as it is clean, stable, and painted with non-toxic paint, it should be acceptable. It is not, however, advisable to buy a second-hand car seat: if it has been involved in even a small impact, it may no longer be safe.

If you have time rather than money to spare, you may be able to contribute to the nursery in a more practical way, by painting the walls or making new curtains, for example. And although not everyone has heirlooms in the attic, you may be amazed to discover what you still have hidden away, particularly if you haven't moved since your own children were small. An old toy box or small chest of drawers could easily be refurbished for the new nursery.

An activity mat will give hours of fun. Choose one that is bright and includes some sounds, as well as several tactile experiences—soft, fluffy, bumpy, and so on.

An unbreakable mirror to go inside the crib, beside his head, will help develop his fascination for faces. A colorful line of soft or plastic teddy bears strung across his carriage or crib will give him something to look at, and if they rattle, he will like them even more. After a few months he will be able to hit them hard enough to make a noise, and if you rattle them yourself in the early days, he will be intrigued by the sound.

By about three months, he will be able to hold a rattle if you put it into his hand. Choose a variety of shapes and ones that make different sounds. Chewable rattles come into their own from about four months, when the gums become sensitive and teething begins. All these should be ready. Avoid making anything too lacy—tiny fingernails can easily catch in the holes.

Don't forget the baby's head, hands, and feet. Babies need hats (against sun and cold), mittens, and bootees or socks. They don't need shoes until they start to walk.

Toys

Babies do not really appreciate toys until they are about six months old, but they do respond to anything that stimulates the senses. A cuddly toy for a newborn should be small, squeezable, and soft to the touch; toys that squeak have added interest. All toys are sucked regularly, so make sure they are non-toxic, washable, and colorfast. Toys with small detachable parts are always clearly labeled "Unsuitable for children under 36 months," so look for this warning.

lightweight, so that he won't hurt himself if he hits himself on the head with them.

A cassette player and a tape of nursery rhymes or lullabies is a good gift, since babies love to be sung to. Or buy a musical toy operated by pulling a string or pressing a button. He will be able to work it himself by the time he is about six months old but can enjoy listening to it from the beginning.

Practical gifts

If you visit regularly and don't want to arrive empty-handed, why not spend some time in the drugstore and arrive with a bag of disposable diapers, premoistened wipes, creams, and other consumables? It may not be glamorous, but the parents may be more grateful than if you buy another cuddly toy.

Financial gifts

Making your grandchild's future financially secure

Bringing up children is an expensive business; if you can afford to, you may want to help provide for your grandchildren's future. Don't worry if you cannot spare a great deal—many savings plans allow for small, regular investments as well as for lump sums. Some people, understandably, also find helping in this way more satisfying then adding to a grandchild's seemingly bottomless toy box.

For up-to-date, comprehensive information on investments, it is best to go to an independent financial planner. Next best are banks and insurance companies, although they will advise only on their own products. A word-of-mouth recommendation is frequently a good starting point; always check the individual's credentials and get more than one recommendation, if possible, when choosing a financial planner. (Your accountant or lawyer may be able to recommend someone.)

Some financial planners, whether independent or attached to a company, earn their living on commission from the companies whose policies or investments they sell, not by charging fees to their clients. Others are independent and charge a flat fee.

If you are thinking of an investment for your grandchild, some of the options are discussed below.

COLLECTIBLES

It is not only financial investments that increase in value with the passage of time. Any number of more tangible gifts may also be seen as assets. Paintings or prints, furniture, books, dolls and dolls' houses, china or porcelain, and wine or port—all these may be worth appreciably more by the time your grandchild grows up, as well as being desirable possessions in themselves. But if you are not well informed, be sure to ask the advice of an expert before investing in any of them.

A leather-bound book of Victorian poetry may feel like a precious antique, but if it turns out to be one volume from a six-volume set, it is unlikely to interest a connoisseur. You may prefer to buy a first edition of a current novelist you admire in the hope that the work will become better known. If you want to buy a bottle of wine or port that can be enjoyed on your grandchild's 18th birthday, consult a reputable wine merchant to ensure that you buy a vintage that will still be drinkable then.

Bank accounts

You can open a custodial account in a child's name, in which case he pays no tax on interest earned, up to a specified amount. Bank certificates of deposit (CDs) guarantee a set interest rate for a specified term of years, and since banks are insured by the federal government, your investment is secure.

Bonds

U.S. government savings bonds are an extremely safe investment. Zero-coupon bonds are worth considering, too. You buy these for a fraction of their ultimate redemption value, and they accumulate at a guaranteed rate of interest over a period of years. You know when they are going to mature and, unlike conventional bonds, you know what your return is going to be.

If your grandchild is your dependent for tax purposes, series EE savings bonds are another safe long-term investment: provided your income is below a certain level, these are not taxable if the proceeds go toward the education of a dependent.

Mutual funds

Mutual funds are a popular way for small investors to put money into a professionally managed portfolio. There is a wide range of mutual funds available; some invest solely in stocks, some in bonds, some in both. Some specialize in a geographical area or in a sector of industry, for example. The choice is yours.

Most funds perform better than the market average over a period of years, so mutual funds are usually a good choice for longer-term investment.

Be honest about your circumstances, what you can afford, and how long you are willing to have money tied up. A reputable financial adviser should have a choice of plans to meet your precise needs.

College plans

A number of states have prepaid tuition plans whereby grandparents can contribute to their grandchildren's college fees (in total, or a specified percentage of the cost) by paying now at today's rates. These payments are tax exempt, but there may be complications if, for example, the child chooses to go to college in another state or not to go to college at all. Many plans are transferable from state to state, but the money will become taxable if it is withdrawn from the plan rather than used to pay college fees.

Paying large expenses, such as medical bills, rather than giving direct gifts of money is a good—and perfectly legal—way around the restrictions on taxable gifts over $10,000.

Thinking ahead

A good rule of thumb is that the longer you intend to leave money invested, the more risks you can afford to take. If you want a quick return, go for safety. But whatever you decide, and however much you feel you can afford to put aside, bear in mind the possibility of future grandchildren and calculate whether you can do the same for them. It is better to be less generous now and give everyone a fair share in the long run than to make promises you may not be able to keep or to offend the parents of your second and subsequent grandchildren by appearing to favor the first. If no other grandchildren come along or your circumstances change, you can always make further provisions at a later date.

Gifts for new mothers

Congratulating the new mother of your precious grandchild

Once the excitement of bringing the baby home amid congratulatory flowers and champagne is over, it is easy for new mothers to suffer an identity crisis. Strangers talk to the baby and ignore the mother completely or view her only as an extension of him, asking how old he is and what his name is. Friends who do not normally give the parents presents arrive laden with cuddly toys or clothes for the baby. The mothers who view their baby as an extension of themselves will revel in this. Others will not.

It is important therefore to remember that a mother is still a person in her own right. She is also in a new and possibly frightening situation, and she needs pampering. Send her a glorious bouquet three weeks after the birth, when most of the initial deluge of flowers has died.

Arrange a massage or a half day at a health club if she is willing to leave the baby for a length of time. (If you offer to look after him, you have the added bonus of having your grandchild to yourself for a while.) Or treat her to a series of yoga classes to help her get back in shape—and offer to go with her to keep her company. Some hair loss is common during and immediately after pregnancy, so being treated to a visit to the hairdresser is another good morale booster.

The essential oils used in aromatherapy, which she can put in the bath or use for massage, feel and smell wonderfully luxurious. They interact with the systems of the body in various ways—stimulating, calming, or healing, depending on the oil. Among the most common: bergamot and lavender will relax her after a stressful day—and lavender also helps to heal stretched or stitched tissues; rose, jasmine, and ylang-ylang are also relaxing; and rosemary is reputed to be a great tonic for general fatigue.

Pregnancy makes some women feel unattractive, and almost all have to adapt their wardrobe to their increased size. Buy her something feminine such as perfume, silky lingerie, or a lacy nightgown or robe. These are not things she is likely to buy for

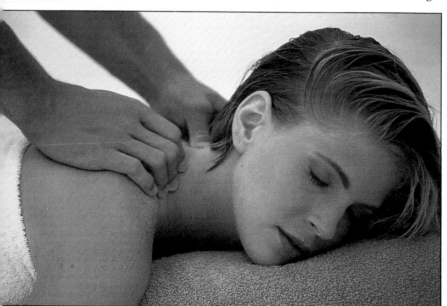

A bottle of her favorite perfume is an instant antidote to baby wipes and lotions, and can be sprayed on whenever a mother is feeling low. A massage (left) will soothe away tension and the minor aches of the first few weeks after the birth, allowing a new mother to focus on her own body rather than her baby's.

A warm bath filled with fragrant oils or essences (right) will revive tired limbs—or help a new mom relax enough to get a few hours of much-needed sleep. Silky lingerie (below) will remind her that she is still a woman as well as a mother.

when needed. If she is breastfeeding, avoid anything too spicy, which might upset the baby's digestion. But don't worry too much about calories, as breastfeeding will help her to lose some of the weight she has gained during pregnancy.

However she chooses to feed her baby, a new mother is going to spend a lot of the next few months doing it. A comfortable chair that gives adequate support to her back—her feet should touch the floor—is essential. If she has one already, you could buy a large, cheerful pillow for it. She can either put this at the base of her spine for added support or use it to hold the baby at a comfortable level for feeding. Make sure the pillow is washable.

A new parent wants to record her baby's every gesture. Photograph albums fill up quickly, and it doesn't matter if she is given several. If she is an avid photographer, some accessory for her camera, or even a new camera, may be a welcome present. Consult her or her partner first, though; don't spend a lot of money until you are sure you are buying the right thing. Record books of the "baby's first smile, baby's first tooth" variety can be fun, and many of them have room for photographs too.

A few CDs or tapes of music you know she likes or some not-too-demanding books that she would enjoy might encourage her to find some time for herself. Child-care experts believe that even half an hour a day spent relaxing and looking after her own needs (and not feeling guilty about it) will help keep the new mother on an even keel—which is as beneficial for the baby as it is for her.

It is also important for new parents to spend time together as a couple. Offer to babysit occasionally so that they can go out—or even have an uninterrupted meal in another part of the house—secure in the knowledge that their baby is in good hands.

herself at this time, but they may help her feel better about herself. Or take her shopping (the baby can come too) and buy her a new dress or a sumptuous sweater. If you have a piece of jewelry that belonged to your own mother, this might be the time to pass it on. But if you have other daughters or daughters-in-law and are likely to have more grandchildren, consider whether you are going to be able to make similar gestures every time.

Practical gifts

Although they frequently don't have the time or energy to cook much, new mothers (particularly those who breastfeed) need to eat well. Make some of her favorite meals that can go in the freezer and be defrosted

Then and now:

Breast or bottle?

Arguments in favor of breastfeeding and bottlefeeding wax and wane in popularity. The best way to feed a baby is the way a mother feels comfortable; whatever her decision, supporting her is in everyone's interests, above all the baby's.

THEN

In the 1990s the experts are unanimous: Breast is best. After a generation when bottlefeeding was the norm, breastfeeding is returning to popularity in many parts of the world, coinciding with the emphasis researchers and parenting experts place on bonding between mother and baby, and also perhaps with the massive upsurge of interest in natural foods and medicines.

Bottlefeeding last became fashionable in the 1960s, when an increasing number of women began returning to work soon after giving birth. Breastfeeding came to be seen as something primitive or faintly distasteful. In a manner strangely reminiscent of Victorian times, many newborn babies were carried off, not to wet nurses but to be bottlefed so that the new mother could either rest or get on with her life.

One respected baby expert writing in the mid-1970s put this question to his readers: "Why bother to understand the complexities of breastfeeding when bottlefeeding is a perfectly good alternative and when breastfeeding seems to be so exhausting, restricting and difficult?" Although he goes on to give a sympathetic and balanced account of the benefits of breastfeeding, it is a question that would hardly occur to mothers and child-care experts today.

Why breastfeed?

The arguments in favor of breastfeeding are compelling. Breast milk is easier to digest than formula milk, so breastfed babies are less likely to suffer from constipation or gas. They also produce less waste, because a higher percentage of the milk is absorbed into the system. It is difficult to overfeed a breastfed baby, so the risk of obesity is lessened. Breastfeeding also stimulates the production of the hormone oxytocin, which helps the womb to return to its previous size and shape, allowing the new mother to regain her figure more quickly.

Breast milk contains some of the mother's immunities, which help a baby to fight off infection. It is also thought that breast milk can be useful in the prevention of allergies. Recent research in the United States suggests that it can also protect against otitis media, a common childhood infection of the middle ear.

Breastfeeding is more convenient, with no bottles or sterilizing units to worry

NOW

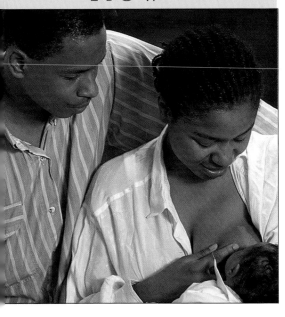

Bottlefeeding (far left) has tended to be associated with feeding on a schedule; today mothers are more apt to feed when their baby clearly needs milk or comfort (left). This approach also reduces the likelihood that a mother will not have enough milk, one of the major reasons for giving up breastfeeding.

about. The milk is always available and at the right temperature for the baby—and even becomes thinner in consistency when the weather is hot.

Learning to express milk is not difficult. Stored breast milk can be given to the baby while his mother is at work. It also allows the father to feed the baby in the middle of the night, so that his partner can get a few hours' unbroken sleep and he does not feel left out of this intensely personal relationship.

Bottlefeeding

On the other hand, bottlefeeding gives the new mother more freedom. She will not have the uncomfortably heavy breasts associated with breastfeeding, for if the breasts are not stimulated by the baby's suckling, their unused milk supply will soon dry up. (However, once the supply and demand of breastfeeding has been established, her breasts will not overproduce and discomfort will be less of a problem.) She will not have to express milk if she has too much or if she is going to be unable to feed the baby herself for a while. Nor must she face the emotional

distress of "failing" at breastfeeding, which many new mothers find difficult at first if they do not get the support they need. She will not suffer from sore nipples or potentially embarrassing leakages or have to deal with the disapproval of strangers if she feeds her baby in a public place. There also need be no concerns about how the baby is to be fed when the mother is ill.

The father of a bottlefed baby can be involved from the start, which reduces the risk of his feeling jealous of the intimate relationship between mother and baby; and it means that he can do some night feedings.

But formula cannot duplicate colostrum, the thin, watery fluid containing antibodies that help build up the baby's resistance to disease, which is secreted by the breasts in the first few days after childbirth. It is widely believed that a new mother should breastfeed for the first few days in order to give the baby this benefit, whatever her plans for feeding thereafter.

Personal choices

If your daughter or your son's partner opts for bottle when you believe in breast or vice versa, do not be alarmed. How to feed her baby is a choice that every woman has to make for herself, unless she is advised not to breastfeed because of a problem of her own, such as heart or kidney disease. Breastfeeding gives a baby all the nutrients he needs; but continued research and development has meant that formulas today are almost as good. As long as the mother (or whoever is giving the bottle) is relaxed and both parties are comfortable, feeding by whichever method should be an intimate and satisfying experience for all concerned.

I don't love the baby
Coming to terms with negative feelings about the new arrival

There is an assumption in our society that everyone loves babies. But in fact, many people do not; babies can do little, cry a lot, get sick all over your clothes with monotonous regularity, and can wear the nerves of the most committed carer to shreds in a very short time. Naturally, your child loves his or her new baby and assumes that you will do the same, but circumstances and your own personality may make this difficult, initially at least.

If you live too far away for regular contact, you cannot be expected to bond with him as you would if you saw him frequently, nor can he be expected to react to you with pleased familiarity. Take heart from the positive side of this situation: you only see his good points—blissfully asleep in a photograph or smiling at the camera.

People unused to dealing with babies—and many of today's new grandfathers in particular had little to do with bringing up their own children—are often uncertain around them. If your grandchild senses this, he is more likely to cry when you hold him and reinforce your awkwardness. If you are uncertain, don't insist on having your turn

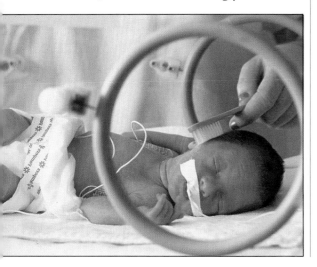

to cuddle him. In fact, many babies show by crying how much they dislike the kind of pass-the-baby routine that tends to go on with newborns. The new parents—especially if they aren't confident themselves yet—may prefer to get used to handling him before they allow others to do so. Certainly, most new parents are likely to prefer your reticence to your insistence on swooping the baby up in an I-know-best manner.

Try not to worry. There is no law that says you have to love your grandchild from the moment he is born. Lots of people find tiny babies uninteresting; you may be one of those who starts to respond when he responds to you. You may find it reassuring to know that many new mothers don't immediately fall in love with their baby, but say that the bond grows over the first weeks and months of his life. And it will between you and your grandchild.

If your grandchild is premature, you may first see him in an incubator, linked up to monitors and tubes. The fact that you cannot hold or cuddle a baby at this stage makes getting to know him more difficult. But providing there are no additional complications, he should be out of special care in a matter of days or, at worst, weeks. Then you can belatedly get on with the important business of being close to him.

Some babies are born with conditions that need almost immediate surgery. In these circumstances you are unlikely to be

Most adults are overwhelmed by feelings of protectiveness toward premature babies, but in these circumstances getting to know a baby can be hard. Everyone's undoubted concern for his well-being to the exclusion of all else may make for a less-than-ideal start to your relationship with your grandchild.

An irritable grandchild who cries a lot, even when he is clean and fed, will not necessarily bring joy to the heart of every grandparent. Don't worry if initially you feel only relief as you leave his home: with time, you will come to love and appreciate him.

able to relate to your grandchild for the first months, or perhaps even for most of the first year of his life. Everyone's attention is concentrated initially on simply keeping him alive, then on helping him start to catch up. Most babies who go through this traumatic start go on to live perfectly healthy lives; many of them become very tough, having learned to fight from such an early age.

Some babies are born with problems for which there is no cure. If your grandchild has special needs, you may have to draw on all your inner strength to accept his unique place in your family (see pp. 60–61).

CASE HISTORY

My first grandson was born abroad and was over a year old when I saw him for the first time. I was excited at the idea of having a grandchild and liked looking at the photographs my daughter sent regularly, but in fact his birth had no day-to-day effect on my life.

By the time my second grandson was born, my daughter and her family were back in this country, but too far away for regular visits and I was still not really involved in their lives. I wasn't disappointed, exactly, but my husband and I had a business, so it was difficult for us to go away anywhere. I accepted the fact that I simply didn't see enough of the boys to get to know them and feel close to them.

I've never been the type to peer into carriages and coo at other people's babies. I even found my own children more interesting only as they grew older and we were able to have real conversations. I tried not to worry too much that I wasn't closer to my grandchildren and was sure that in time a relationship would grow.

A couple of years ago we sold our business and retired. Our first treat was to go for an extended visit to my daughter's. We took the boys to school some mornings, helped with homework, spent hours chatting, read to them at bedtime, and took them out—both separately and then together—for a burger. I think that visit marked the start of our real relationship with them.

The children are seven and nine now, very bright, with great senses of humor. We see them fairly often, and I feel I appreciate them as people, whereas I couldn't respond to them as babies.

Sharing the baby

Giving all the family time to spend with the baby

After your grandchild is born, it's understandable that you want to spend as much time as you can with him. But however much you love him, it is important to remember that he is not your baby. His parents need to spend all the time they can with him in the first weeks, learning to deal with his needs, adapting to the changes in their family, their relationship with each other, and their sleep patterns.

New mothers are often amazed at how much time caring for the baby takes, and how difficult it is to accomplish anything else. You will give valuable support, and may be more appreciated, if you offer to do the ironing or cook the dinner rather than to look after the baby.

It is also important to remember that other friends and relatives feel they have a claim on your grandchild: the other grandparents, of course, but also uncles, aunts, and close friends all want to get to know him. Too many visitors, or one who stays too long, can wear out both parents at a time when they need all their spare

New fathers are sometimes reticent about handling their babies, as if somehow their partners know how to do it better. By encouraging your son to care for his child from the start, you are helping him to lay the foundations of a close, loving relationship.

energy. If you live close enough to visit regularly, limit yourself to an hour at a time, unless you are invited to stay longer—in which case, make yourself useful.

If you are staying with the new parents, you will be there to help and should not expect them to entertain you. Do not be offended if they leave you alone all evening because they are looking after the baby or if they collapse hours before you are ready

It is only natural to want to get the whole family together to celebrate the new arrival, but consider carefully whether this will put undue strain on the parents. Keep any gathering short and informal, and be prepared for the parents to leave once everyone has seen and cooed over the baby.

to go to bed. If there is little else for you to do, indulge yourself with reading, sewing, or watching television, and be ready to talk or lend a hand when required. You may be rewarded later in the evening by a cozy hour's chat with your son or son-in-law after mother and baby are asleep.

Try not to be possessive or to feel neglected if you hear that someone else has been invited to visit when you were not. This is especially important if you are the parents of the new father. A new mother is likely to be more eager to have the support of her own mother and/or sisters or female friends her own age who have children and can share recent experiences.

It is easy for the paternal grandmother to feel left out, but important that she should not give way to hurt or jealousy. Enough powerful emotions are at work at this time without adding to them. If you are cheerful, helpful, and understanding now, your visits will be all the more welcome later, when things have settled down.

A new father oftens feel neglected because his partner has to give so much time and energy to the baby. The father's parents can play a useful role here, reminding him that the baby is helpless and does indeed need all the attention the new mother is giving him, but that this does not mean that anyone loves or appreciates the new father less. Encourage him to learn how to care for the baby, too—cuddling him, changing his diaper, washing him, and getting him ready for bed.

A single parent will appreciate all the help you can offer, but don't limit yourself to babysitting. It may also be useful to get the numbers of support groups she can contact or help her find out about local child-care arrangements.

SINGLE-PARENT FAMILIES

If your daughter is a single parent, you may be called upon to provide the emotional and practical support that would otherwise come from the father. This might encompass anything from doing the shopping or accompanying her to postnatal checkups to simply being there—in person or on the phone—if she needs you. If you find it difficult to accept her situation, try to discuss it calmly. The future well-being of mother and baby is what matters, and if you alienate your daughter by expressing disapproval, you may miss out on one of life's most rewarding relationships.

Many child-care experts give the grandfather a special role in a single-parent family. He can introduce the baby to the idea that there are people who look and dress differently from his mother and have deeper voices, but who are still friendly and trustworthy. Other experts point to the danger of a single mother's desperately trying to provide for her baby's every need in order to compensate for the lack of a father. This may give the child unreasonable expectations from other people later in life. Grandparents can ease the burden here, by providing loving and reliable support for mother and child.

A single mother may experience more financial hardship than one who is part of a couple, simply because she is trying to do two jobs at the same time and is likely either to have to give up work or to pay for child care. If you can look after the baby on a regular basis while she is at work, this will help her enormously. But don't feel guilty if you can't: you might have a full-time job yourself, have other commitments, or lack the energy or health to be a full-time caregiver. In addition to all the emotional support you can give, help her find out about the financial support to which she is legally entitled and the most effective ways to obtain support from the child's father, if she is unable to do this unofficially.

Common dilemma: Am I interfering?

Knowing when and how to offer support and help

The line between giving sound advice and interfering is a fine one. Your common sense and the nature of your relationship with the new parents are your best guides. Attitudes toward many aspects of childrearing and toward working mothers have changed enormously since you were a new parent; while no one is saying that your way is wrong, it is not necessarily the only right way either.

When you were raising your children, it is likely that you were given firm instructions about how to deal with your newborn baby: feed him every four hours, no more, no less; don't pick him up every time he cries, or you will spoil him for life. Today's thinking is much less rigid, with many experts believing that it is wrong to leave a newborn baby to cry. Watching as your daughter or daughter-in-law cuddles her crying baby may bring back unhappy memories of not being "allowed" to do the same for yours, but you must not let this form the basis of a criticism. Talking to her about your feelings may deepen the understanding between you, but it will not do so if you show resentment at her having a more rewarding time than you did.

Whether she chooses to breastfeed or bottlefeed is up to her, and whatever decision she makes deserves your full support, regardless of your views on the subject. Pointing out the advantages of formula if she is convinced that she wants to breastfeed but is having temporary problems, for example, is less helpful than suggesting she call a breastfeeding counseling service for on-the-spot advice. Similarly, if she has tried breastfeeding and given up, don't add to her possible feelings of guilt at having "failed," but praise the fact that her baby is now clearly more settled and obviously thriving.

Your son's priorities will of necessity change once he is a father. If he normally visits on weekends to help you in the yard, for example, he may find he hasn't time now. Ask someone else to help for a while, so that you are not adding to his already overstretched schedule.

The new mother is probably reading books or brochures that were not available in your day. Ask if you can read them, too. They may give you a clearer idea of the thinking behind current approaches to childrearing.

Household arrangements

You may be surprised by the extent to which the new father is involved with the baby. Many men feel left out of the intimate mother-baby relationship and need to find ways of bonding with their child. Getting up early, changing the baby's diaper, and spending half an hour alone with him before the mother wakes up may be a special time for a father, not a sign that his partner is lazy or taking him for granted.

The same applies to household chores. Most women find it hard to stay on top of the housework when they are coping with the demands of a new baby, however immaculate their house used to be. You may not like to see your son having to prepare his own meals or do his own laundry, but many couples share household jobs anyway, and he may regard this as normal. The worst thing you can do at this time is sow seeds of discontent between the new parents. At a time when they are adjusting to a new situation, and not getting as much sleep as they are used to, criticizing the new mother to her partner—even if he is your son—is not going to help.

It is also up to the new mother and her partner to decide whether she will go back to work. She may have to do so for financial reasons and may feel guilty about "abandoning" her baby. If you were a full-time mother, your daughter may feel she is unable to live up to your standards or that she has to compete with you to prove that she, too, is a good mother. Don't let any disapproval of yours reinforce these unnecessary and negative feelings.

If you don't live close to the new parents or don't see them regularly, you will find that you see them even less and that they telephone less frequently. Try not to be hurt. Ask if there is a particular time of day that is convenient for you to phone, but don't take offense if you call and find the baby screaming and the parents too harassed to talk. Don't make demands on the new parents: they are busy with their new child, and that must be their first priority.

Postnatal depression

You may be the first person to recognize any emotional problems the new mother is having. Most people think of postnatal depression as occurring in the first few weeks after giving birth, but this is not necessarily the case. A new mother can feel tearful, unable to cope, alienated from the baby, or terrified that something is going to happen to him at any time during the first year of his life. She may manage to look after the baby's needs but be totally incapable of running her house or the rest of her life.

Clearly she needs help. Offer to take on some of the daily chores that are getting too much for her. Look after the baby for an hour so that she can go out and get some fresh air or take a nap; encourage her to talk about her feelings. Depression is often at its worst first thing in the morning, so if you can be there to make breakfast or deal with the older children, she may be better able to cope later in the day.

Encourage her to seek help from her doctor, or a counselor or psychotherapist if the depression lasts more than about 10 days. If her doctor thinks tranquilizers or antidepressants are appropriate, he or she will prescribe ones that won't harm the baby if she is breastfeeding.

Offering to take the baby out for a couple of hours gives new parents the opportunity to catch up on some sleep or have an uninterrupted meal together—and gives you some time with your grandchild. But don't volunteer too often; it is also important for the new parents to spend time together with their baby, simply learning to be a family.

From a distance

Establishing a relationship when you don't live nearby

If your grandchild lives too far away for you to visit regularly, it is inevitable that you will miss out on some of the pleasures of grandparenting. But there are many ways in which you can compensate for the distance between you, right from the start.

The telephone is the closest thing to first-hand contact you are going to be able to have on a regular basis. But you will have to accept that, initially at least, the new parents are going to be tired and busy, and it may not always be convenient to talk. Be understanding about this—things will calm down in a few months, the baby may settle into a routine, and you can establish what is likely to be a convenient time of day for you to phone. Even quite young babies are fascinated by the telephone, and your grandchild may be able to gurgle to you from an early age.

If you think or know that they would call more often if they could afford it, offer—tactfully—to pay (or contribute to) their phone bill. Explain that they will be doing

you a favor, keeping you in touch with them and your grandchild. And if you can't afford to phone often, be meticulous about birthdays and other special occasions. Get several members of the family together so that everyone can have a quick turn to talk—you will feel you have been in touch more closely than you can be by letter.

You are likely to find that even regular correspondents write fewer letters when there is a new baby in the house. Remind yourself how busy they are and don't take offense. Keep writing to them. There is nothing to stop you from writing to your grandchild long before he is able to read. If he has been receiving letters from granny and granddad for as long as he can remember, it may become a natural thing for him to start writing to you as soon as he is old enough.

Photographs and videos will also help you stay in touch. Encourage the

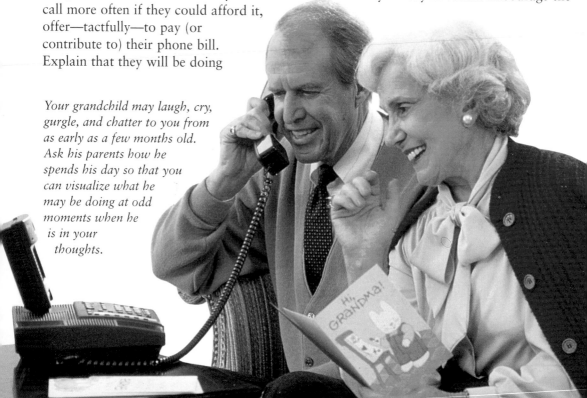

Your grandchild may laugh, cry, gurgle, and chatter to you from as early as a few months old. Ask his parents how he spends his day so that you can visualize what he may be doing at odd moments when he is in your thoughts.

CASE HISTORY

*A*fter my marriage broke up, I was transferred to an office in my home town, 300 miles from my ex-wife and teenage daughters. I managed to keep up a good relationship with both my daughters, who came for long visits during college vacations. But when they started to work, they had a limited amount of free time. I was still working myself, so although we kept in touch by phone we saw a good deal less of each other.

Then Jenny got married and had a little boy. I took a long weekend to go down and meet James when he was three weeks old. He was delightful, and I was so proud of him—it was good to have a grandchild, and a boy in the family at last! But I knew I wouldn't be able to visit on a regular basis, and they were often too busy or too tired to talk on the phone. I was also aware that my ex-wife saw a lot of them, and I was jealous. I felt I was missing out on something special.

After six weeks of sulking, I decided to buy them a video camera and asked them to film James whenever they had a spare moment. I wasn't expecting them to have much time at first, but in fact when the baby was just over three months old they were able to send me an hour-long film that I can watch whenever I like. It ends with a close-up of James smiling at the camera, and it always makes me smile back.

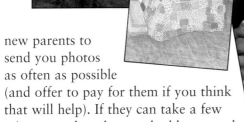

new parents to send you photos as often as possible (and offer to pay for them if you think that will help). If they can take a few minutes to date them and add a note about where they were taken and who else is in the picture, it will make them more meaningful for you. Make a point of putting the photos in albums or display folders and captioning them so that they become an accessible source of enjoyment, rather than a haphazard collection of pictures.

If the new parents don't have a camcorder, consider renting one for them for a week or two so that you can have moving pictures of your new grandchild. (You could also arrange to do this on special occasions, such as his first Christmas.) Make sure your video systemps are compatible: they are not, generally, between North America and the United Kingdom, nor between Britain and parts of

mainland Europe. Find a reliable company that will convert one system to the other for you (look in the Yellow Pages under Video Services).

You will find that you rapidly become an expert on presents that can be mailed. This is easy with babies, whose clothes and toys tend to be small, light, and unbreakable anyway. And if you and your grandchild live in different countries, always ask his parents if there is anything in particular they would like from "home" before sending presents. Even in these days of globalization, there may be a favorite item from a particular store that is unavailable on the other side of the world.

CHAPTER TWO

Older Babies
3 to 15 months

You will find the period between 3 and 15 months one of the most enjoyable of your grandchild's life. In the space of a year, she will change from a helpless baby into a self-motivated little person. Her development into an individual with character and looks all her own may seem to come about overnight. So much happens, in fact, that you may feel that it all goes by too quickly; you are likely to be surprised by how soon she walks, plays, and generally wants to communicate with you.

Even if you don't live close by, and there are other grandchildren clamoring for your time and attention when you visit, make a special effort to notice as much of what she achieves as possible. Take mental pictures of her early steps, sounds, and words, and enjoy getting to know her. Talk to her whenever you are involved in such everyday activities as diaper changing, bathing, and feeding. And tell her about yourself, your family, and her place in it so that she gets to know the sound of your voice.

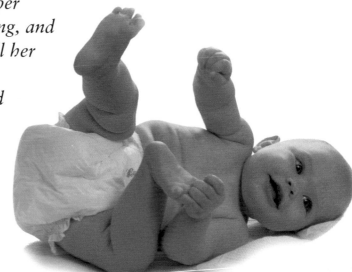

Basic baby skills

What you can expect your grandchild to do at this stage

One of the most exciting and rewarding periods of babyhood occurs when a child is past being a completely helpless bundle and begins to communicate and develop as an individual.

You will probably find that your grandchild has learned something new each time you visit. Enjoy everything she does, but don't compare her development with that of your own children. It is upsetting for parents to be told that other people's children have walked sooner or spoken earlier, because it implies that their child is slow or inferior in some way. Moreover, memory is selective: we all have a tendency to improve on the facts when it comes to our own children.

You may be able to spend as much time as you like enjoying the baby's new skills without feeling guilty about what else you should be doing, a luxury her parents may not have. Join her as she explores the textures on her activity mat, stacks her blocks, and sorts her shapes. Share her delight in repetitive games, such as throwing an object out of her sight, looking for it until you find it, and giving it back: this is fun and is teaching her important facts about her world. Until she knows that something exists even when she cannot see it, your grandchild does not know that mommy or daddy will be back soon, or that her teddy bear will be where she left it.

Talking to your grandchild

When you speak to a baby of this age, you introduce her to the way in which language and communication work. Don't be self-conscious about it or perturbed that, initially at least, you may not get much response. Almost before you know it, you will be having "real" conversations.

Before she can sit up, a baby watches your face when you hold her close, and if you purse your lips and make a face she will imitate your action. When your grandchild starts making cooing noises to you, follow your instincts and coo back so that she knows that her efforts to communicate have received a response.

Make a time when the house is quiet, so your grandchild has your undivided attention. Talk about anything you like, but leave pauses for her to join in, even if it's just to raise her hand or babble.

Don't sit your grandchild in front of a TV while you do something else. Television will hold her interest because of its fast-moving images, but she will soon learn that there is no point trying to communicate with it. Taken to extremes, this will inhibit her ability to focus on one speaker.

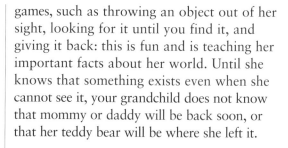

When you are out for a walk, if you point to the birds and tell your grandchild what they are, he will soon point the birds out to you and make what for him is an appropriate sound to identify them.

How your grandchild develops

The chart below indicates what your grandchild may be able to do at different ages. Of course, all babies are different. Use this chart only as a guide. Some babies will reach these stages sooner, others later.

PHYSICAL SKILLS	MANIPULATIVE SKILLS	SOCIAL SKILLS	LANGUAGE SKILLS
FOUR MONTHS She can sit without her head wobbling as long as she is supported. Between four and five months, she may roll over from front to back.	She is developing hand-eye coordination and will examine her own hands and feet, other small objects, and her reflection in a mirror. She can reach for objects and may put them in her mouth.	If you are a frequent visitor, she will be able to distinguish your voice from others. She wriggles to attract attention, and enjoys new faces, toys, and places.	She "talks" to objects and people and can pronounce the sounds *h*, *b*, *p*, *f*, and *n*. She laughs in response to the sound of your happy speech and/ or laughter.
NINE MONTHS She rolls, crawls, and shuffles around to get to toys she wants or to you. She tries to pull herself up and uses the furniture and your legs as props to help in her explorations of her surroundings.	She examines objects, and turns them around to view them from all angles. She starts to pick things up, using her thumb and forefinger.	She may be clingy and wary of strangers. She shouts to make you pay attention. She is happy to sit playing alone for up to 10–15 minutes. She loves interactive games such as dropping and throwing objects away. She is delighted when you applaud her actions.	She knows your name and under- stands some simple commands, but does not always respond to "No" and "Give me." She babbles in a mixture of her own language and words she hears around her.
FOURTEEN MONTHS She can sit from a standing position and totter quite fast, often falling down and getting up again in quick succession. She is becoming aware of the danger of walking downstairs and falling off things and needs close supervision. She can see and follow fast-moving objects.	She loves pushing items into holes and hiding things from you. She understands the concept of hide-and-seek games and will concentrate on shape sorters for up to 20 minutes.	She can express feelings of fear, annoyance, and jealousy through shouting and crying. She may have a favorite comforter. She points a lot to show things to you.	At one year, she has a vocabulary of about three words, or signs or sounds, and more than 20 by 18 months. "Kitty" may refer to all animals. She under- stands short sentences like "Give me the teddy bear," and uses single-word sentences like "Ball" to make her needs known: "I want my ball."

Toys for older babies
Choosing play materials to help your grandchild's development

Today most people are aware that play and learning are synonymous. Manufacturers have caught on to this idea too, and almost everything is now described as an "aid to learning." Don't let this tempt you to buy more sophisticated or expensive toys than you think suitable. In her first year or so, your grandchild will be delighted and stimulated by the most basic toys as long as she also has company. This does not mean you should do everything for her, but be nearby and take an interest in her endeavors so that she can play with increased confidence.

TYPE OF TOY	PLAY VALUE
BLOCKS Good-quality colored wooden blocks, kept in a box or wagon, are sturdier and last longer than plastic. Wooden blocks can be used in many ways and will be enjoyed by your grandchild well into her school years. Soft cloth blocks are a good choice for those under six months.	Blocks can be used to identify and name colors. From about the age of 12 months, stacking blocks aids hand-eye coordination, the ability to concentrate, and the understanding of spatial concepts. Building and knocking down promotes feelings of control and is fun. The wagon provides storage and is a push-along aid to walking.
ACTIVITY MAT This can be rolled up and moved to different places to offset baby boredom. It must be washable and made from high-quality materials, with no sharp edges.	The mirror, flaps, and rattles encourage babies to discover and explore using their pincer-grip and fine-motor skills. Different textures encourage tactile development. Bright color contrasts stimulate visual interest.

SHAPE SORTER
Large wooden or plastic pieces endure even when sucked and are easy for the baby to grasp and manipulate.

Inserting different pieces helps the baby learn about shapes, sizes, and the relationship between objects. At first, the fascination is in making the pieces disappear and retrieving them. Placing the correct shape into each hole comes later, as does identifying and naming the shapes.

CONSTRUCTION SETS
Concentrate on one kind. Select a set that will be compatible with more sophisticated components as the baby gets older. A foundation board allows the baby to anchor pieces firmly, avoiding frustration.

Large pieces encourage the development of the building skills she will acquire throughout her childhood. Additional pieces that fit, such as people, cars, and trains, expand imaginative play.

STUFFED TOYS
Large numbers of stuffed toys are unnecessary, but a few are invaluable. Make sure they are washable, and if you can, buy two alike to minimize distress in the event one is lost.

A stuffed toy is a comfort object first and foremost; as she gets older, some will be useful as props—for guests at a tea party, an audience for a story, and patients to be nursed.

The treasure basket

Find a clean basket with no sharp edges that is big enough for the child to dip into without being able to see everything inside—but not too big. Fill it with a collection of safe objects for your grandchild to touch and explore. Include wooden or plastic spoons; plastic blocks; squares of fabric of different textures—cotton, corduroy, felt; small plastic containers; plastic measuring cups that fit into one another; a toy hand mirror.

A treasure basket has a touch of the grown-up world your grandchild loves: why else does she always want to hold your car keys and fiddle with the remote control? Add new items every so often to provide an endless source of interest and delight.

TYPE OF TOY	PLAY VALUE
BOOKS Choose books that are laminated board, cloth, or vinyl, which can easily be cleaned.	It is never too early to sit with a baby and encourage her to turn the pages. Point out shapes and colors, and she will do the same. Let her take one or two softer books into her crib with her at night so that they become "friends."
BATH TOYS A set of buckets with holes and strainers make bathtime a pleasure.	Water is a fascinating medium with a texture unlike anything else a child plays with. She can explore filling and emptying, pouring and straining. Demonstrate how to use the toys to excite her curiosity, then let her experiment.
ACTIVITY CENTER This can be anchored to the bars of her crib. Vary its position for maximum interest.	Dials, pull cords, and squeezy buttons teach the baby that she can elicit a reaction and a sound. Mirrors encourage the baby to focus and concentrate.
BOUNCING CRADLE TOYS These have taken over from the old-style row of beads or animals that were strung across large carriages. They clip onto the front of the baby rocker or bouncing cradle and are inexpensive; buy more than one set for variety.	The baby can finger the toys and move them from side to side and will soon learn that if she reaches out to hit them, she will make them turn over. Later she may start to babble to them.
CRAYONS For babies 15 months and over, use thick, non-toxic crayons or washable markers.	At about 15 months babies enjoy watching you draw shapes of things they recognize. They will begin to make their marks on paper and experiment with different colors and textures.

Then and now:

Day care

As it becomes more common for both parents to work outside the home, and for single parents to combine parenting and a career, your grandchild's early life is likely to include at least one professional caregiver who is not a member of her immediate family.

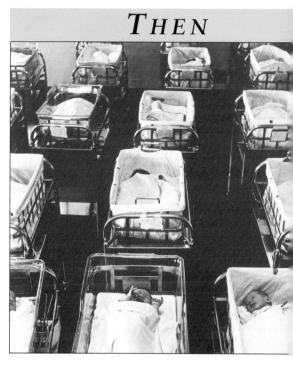

THEN

If you and your partner both had full-time jobs when your children were babies, you were in a minority; most mothers stayed home with their children. Even just 20 years ago, many mothers who worked had only two choices for a caregiver: a family member or—for those who had the means—someone to live in and look after the children. Professional day care was rare and different in approach from what we now know that babies need. Babies who had professional day care led regimented lives with set feeding times, enforced naps, daily "airings" in all weather, and even prescribed times for toilet training at a very early age.

Working parents today can choose among a number of options: a day-care center, a live-in or daily nanny, an au pair, family day care, a workplace nursery, or a family member. Moreover, professional child care is more child-centered. A baby may be encouraged to sleep at a given time—say, after a meal. She will also be placed in her crib when she shows signs of needing a rest, but kept stimulated, and played with if she shows no desire to sleep. Nor are babies

forced into toilet training. Rather than following rigid rules, caregivers listen to parents' wishes and take cues from the baby.

In the past, babies were often left to amuse themselves for long periods. Now we know that babies need stimulation. Toys and play equipment that help the baby's development are an important part of any day-care center, and professional nannies and caregivers receive instruction about this during their training. Day-care centers may copy the home environment, with cozy furniture, pictures, and colorful mobiles instead of the sterile, hospital-like appearance formerly found in day-care centers or nurseries.

Some employers now provide nurseries for the children of employees. These are run along lines similar to day-care centers, and the parent may be encouraged to drop in for short visits during the day.

Home-based care

Care in a home environment—whether it is your grandchild's home or that of a sitter—has many advantages. A nanny or sitter can have the sort of one-to-one

NOW

Although babies often received loving care in large nurseries, the stimulation of one-to-one contact was missing (far left). Care in the home, whether by a sitter, nanny, or au pair, is often more fun for children and more rewarding for their caregiver.

concern the parents. In the unlikely event that the caregiver is acting negligently and putting your grandchild in danger, you must inform the parents immediately.

Doing it yourself

It used to be that the first person a working mother turned to for help with childcare was her own mother. But today relatives rarely live close enough for this to be an option. In cultures in which grandparents automatically assume the day-to-day care of their grandchildren, there is often an extended family of aunts, uncles, and others as well.

If you are asked to be wholly responsible for your grandchild, weigh the pros and cons before committing yourself.
• Do you feel physically able to cope?
• Are you ready to give your time to what most people admit is an exhausting job?
• Will you be able to make your ideas on childrearing blend amicably with those of your grandchild's parents?
• Can you discuss objectively what you will be paid, if anything, for your services?

relationship that your grandchild's parents have with her. Toys are smaller in scale and activities geared to a few children, rather than the larger pieces of equipment and group activities that nurseries or day-care centers need for the many children in their care.

Regardless of how close you live to your grandchild, you must appreciate that the caregiver is being paid to look after the child and is a professional. It is acceptable to visit your grandchild occasionally during the day if you have arranged it with the caregiver in advance, but do not drop in whenever you feel like it or take your grandchild away from the house on your own. In doing so, you would put the caregiver in a difficult position, and would undermine the parents' arrangement as well.

If you witness things involving your grandchild and her caregiver that you do not approve of, you must decide whether it is important enough to inform her parents. You may, for example, feel that a caregiver's manner or vocabulary when speaking to your grandchild is unsuitable, but this may be something that does not

REASSURANCES FOR YOU

The number of children a caregiver can be responsible for in her own home is often restricted by law. A caregiver's home may be inspected periodically to make sure that it complies with safety standards; it should be licensed. Some caregivers have special training in family day care. All caregivers should have references, which your grandchild's parents will have checked.

To be licensed, day-care centers, including those in the workplace, need to satisfy a number of criteria in such areas as staff-to-children ratio, and building and safety regulations.

Basic baby care

What you may have forgotten about caring for babies

Trends in child care change. Depending on your age, you may find your grandchild is changed and fed in much the same way as you looked after your own children's needs or you may find her care very different. In case some things are new to you or if you have merely forgotten some details in the intervening years, these pointers will help you to look after your grandchild.

Changing diapers

Volunteering to change the baby's diaper may be the best-received of all your offers of practical help, and it is a good way to get used to handling your grandchild.

Put her on a flat surface that is the right height for your back. Fasten the straps on the changing table (you don't want her to perfect her ability to roll over when you are changing her). If you use cream to prevent diaper rash, be careful not to get it on the tapes of a disposable diaper—they won't stick if you do. Many professionals advise against baby powder, as the fine particles may exacerbate breathing problems in some babies.

Baby foods

Most parents start to think about introducing solid food into their baby's diet when she is four to six months old. Your own children may still have been totally bottlefed at this stage. A baby's digestive system is better equipped to deal with breast milk and formula than anything else, so if you find the parents need reassurance in deciding to delay solids, you can certainly back them up. There is no hard evidence to suggest that introducing solid foods makes a baby sleep through the night, and certainly babies need breast milk or formula above all else until they are at least six months old.

If your grandchild is bottlefed, you can feed her to give her parents a rest. Sit comfortably and communicate with her by using lots of eye contact. Don't waste this precious time watching TV or carrying on conversations. Bottlefeeding can be a very cozy and satisfying time for you and the baby. Stories abound of putting a little extra formula into babies' bottles as a way to fill them up so that they sleep through the night. Don't do this. Nor is it safe to reheat a bottle in the microwave: it causes hot spots in the milk, which can scald a baby's mouth.

Once solid food has begun in earnest, you can give lots of help in what can often be a frustrating business. If you are able to

Changing diapers is not a chore to be rushed. Spend this time talking to your grandchild and making eye contact with her. Consider hanging a mobile above the changing table for her to look at. Most babies enjoy being without a diaper for a while and simply kicking their legs.

WHICH DIAPER?

• **Disposables** are convenient, and since you buy them as needed, they do not involve a large initial cost, although they can be expensive in the long run. But disposables do have ecological drawbacks: it takes years for a disposable diaper to begin breaking down in a landfill site, and a lot of trees are felled to provide the wood pulp needed to manufacture them in the first place.

• **Fitted reusables** are made from cloth and are shaped like disposables; they fasten with Velcro at the sides. They are used with liners, and unlike other cloth diapers, there is no folding or pinning. They are expensive but long-lived and can be handed down within the family.

• **Cloth diapers** have to be washed and dried and are expensive to buy initially. But even taking these factors into account, they are more ecologically friendly and economical than either of the other two options in the long run.

The easiest fold is probably the kite: place the clean diaper on a flat surface in a diamond shape with points at north, south, east, and west. Bring west and east into the center so that lines southwest and southeast sit side by side. Bring the north point down to the middle of the kite, then fold up the double layer at the south until the diaper is the right size for the baby. When you visit, you could offer to fold a stack of these so that some are always at hand.

In addition to contributing to the initial cost of the diapers, you may wish to help, either by laundering some of them yourself or by paying for a diaper-laundering service to save the parents work.

take a turn at feeding the baby it will give her parents a chance to see that there is nothing personal in her habit of turning her head aside when the spoon is heading her way or in throwing the food on the floor.

If her parents usually prepare home-cooked food for your grandchild, you should do the same. Purée (when she is very young) or mash (as she gets older) some vegetables or fruit you are going to eat with your own meal. As long as you leave out salt and sugar and use fresh ingredients you will be doing what is best for your grandchild. Once she reaches 9 or 10 months, add some some finely chopped meat or chicken to the vegetables and include some finger foods that she can pick up and eat herself.

The advertising touting prepared baby food is powerful and has taken away some new parents' confidence in their ability to make fresh, healthy food for babies. If you are careful not to comment on the parents' choice, you may be able to persuade them that in this case the old ways are the best.

Under six months
The most suitable foods for babies under six months are: baby rice (specially manufactured and gluten free) mixed with cooled, boiled water, formula, or expressed breast milk; puréed or mashed fruit; and puréed or mashed vegetables.

Until she is at least six months old (many doctors recommend at least a year), do not give your grandchild eggs; wheat products, such as bread and cereals; cheese, yogurt, cow's milk; citrus fruits; onions, peppers; high-fat or fried foods.

Your adopted grandchild

Welcoming a child who is not a blood relative into your family

Although a couple may receive little advance notice that a baby or child is ready to be transferred to their care, adoption does not happen overnight. Months, even years, may pass after a couple files their application, giving you and other family members time to become accustomed to the idea of the new addition.

The legal and social circumstances surrounding adoption have changed a great deal in recent years, so your child and his or her partner will usually be aware of the baby's or child's circumstances and birth history. Social workers encourage adoptive parents to make a scrapbook, with photographs where possible, to explain the child's origins to her as soon as she is old enough. Contact with her natural parents will also usually be permitted. All this differs completely from the secrecy that used to surround adoption. However uncomfortable you may feel, such openness has been shown to be best for adopted children in the long run.

A wholehearted welcome

If your grandchild has not yet been adopted, you may be involved in what can be a long and tense legal process. Be on hand, if that is at all practical, to support the waiting parents and empathize with what they are going through.

When your grandchild arrives, you will start getting to know her. In some ways this will be similar to when you first met your natural grandchildren; in other ways it will be different. First of all, accept that this baby or child is a wanted and loved member of the family, just as if the new parents had conceived her. On the one hand, this is easy because she is an innocent child; on the other, it can be difficult, since she comes with a background and family that are not your own. Accepting her origins without judgment is the key to being able to love her without reservation.

In the days and weeks after her arrival, there will be great excitement on the part of the parents and any siblings. Enjoy everyone's happiness and take your time to become familiar with the new child. It may be very apparent that she bears no resemblance to your family, as other new arrivals have. Don't let this concern you; it won't concern the new parents.

What you can do

You must be scrupulously fair in your dealings with all your grandchildren. Work on any negative feelings about the new baby before they start to cause problems. If you are worried, consult an outsider instead of

Acknowledge racial characteristics that differ from your own as you would the fact that your grandchild's hair is red and yours blond. Such traits will make no difference to her parents and other members of the immediate family.

Many couples adopt because they are unable to have children of their own. The arrival of an adopted baby may signal the end of a period of unhappiness and is an occasion for celebration.

the parents. Your family physician can put you in touch with a counselor if you wish.

It may help you to look outside yourself and see how your other grandchildren are coping. However excited they seem at the prospect of such an addition to the family, when the reality hits home, they may experience a mixture of emotions, which the parents are too busy to appreciate fully. Some children may see the newcomer as a usurper of their parents' love in the same way a biologically related sibling might be seen, except more so, because the parents made a more active choice over this arrival. Give extra time and attention to your existing grandchildren, while leaving time to get to know the new child. Never imply to other grandchildren that they hold a superior position in your affections: you will hinder their acceptance of their new sibling.

Most people treat the arrival of an adopted child as they would a birth, with gifts for the baby, siblings, and parents. Since the new mother has not been through pregnancy, she is likely to be less exhausted than if she had given birth and may be willing for you— and perhaps the other grandparents—to organize a party to help integrate this much-wanted child into the family.

Foster care

Some couples offer their home on a short-term basis to children whose families are temporarily unable to care for them. You probably won't get to know the children in your child's foster care well. But these children need your love and support as much as your grandchildren do. Lacking a stable family structure themselves, it is important that they know that happy family relationships still exist.

CASE STUDY

My daughter, Clare, is an only child, and once she reached her 30s, I did drop hints about being a granny. But she didn't want to settle down. I was astounded when she came back from a trip abroad with a photo of a baby she was going to adopt. She had visited a friend who was a doctor at an orphanage, seen this boy, and knew instantly that he had to be hers.

I thought it was a ludicrous idea and assumed she would come to her senses. We knew nothing about this child; the country was unstable, and his parents were missing or dead. And my daughter would be a single mother. When I realized Clare meant to go through with it, I was terrified for her.

When Clare brought Mikael home, I knew I should be pleased, but I couldn't accept that she was bringing a stranger into our family. He was about two but looked younger; he was small and thin, but had the eyes of an old man. His stare made me uneasy, but I could see that he needed looking after and began to understand part of what had moved Clare so much.

That was two years ago. Mikael didn't say a word for six months, but he gradually started to talk and to fill out and grow. He's a nice boy, although I still find it hard to accept that this is my grandchild. But I know my daughter is happy, and I'm very proud of what she has done.

Naming ceremonies

Christenings and other special ways to welcome a child to the world

Many people with religious beliefs mark their child's entry into the world with a spiritual celebration. For Christians, this usually takes the form of a christening; other faiths have different customs (see p. 51). Sometimes these celebrations cause conflict within families.

Practical arrangements

If you have a family heirloom christening robe you would like your grandchild to wear, show it to the parents but do not put pressure on them to accept it. The other grandparents may also have a gown they would like to see worn. Despite the importance this issue often assumes, the gown your grandchild wears at her christening will be quickly forgotten as she reaches other milestones in her life.

If there is no family gown, you might contribute to the event by making one or having one made. Many families embroider the name of each child who wears the gown into the hem to make it a unique heirloom. Alternative keepsakes are a shawl, a needlepoint or embroidered sampler with your grandchild's name and date of birth, or a porcelain plate including these details.

The parents of course will choose the godparents and will decide who is invited to the event and to any party. But you could offer to make or buy the cake or, if your house is larger than theirs, offer to host the party. Or simply ask the parents what you can do to help them enjoy the event.

Many parents feel they should organize everything to do with this first milestone in their child's life themselves. If you have to take a back seat, look for something imaginative to do to be involved in the proceedings without stepping on anyone's toes. Taking informal photographs during the day and making albums for yourself, the parents, and the other grandparents to keep will be greatly appreciated. You could

A priest sprinkles the baby's forehead with water, symbolizing Christ's baptism in the River Jordan. The ceremony allows other members of the parents' church to welcome the newborn into their community.

The imposing setting of a Greek Orthodox christening emphasizes that this is an important rite of passage for both baby and parents.

NON-CHRISTIAN RITES

Almost all faiths mark a baby's entry into the world in some way, but the rituals vary considerably.

Jewish ceremonies
Nowadays both boys and girls are named and blessed in the synagogue, followed by a family party. In addition, Jewish boys are circumcised before the baby's eighth day. The operation is conducted by a mohel in the presence of the parents, family, and a rabbi. Prayers are said by the rabbi, and the child is given a Hebrew name in addition to the name he will be known by.

Humanist ceremonies
A naming ceremony without religious content can be arranged through humanist societies. Two or more adults promise to act as guardians to the child. Appropriate poetry may be read, either by a representative from a humanist society or by the parents, to welcome the child into the world. The ceremony is often concluded by planting a tree for the child in the family garden.

Buddhist ceremonies
The oldest members of a Buddhist family prepare a crib and clothes for the baby. Then the newborn is laid inside, along with tools and books if the baby is a boy, and needles and thread for a girl. When babies are a month old, their heads are shaved, and sacred threads tied to their wrists to welcome the spirit that will care for the baby. Monks may be invited to this ceremony.

Taoist ceremonies
Although the date and time of a Chinese baby's birth are recorded, so that a horoscope can be worked out, no announcement of the birth is made until the baby is one month old, when the Mun Yiu (full month) ceremony takes place. Relatives and friends bring money in red envelopes, and eggs dyed red are eaten for good luck.

Islamic ceremonies
New life is seen as a gift from God, in recognition of which the baby's family gives food, money, and clothes to the poor. Allah's name and the *adham* (prayer) are whispered into the ear of the newborn and on the seventh day the baby is named and the head is shaved to remove the uncleanliness of the birth and encourage the hair to grow thicker. A feast, to which relatives and friends are invited, is held at the naming ceremony.

also make a video of the event. But since that is more intrusive than still photography, you should make sure that the parents want you to do it.

Christenings often bring to the fore any debate concerning family names. You may not have been aware of the parents' wish to use or exclude traditional family names. Remember that there are two families and that passing on everyone's "traditional" name might not be an option. You may indeed find the choice of name odd or not to your liking. Vogues for names come and go, so it is unlikely that parents will pick names that would have been your choice.

Silver is a traditional material for christening gifts: photograph frames and tooth fairy containers are popular. But china mugs and money boxes are also perennial presents.

Nonreligious parents
If you have strong religious beliefs and the parents do not, you may find it hard to accept that your grandchild will not be christened. You may find it helps to talk to your priest or minister about your feelings: he or she will be able to offer you some consolation. It may help to bear in mind that your grandchild will be able to choose for herself, when she becomes older, whether or not she wishes to be baptized.

Toddlers
15 months to 3 years

It is easy to forget how quickly children grow. In what seems no time at all, your "baby" grandchild has learned to walk and begun to talk to you in recognizable words or signs. He has become a (sometimes willful) little person with a mind of his own. Life for a toddler is one big adventure, which he will be delighted to share.

You may be surprised at the speed with which your grandchild masters new skills. In the toddler years, he will progress from tottering on unsure feet to climbing stairs with confidence; from calling every man he sees "Dada" to being able to name clearly most of his family and friends. He will advance from throwing—in frustration—a block that won't fit a shape sorter to sitting and completing a jigsaw puzzle. His artistic efforts will develop from crayon scribbles to pictures with named elements, such as the sun or Mom.

Toddlers love life, and if you can provide a few props and an interested presence, these years will be full of fun for you both.

What toddlers like doing

Games, toys, and activities to satisfy the most energetic grandchild

Whether you see your grandchild regularly or only occasionally, you want the time you spend with him to be enjoyable and special. Obviously, what you do together depends to some extent on your circumstances and how active you are. Fortunately, young children enjoy simple indoor and outdoor activities, so entertaining them does not need to be costly or sophisticated. And because children learn by imitating the actions and behavior of other people, as well as through play and exploring the world around them, the time you spend doing things with your grandchild can enhance his physical, mental, and social skills.

Make sure that the activities you plan are suitable for your grandchild's age and stage of development (see pp. 58–59). Allow for the fact that toddlers seem to have boundless energy and can be demanding and tiring. Bear in mind, too, that although they may have a short attention span when doing some things and grow bored easily, they also have an amazing capacity for repetitive action in other games. Plan a variety of things to do that will suit both your paces, and include active and passive pastimes during the day.

Outdoors

One of the simplest and most enjoyable outdoor activities you can do with your grandchild is to go for a walk. Once he has found his feet, he may not want to sit in his stroller, but take it with you if you are going any distance (you may have to carry him otherwise). Depending on where you are going, consider using a harness and reins for safety. If you need to be somewhere by a certain time, allow for the fact that toddlers love to dawdle when walking.

Point out objects of interest, such as a bird, squirrel, or dog, or items in store windows. Look out, too, for things which you can take home and use later, such as an interestingly shaped stone, pebble, or shell, acorns, feathers, leaves, or pine cones.

If your grandchild is used to traveling by car, he will find it a treat to go for a ride on a bus or train. And take him to a child-friendly restaurant and let him choose his own drink or something to eat.

Toddlers also love gardening; donate some ground for him to dig with his own miniature tools and perhaps sow with seeds, or ask him to help you rake leaves. You could set up a swing, make a little house to play in, or provide a sandbox or wading pool (for safety, see pp. 66–69).

• Weatherwise

Toddlers usually need to work off some energy outdoors, so unless the weather is really bad, don't let it prevent you from donning suitable clothes and going out,

Farms are fun, especially when there are baby animals to see and hold. Toddlers find many activities exciting: going to the park to feed the ducks, to run around, or to play on the slide or swings; a trip to the beach; or even a trip to the store to buy a newspaper or some groceries.

This is the stage at which your grandchild may have unbridled energy and a boundless capacity for fun. If you can find an outdoor activity you all enjoy, you will have hours of pleasure together.

even for just a short time. On rainy days, children love wearing galoshes and splashing through puddles. Point out the different-shaped clouds or reflections in puddles, and look for a rainbow. In the snow, take your grandchild for a sled ride, build a snowman together, look for icicles, or let him help you clear a path.

Indoors

Playing with household items will give your grandchild hours of fun, and you can do many activities together around your home. Talk to him and involve him in what you are doing. If he is old enough to understand, make up simple stories with him as the hero or tell stories about your childhood. He will also love to hear you sing funny ditties or nonsense rhymes.

• Helping you

From the age of about 18 months, your grandchild will love to mimic what you are doing. Helping around the house—dusting, clearing up, drying dishes—or washing the car will be fun for him, and you can also help him learn. When dusting, identify the types of furniture; when drying, tell him the names and colors of the dishes, and say whether a plate is large or small.

• Water play

Let your grandchild help you wash small dishes or flatware, or his own tea set. Be careful not to give him sharp knives or anything precious. Give him a bowl of water with some clean plastic containers, such as liquid detergent bottles, food containers, or cups to play with.

Add some glycerin to detergent and water to make soap bubbles to blow. Make a simple blower by twisting the end of a thin piece of wire or a pipe cleaner into a ring.

• Make-believe

If you provide a few basic props—such as cardboard boxes, curtains, blankets, and pillows—and a corner of a room, your grandchild will be able to use his imagination to entertain himself and you. He will also enjoy activities such as inviting you for tea, "cooking" with a saucepan and wooden spoons, or playing store with a few cans, empty packages, and plastic bottles.

• Creative play

Dried pasta can be threaded and used as jewelry; pieces of colored construction paper can be used for drawing or finger painting; pictures can be cut out of magazines with blunt scissors; a saucepan or box can be beaten with a spoon to make a drum and containers with tight-fitting tops can be filled with raw rice, dried peas, or lentils for shaking.

• Other activities

Toddlers carry their enthusiasm for some activities through to their preschool years and beyond. Dressing up, baking, and all sorts of drawing and writing are obvious examples of skills that, once learned, are perfected over the years (see pp. 76–79).

What toddlers like doing

Books for toddlers

It is never too early to encourage a child's interest in reading. Most children love looking at books from an early age. If your grandchild is coming to visit, ask his parents to bring some of his favorite books. Make a point of sitting down with him at least once a day and looking at books, if only for a few minutes. Point out objects or read him a story. You may also want to keep a small selection of books in your house especially for your grandchild to look at.

Books also make ideal presents for toddlers. Look for books that have moving parts or make a noise, that have lots of pictures to encourage talking, and perennial favorites, such as simple fairy tales and nursery rhymes that you can teach your grandchild to recite.

Choosing toys

Your grandchild learns many skills through playing, so if you like buying him toys, it makes sense to give him ones that will help his developing skills. Playing with different types of toys can help him distinguish between shapes, sizes, colors, and weight; stimulate his imagination and creativity; and help to develop spatial awareness, manual dexterity, and other skills.

To be beneficial, a toy needs to be appropriate for your grandchild's age, personality, and stage of development. Avoid buying expensive porcelain dolls or complicated train sets, for example, until your grandchild is old enough to appreciate them. Choose toys that are fun and have plenty of play potential, with lots of features and bright colors. Remember, too, that many boys enjoy playing with dolls and many girls like construction sets.

Toy safety

Many children stop putting everything in their mouth once they are about a year old, but others persist well into toddlerhood. For this reason, checking for safety measures when buying toys is vital.

A walk on the beach is an opportunity for splashing and playing in the water, as well as hunting for shells, seaweed, and other marine treasures. It is never too soon to teach a toddler the names of different shells or to listen to the calls of some of the seabirds. He won't remember them all, but you are sowing the seeds of what may develop into a lifelong interest in the world around him.

Check with her parents before buying your grandchild a large piece of outdoor play equipment, since many yards are simply not big enough. Children also outgrow such items fast, although this is less of a problem if you have a big family and can pass them on. Make the most of what is available in parks and playgrounds.

• Buy toys from reputable manufacturers. Electrical toys should have a seal saying UL (Underwriters Laboratory) Approved. The U.S. Consumer Products Safety Commission has a hotline—800-638-CPSC—which gives safety tips and provides news of recent recalls of products with potential hazards.
• Whenever possible, take a toy out of its box and check that it is sturdy and well built before you buy it.
• Take safety messages such as "Not suitable for children under three years," or their equivalent symbol, seriously.
• Make sure that the toy has no sharp edges or detachable small parts.

Detachable pieces and sharp edges on plastic toys are common. Small pieces are easy for a child to choke on. Many toys—such as dolls—are not dangerous in themselves, but their accessories, such as shoes and combs, can be.

TEMPER TANTRUMS

The majority of children of between one and four years old have occasional tantrums; some two-year-olds have one or more every day. Often, these are short outbursts that are quickly over, but in some situations they develop into full-blown episodes.

At their most extreme, children lie on the ground, scream and kick, or throw things. If your grandchild has tantrums when he is with his parents, do not undermine their authority by interfering or criticizing.

If he has a tantrum with you, try to figure out why and as far as possible avoid these trigger situations. Tantrums are more common when a child is tired, hungry, or overexcited; the most usual causes are not being allowed to do something he wants to do, being made to do something he doesn't want to do, or simply frustration at his limited capabilities.

How you deal with a tantrum depends on the age and temperament of your grandchild. If his parents have a method that works, follow it. Whatever you do, stay calm and avoid bribes, spanking, or threats.

Diversionary tactics may prevent a threatened tantrum or halt one. Choices ("Do you want to go to the park or do some painting?") are better than open-ended questions ("What shall we do now?"). If this does not work, try ignoring the child, put him in a different room until the tantrum is over, or leave the room so that he does not have an audience.

If you are in a public place, decide whether to stay put until the tantrum blows over or remove him from the scene. If you can't pick him up and take him to the car, for example, hug him; this works well with some children.

Once the tantrum is over, tell him that you still love him even if you do not approve of his behavior, then let the matter rest.

What toddlers like doing

How your grandchild develops

You will take pride in watching your grandchild acquire new skills, but avoid comparing his development with that of other children. All children develop at their own rate, and there is a wide range of average. The majority, however, will have acquired certain skills by the time they reach a particular age. Here is a guide to the stages of a child's development at different ages, with suggestions of suitable toys to buy and activities to do. Remember, most toys and activities apply to more than one age range.

PHYSICAL

15–18 MONTHS
Walks around furniture or alone with hesitation
Explores and is into everything
Can throw a ball and push a large toy
May place one block on top of another
Starts to climb on chairs and scramble up stairs
Drinks from a cup without spilling and feeds himself with a spoon

MENTAL AND SOCIAL

Jabbers and says a few words
May start temper tantrums
Carries objects around
Knows some body parts, such as nose or eyes
Understands simple commands, such as "Shut the door"
Puts simple shapes into shape-sorting box or puzzle

18 MONTHS–2 YEARS
Walks steadily
May have started running
Climbs on chairs
Squats to pick up a toy without falling over
Walks up stairs with helping hand

Starts to say words in phrases
Looks at books and points to items he recognizes in the pictures
Copies adult activities
Favorite word is "no"
Tries to join in nursery rhymes
Can be quite aggressive and likes his own way
Unscrews lids and turns door handles
Takes off shoes and socks

2–3 YEARS
Runs everywhere
Kicks a ball firmly
Jumps
Climbs easy playground apparatus

Joins in nursery rhymes
Vocabulary expands; he can make sentences
Copies circles and lines
Knows some colors
Can count to five
Usually dry during the day
Helps dress himself

3 YEARS
Climbs with increasing agility
Rides a tricycle using pedals and steers around corners
Hops and stands on tiptoe
Kicks a ball forcefully
Dances
Catches a ball with both hands

Many who, what, why questions, but grammar may be incorrect
Builds tower of nine blocks
Knows several nursery rhymes
Counts up to ten
Cuts with blunt scissors
Draws person with head
Gives name, age, and gender
Eats with a fork and spoon
May have an imaginary playmate

During the toddler years the world becomes a fascinating place for children. A walk often beomes a nature trail as you pick up leaves, examine plants, and see how many birds you can spot.

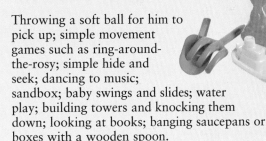

SUITABLE TOYS INCLUDE

Baby books; kiddie cars; stacking toys; simple insert toys such as shape-sorting boxes to aid manipulation; toys that make noise, such as drums; small set of wooden building blocks; push-and-pull toys to aid balance; chatter telephones to help speech; coloring materials; large, soft balls; handbag or box full of safe interesting objects to rummage through.

Tea sets for pretend play; blocks for building; picture books with simple stories; child-size household objects such as brush and dustpan; musical toys with nursery rhymes; jack-in-the-box; crayons, paper, play dough or modeling clay (supervise closely); simple dolls; simple puzzles; balls; wheeled toys; stacking toys.

Finger paints; play-house; push-and-ride toys; first jigsaws and large puzzles; large beads for stringing; construction toys; simple climbing toys; sandbox; bucket and shovel; dolls and teddy bears; wooden train.

Dress-up clothes; blunt scissors and magazines for cutting up; crayons, washable markers, coloring books; toy tools, tricycle, or pedal car; picture books; glove puppets; toy farms; powder paints and chunky paint brushes; chunky chalks and chalkboard; chef set; fix-it kit; doctor's set; easy musical instruments; shopping basket, play money, cash register; accessories such as handbags and hats.

ACTIVITIES INCLUDE

Throwing a soft ball for him to pick up; simple movement games such as ring-around-the-rosy; simple hide and seek; dancing to music; sandbox; baby swings and slides; water play; building towers and knocking them down; looking at books; banging saucepans or boxes with a wooden spoon.

Kicking or rolling balls; simple chasing; household "cleaning," such as sweeping and dusting; simple puzzles; make-believe play, such as having a tea party with a miniature tea set; talking on a pretend phone; singing nursery rhymes; being read simple stories; singing songs with simple actions; splashing through puddles; feeding the ducks.

Musical games; going to a park to play on under-fives' equipment, or to a beach with bucket and shovel; filling and pulling a small wagon; simple ball games; doing puzzles; pretend play; dressing up; painting; telling stories; printing with potato pieces; hiding a few toys or edible treats for him to find.

Helping with baking; gardening; dressing up; going for rides on tricycle; playing simple card or board games; cutting out pictures; making dough models; playing ball; coloring pictures; gluing pasta or paper shapes; cutting up vegetables for block painting; pretend play; trips to the library; nature activities.

Your special-needs grandchild

When extra love, caring, and support are required

If your grandchild has special needs—a term that covers minor physical defects, learning problems, allergic reactions, chronic illness, and permanent disability—your role is to give extra love and support to your family and to the growing child.

In the case of severe disability, you may need to call on all your inner resources to help you support your grandchild's parents and siblings. If the disability is not life-threatening but something to be accepted, you must be positive in your comments and attitude in order to give your best to the child.

Find out all you can about the disability so that you can assess how best to help your grandchild and his family. His parents may be wrapped up in the medical aspects of his condition, initially at least. If you want to contact the parents and families of other children who share your grandchild's special needs, get in touch with an appropriate support group or a sympathetic doctor. Today we tend to expect that all children are born perfect, and it is hard to accept that your grandchild is not. It may help to remember that one in five children has special needs at some point in childhood.

When you are first told of your grandchild's condition, you may feel frightened for his future. This is natural, but all you really need to bear in mind as he reaches the age at which other children are walking and talking is that normal development may be slower and the milestones you remember in your own children's childhood could happen later. This does not mean that you should not have high hopes for him, however: the key lies in maintaining a positive outlook.

Other people's reactions

You may find it difficult to cope with some people's reactions to your grandchild. While it is charitable to be tolerant of others' ignorance, don't waste energy educating casual acquaintances unless you think it a matter of principle that they not be allowed to offer condolences or make crass, ill-informed comments. In such situations, you will probably make new friends and find support from surprising sources. The important thing is not to let the strength you need for your family be sapped by people outside it.

Your role in the family

Assess whether your grandchild's parents need extra practical support—around the house, for example—or someone to listen to their concerns and fears, or whether you can be of more use making sure any financial help or other benefits to which the family is entitled are forthcoming.

Many toys need little or only slight adaptation to suit children with developmental delay. The families of children with the same condition as your grandchild may be able to tell you what they have found useful. Check, too, whether there are any toy libraries in your area; these are often a good source of special toys.

The temptation to step in and help a child with special needs can be overwhelming. But like all toddlers, your grandchild wants and needs to learn to do things for himself. Give him the chance to be as independent as possible from toddlerhood onward.

It is important to remember that a special-needs child is only one member of the family. Don't overlook the needs of the other children: they may be overwhelmed by their new sibling's demands. Perhaps you can give them the extra time and attention that their parents can't provide. If, however, he is their firstborn, his parents may opt for counseling if they wish to have a second child. When a sibling arrives, your role will be the same as that of any grandparent—to let the firstborn know he is still special to you.

Even when they have accepted their situation, and adjusted and organized things accordingly, the parents of children with special needs often cannot find time for themselves. When you feel confident that you can care for your grandchild, offer the parents a short break. Undoubtedly they will need some persuading, but you will be contributing to their inner resources considerably if you can release them from their daily burden of care for a time.

Above all, your special-needs grandchild should be treated liked any other child—loved, kissed, hugged, played with, talked to, and (perhaps most difficult) taught reasonable limits to which he must adhere.

THE DEATH OF A CHILD

A child's death is devastating. Parents, grandparents, siblings, relatives, friends, the doctors and nurses who cared for him—everyone who knows you and your grandchild will be affected by this unnatural course of events. However much we grieve when elderly people die, we also know, and ultimately accept, that that is a part of the life cycle; but when a child dies, there is an unbearable sense of waste and injustice.

If your grandchild has severe disabilities, his parents may have been warned—and told you—that he might not live long, but this will not ease your grief and loss when the time comes. Do not try to offer your grandchild's parents consolation along the lines that their child was suffering and could not have led the life of other children, unless you know that is what they believe. And do not feel obliged to be comforted by this knowledge yourself. You and everyone else who knew him have the right to grieve over the loss of a child, whatever his state of health.

Research suggests that families who are close and loving recover from this kind of loss more quickly than others; this is obviously a time for binding together and sharing the pain. However bereaved you feel at what has happened, don't let your grief dominate your contact with the parents. Be led by their feelings and save your own extremes of grief for a close friend or appropriate support group. If you are the parents' sole emotional support, you may feel the need to contact a grief counselor as an outlet for some of your own sorrow.

You will also need to keep a watchful eye on any siblings, who may find the whole business frightening and bewildering. Children feel grief deeply, but they express it differently from adults—perhaps through behavioral difficulties, regression to outgrown baby habits, or as fear concerning their own mortality. Because of the powerful feelings they are witnessing, it may also seem to them that everyone loved the dead child more than the children who are living. Parents may be too distressed themselves to fully notice their other children's difficulties; it may be left to you to provide the reassurance that is needed.

What toddlers wear

Choosing clothes for your toddler grandchild

Like many grandparents, you may enjoy buying clothes for your grandchild, especially if your children were girls and your grandchild is a boy, or vice versa. Perhaps money and the choice of clothes available were more limited when your children were young. Today you may be overwhelmed by choice and find it difficult to select something appropriate, particularly if you do not live close by and have only a vague idea of what he usually wears or how extensive his wardrobe is. Picking the right size may also be difficult, as some clothes manufacturers use the child's height as a measurement and others use the age. Always check with your grandchild's parents what your grandchild's current size is and what kind of clothes he needs before you buy.

Practical clothing

Most of the time your grandchild probably wears practical clothes, such as sweaters, T-shirts, overalls, or pants, which can withstand the rough and tumble of an active child's life and be laundered easily. Much as you may long to dress your granddaughter in frilly dresses or your grandson in a suit, tie, and vest, such clothes are likely to be appreciated for special occasions only. Most parents feel the hand-washing, careful ironing, or dry cleaning they need take too much time for everyday wear. Such clothes are usually expensive, too. If you are intent on buying "special" clothes, it is worth remembering that summer clothes often wash and dry more easily than those for winter.

Hats and caps are useful both summer and winter and are fashionable for both boys and girls these days. Your grandchild may be delighted to receive a trendy baseball cap (which he can wear back to front).

If you enjoy knitting, you may find that making your grandchildren sweaters is much appreciated, especially if you can depict animals or favorite characters on them. (But remember that some characters become outmoded at least as fast as your grandchild grows.) Unless you are knitting for a special occasion, use machine-washable yarn—there is plenty of choice of color and texture available today.

Even at an early age, many children have strong likes and dislikes about clothes, and may refuse to wear certain styles. So don't be hurt if your grandchild sometimes declines to wear what you have bought or made for her. If you don't make a fuss, chances are that the next time you see her, she will be sporting in delight what she once wholeheartedly rejected.

Even the most sociable toddlers are rarely invited to enough parties to make a wardrobe full of special party clothes worthwhile. Check what your granddaughter has already before buying another pretty dress.

Shoes

It is vital for young feet to have shoes that fit well, so it is best not to buy them unless your grandchild is with you for a fitting. Children grow out of shoes quickly, but even shoes in good condition should not be handed down because each child molds the shoes to suit his feet. Although you may prefer that your grandchild wear leather shoes, many children today wear sneakers, which are more comfortable and adequate for growing feet.

If his parents are willing, you may want to take your grandchild shopping for shoes. Choose a time when the store is not busy. Be guided by his parents wishes: if they have requested sneakers, don't be seduced by party shoes. If you can't find what you want at the first store, try another, but if you are still unsuccessful, check your grandchild's reaction. Having been promised shoes, some children are reluctant to go home without them; others are easily bored by shopping and resent going from store to store and repeatedly trying on variations of the same items.

TIPS ON BUYING CLOTHES

If you find the choice in children's clothes overwhelming, these guidelines may help.

- Consider safety and practicality. Avoid clothes with drawstring hoods, which could strangle a child. Try to buy clothes with a flameproof or fire-resistant label. If he is not toilet trained, check ease of opening. If he is, remember that elastic waistbands are easier to manage than zippers, buttons, and snaps.

- Children grow very quickly, so buy casual clothes, such as T-shirts and sweaters, in slightly larger sizes so that your grandchild gets more wear from them.

- On the other hand, take extra care that you have the right size if you are buying an outfit for a special occasion, to avoid disappointment.

- If the parents are on a tight budget, buy clothes that serve more than one purpose: colorful cotton T-shirts can also be worn as undershirts, for example.

- As a treat, buy your grandchild "fashion" clothing, such as items depicting film characters, but make sure they are the right size for immediate use and be prepared for them to be discarded early. Clothes featuring characters from a favorite book are also popular.

- Once they are toilet trained, most children consider gifts of underwear a sign that they are "grown up."

- Colors that you may consider unsuitable for a child—such as black—may be popular with (and suit) your grandchild.

- It is easier for parents to exchange clothes that do not fit if you buy them from nationwide chain stores.

- Buy basic clothes, such as nightwear, socks, sweaters, and T-shirts on sale even if they are a size too big for your grandchild. You can easily keep them until he is older.

- As a general rule, buy clothes that are tough, practical, and easily laundered.

Then and now:

Potty training

Washing and drying piles of diapers was once a chore to be disposed of as quickly as possible, so young children were encouraged to use a potty from the time they could sit upright. Today, attitudes are more relaxed.

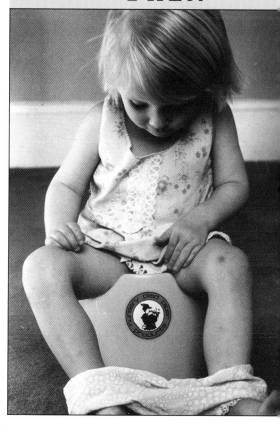

Potty training often became something of a battle of wills as children were encouraged to sit there until they "performed" (above). Today many children treat the potty as another toy, to be carried from room to room for use when they remember or feel the need (above right).

When your children were growing up, getting them potty trained as early as possible may have been considered a desirable goal. Before a child was a year old, parents would often sit him on a potty regularly. Even just a few years ago, children were expected to be potty trained by the age of 18 months to 2 years.

Today, however, it is believed that "catching" a bowel movement or urine by putting a child on the potty from an early age is not toilet training, but just good observation on the part of the parent. For the child himself it is a reflex action. And when he grows older, he may very well refuse to "perform," thereby causing much tension or frustration between parents and child.

Even if you feel that your grandchild has reached the stage when he should be dry—during the day at least—don't comment on it or compare him with other children. If you are involved in potty training, go along with what his parents have said or want to do. It is important that all his caregivers do the same thing, so that he does not get confused by different messages. Similarly, you must know the words he uses when he wants to use the potty.

Tips for successful potty training

Keeping a relaxed attitude is essential if you are involved in potty-training your grandchild or if he wets himself at your house. Although you may be angry by a puddle on your new carpet or upholstery, don't let on. Getting angry may frighten him or make him more nervous about potty training, and maintaining a good relationship with your grandchild is more important. Clean up in a matter-of-fact way, and suggest that next time he wants to use the potty he should tell you.

If your grandchild is coming to stay, remind his parents to bring his potty, or

NOW

diapers, which can be pulled up and down like training pants. As your grandchild begins to be trained, you may wish to buy special underpants as a present.

All children eventually gain control over their bladder and bowels. Some may take a little longer than others, but it is highly unlikely that your grandchild will still need diapers when he goes to school.

POINTS TO REMEMBER

• To become potty trained, a child must be able to make the connection between the physical signals from his bladder or bowels and the passing of urine or feces.

• Early advancement in such skills as walking or talking does not necessarily mean that your grandchild is old enough to be potty trained.

• The earliest time to start potty training is around 18 months, but for most children 2 years is more realistic. Some children may not be ready until nearer their third birthday. Girls are usually ready a little earlier than boys.

• There is no set method of potty training; what works for one child may not work for another.

• Some children learn more quickly than others, so don't compare one grandchild with another or with a friend's grandchild.

• Your grandchild may be unable to urinate on an unfamiliar potty or toilet.

• Young children cannot postpone passing urine until it is convenient.

• Accidents may happen even after the child is trained.

• Even if a child is potty trained during the day, nighttime control can take months longer. Bed-wetting accidents can occur for several years.

• If you go out with your grandchild, don't forget to take spare underwear and clothes in case he has an accident.

take him shopping to choose one for use especially in your house. Buy one with a rigid base to prevent it from toppling, and for boys make sure it has a splash guard. When your grandchild is not using it, keep the potty within easy reach in a warm room. If possible, place it on a washable floor surface or use some waterproof material to cover the carpet. If your grandchild moves the potty, make sure you always know where he has left it: there is nothing worse than not being able to find the potty when he has remembered he needs to use it.

Encourage your grandchild to sit on the potty after every meal and at various times of the day for a short period, but don't make a fuss if he doesn't want to. Praise him when he uses the potty successfully.

Training pants are easier for a child to pull up and down and are more "grown up" than diapers—or consider "pull-up"

When a toddler comes to visit

Making your home safe for your grandchild

The liveliness and curiosity of toddlers make them amusing and welcome visitors. But these qualities also render young children particularly accident-prone. Domestic accidents are the most common cause of injury and even death among children between the ages of one and five. Once they are older, we tend to forget how active toddlers are and how quickly accidents can happen. In addition, the average home today has more potentially hazardous gadgets and appliances than it did when your own children were young. Although nobody can make a house completely accidentproof, once your grandchild is able to crawl and walk, it is essential to make sure your house is safe. Don't view these procedures as simply for your grandchild's sake. As you get older, many of them will also make your home safer for you.

If your grandchild does not visit often, you may find it more economical to rent or borrow larger safety items rather than to buy them. Certain safety measures—removing scatter rugs when he comes, for

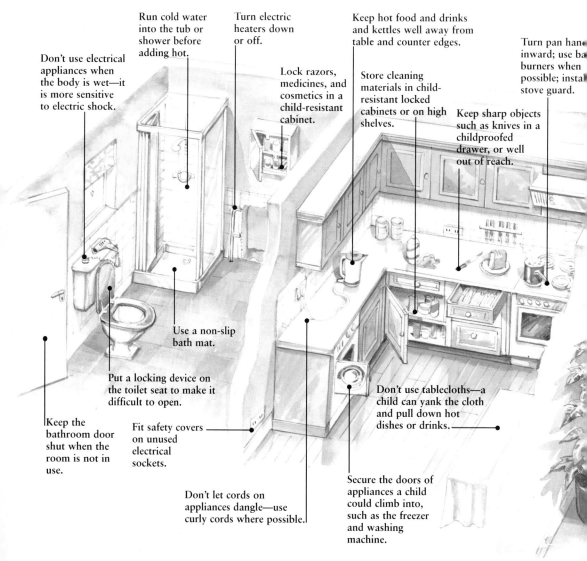

Run cold water into the tub or shower before adding hot.

Turn electric heaters down or off.

Keep hot food and drinks and kettles well away from table and counter edges.

Don't use electrical appliances when the body is wet—it is more sensitive to electric shock.

Turn pan handles inward; use back burners when possible; install stove guard.

Lock razors, medicines, and cosmetics in a child-resistant cabinet.

Store cleaning materials in child-resistant locked cabinets or on high shelves.

Keep sharp objects such as knives in a childproofed drawer, or well out of reach.

Use a non-slip bath mat.

Put a locking device on the toilet seat to make it difficult to open.

Keep the bathroom door shut when the room is not in use.

Fit safety covers on unused electrical sockets.

Don't use tablecloths—a child can yank the cloth and pull down hot dishes or drinks.

Don't let cords on appliances dangle—use curly cords where possible.

Secure the doors of appliances a child could climb into, such as the freezer and washing machine.

example—cost nothing. Several of the larger items, such as safety gates and a car seat, can "travel" with your grandchild.

There are two ways to approach home safety. First, do a room-by-room hazard check. Second, be aware of the most common causes of accidents in and around the home among the under-fives. These are burns and scalds, drowning, poisoning, falls, choking, suffocation, and strangulation.

Burns and scalds

Because young children have thinner skin than adults do, they are more susceptible to burns and scalds at lower temperatures.
• As soon as he is old enough to understand, teach your grandchild not to touch anything in the kitchen that might be hot. This

includes such items as the oven, stove, faucets, saucepans, teapot, and coffeepot.
• Turn the thermostat on your hot-water system down to 55°F (13°C) to help prevent scalding.
• Always run cold water in the shower or tub first, then add hot. Cover the hot faucet with a washcloth, towel, or safety cover.
• Keep matches and lighters out of reach.
• Keep hot food and drinks out of reach; never carry a hot drink and your grandchild at the same time.
• Install, and regularly check, smoke detectors.
• Install a screen around all fires—gas, electric, open—and wood-burning stoves.
• Position movable space heaters so that they cannot be knocked over.

Hide the wires of appliances where possible.

Remove knickknacks or place them out of reach.

Fit protectors on sharp table corners.

Install a fire screen.

Move furniture that can be climbed on away from windows, or fit window locks.

Tie blind and shade cords, which pose a strangulation hazard, out of reach.

Check which house plants are poisonous.

Use a safety gate at the top and bottom of stairs.

When a toddler comes to visit

Keep the toolshed, greenhouse, and yard securely locked.

Make sure gates and doors are securely fastened.

Learn which plants are poisonous and keep a close eye on toddlers. Consider fencing off a safe area for him.

Don't leave tools or chemicals lying aroun

Cover or fence of pools and ponds; supervise children near water.

Drowning

Young children are fascinated by water but can drown quickly in only a few inches of it.
• Don't leave buckets of water around.
• Always supervise a young child in the bathroom. Never leave him in the tub unattended, even for a few seconds.
• If you have a swimming pool, install a self-closing gate that latches firmly. But remain vigilant.
• Always supervise a child near water, even if he is playing in a child's wading pool.
• Cover garden ponds with chicken wire or strong board, or fence them.

Poisoning

• Don't leave medicines in pockets or purses. Adult vitamins containing iron and iron tablets, in particular, can be fatal to young children. Nose sprays for adults are also dangerous.
• Never refer to medicines as candy.

• Buy medicines and other potentially harmful products in child-resistant containers, but remember that these are not 100-percent childproof.
• Put poisonous house plants on high shelves; teach your grandchild not to eat or pick anything in the yard without showing it to you first.
• Keep all potentially harmful products—medicines, pesticides, household cleaners—locked away and out of reach.

Falls

• Remove scatter rugs from polished floors.
• Put up safety gates to stop a toddler from going up or down stairs.
• Be extra-vigilant if you have banisters with vertical bars that a child could squeeze through, or horizontal bars that he could climb over. Consider blocking them temporarily with board or firm netting.
• Keep doors to balconies securely locked.

• Install window locks on all accessible windows, but make sure they can be opened easily by an adult in an emergency.
• Move furniture that can be climbed on away from windows; if the toilet is near a window, use a window lock.
• Keep dark areas, such as landings, well lit.

Choking, suffocation, strangulation

• Do not give under-fives hard candy or whole nuts. Peanuts are especially dangerous, since the oil they contain can also trigger allergic reactions.
• Don't leave small objects, such as coins or round batteries, lying around.
• Buy only those toys suitable for your grandchild's age. Most toy-related choking accidents occur with toys not recommended for under-threes because of small detachable parts.
• Deflated or burst balloons are a hazard for a small child, who may suck one into his mouth and choke or suffocate.
• Keep plastic bags hidden.
• Make sure there are no loose or dangling wires or cords that a child could wrap around his neck.

In the car

Children must ride in the back seat and be strapped in a car seat appropriate to their weight and size or wear a seat belt if they are older. If your grandchild is staying with you, ask his parents to leave you his car seat. See also p. 20.

When to call a doctor

Accidents are not the only potential problem when your grandchild is with you. It is easy to forget how quickly a small child can become sick or how a minor illness may suddenly get worse. If this happens, you may need to decide whether to call a doctor or even an ambulance.

A fever or high temperature is common when a child is sick. To help bring it down, undress him and keep him cool. Sponge him with tepid water and give him plenty of fluids. A child with a fever or mild pain can be given a dose of acetaminophen appropriate for his age. Never give aspirin to a baby or child unless prescribed by a doctor. The use of aspirin by children has been associated with Reye's syndrome, a serious disorder of the brain and liver.
Call the doctor if the child:
• Has a temperature above 101°F (38.3°C).
• Is drowsy, losing consciousness, or cannot be awakened.
• Has a convulsion or seems limp.
• Appears to have severe abdominal pain.
• Has difficulty breathing or turns blue.
• Has prolonged diarrhea or vomiting.
• Has an unusual rash.
• Appears gray or ashen.
• Has a severe head injury, or if a head injury is followed by vomiting or loss of consciousness.
• Has swallowed a poisonous substance.
If you are in any doubt, call the doctor.

SAFETY CHECKLIST

• Are chemicals and medicines out of sight and out of reach?

• Is the hot-water thermostat turned down?

• Are all gates and toolsheds locked?

• Do all fires have protective screens?

• Is there any access to open water?

• Are there any hanging tablecloths, cords, or wires?

• Are safety locks installed on windows and is all furniture well away from them?

• Are glass doors and tables covered with safety glass?

• Are there safety gates on stairs?

• Are all garden tools and other sharp objects out of sight and out of reach?

• Are all small objects out of reach?

Feeding a toddler

Coping with fussy children with minuscule appetites

Your grandchild's eating habits can be one of the biggest sources of friction between you and his parents. You may think that his parents are too strict about not allowing him treats (particularly candy) or too lax in allowing him to be picky. His parents may feel that you are setting him on the road to tooth decay and poor habits by giving him sugary foods or that you are unrealistically strict about his behavior at mealtime.

You may find that you disapprove of the kind of food that your grandchild prefers, or worry that he seems to have an impossibly small appetite or a limited diet of two or three favorite foods. You may also find it difficult not to get upset if your grandchild wastes food, especially if you have lavished time and attention on preparing a meal, or if you remember days when food was less plentiful than it is now.

If it is any consolation, his parents may also be concerned about your grandchild's eating habits, convinced that he doesn't eat enough and might be hungry. They may also have to sit and watch as he enthusiastically eats at your house something he won't touch at home. If this happens, make the dish a treat that he gets only at Granny's house.

Don't allow your grandchild's eating habits to be a source of conflict within your family. Come to an amicable agreement with his parents about what foods are or are not allowed and what constitutes acceptable behavior. Don't let your grandchild hear you discussing any feeding problems or let him know that you are worried—he will revel in being the center of attention.

Common feeding problems

Young children have small stomachs that cannot process large quantities of food, so most toddlers prefer to eat small meals with snacks in between. Make sure that such snacks are healthy; give sugary treats only occasionally. Too many high-fiber foods can also fill children up without providing enough calories; high-fiber low-fat diets are inappropriate for under-fives, who need plenty of calories for energy. Some children who suffer from a poor appetite and low weight gain may be filling up on sugary drinks, which provide empty calories.

Once he is happy in a highchair and can feed himself a spoonful every so often, introduce your grandchild to the idea that meals are social occasions for all the family. He will feel very grown up if you give him the same food you are having, and you may even find that he cheerfully eats foods that he used to throw on the floor.

THE GOLDEN RULES

- Don't fuss over, bribe, or force a child to eat.
- Don't show concern if he does not eat.
- Stay calm if he rejects your lovingly cooked meal in favor of a TV dinner or fast food.
- Expect a toddler to make a mess, and cover the floor with newspaper. Don't demand perfect table manners.
- Don't use candy, cakes, or cookies as a bribe or a reward for good behavior.
- Give small portions, and let your grandchild ask for more if he wants it.
- If he is old enough, involve your grandchild in selecting and preparing food.
- Don't undermine parents' rules about when—or if—candy is allowed.
- Avoid foods that may cause choking: whole nuts, chunks of meat, or popcorn.
- Don't let him fill up on juice.
- Make sure your grandchild sits down to eat; eating while running around presents a choking hazard.

It may also help you to know that almost every family has a tale of a child who went through a phase of eating only cornflakes or baked beans or strawberry yogurt for days at a time. Fads are usually harmless and best left to run their course. If you are worried, find subtle ways of introducing a wider variety of food—blending fruit into a milk shake or adding it to ice cream or jello, for example, or grating some cheese on the baked beans or a hamburger.

Some children are more adventurous about food they have helped to prepare. Let your grandchild stir a cake mix, spread peanut butter or honey on his sandwich, sprinkle cheese on his pizza, and select the fruit and vegetables in the supermarket.

The food groups

If your grandchild eats something from each of the food groups listed every day, or over several days, he will get a balanced diet. And if he is growing normally and has plenty of energy, he is getting enough food.
- Proteins such as meat, poultry, fish, eggs, beans, lentils and other legumes, tofu.
- Starchy foods, such as bread, pasta, rice, corn, millet, oatmeal, yams, potatoes, breakfast cereals.
- Fruit and vegetables, both fresh and frozen; check the salt and sugar content of canned fruit and vegetables, and choose fruit canned in juice instead of syrup.
- Dairy products, such as milk, cheese, yogurt, butter.

Healthy snacks
- Milk shakes with no added sugar.
- Sandwiches filled with smooth peanut butter, cream cheese, or fruit spread.
- Slices of apple, banana, peach, nectarine, strawberries, or seedless grapes.
- Frozen or regular yogurt.
- Bagels, muffins, chapatis, pita bread.
- Small pieces of steamed, cooled carrot sticks or broccoli florets.
- Soft dried fruits.
- Breakfast cereals with no added sugar.
- Cubes or slices of cheese.
- Pieces of homemade pizza.

The vegetarian toddler

There are two concerns with a vegetarian diet for children. First, vegetarian foods generally have a high fiber content. To make sure that your grandchild gets enough energy, give him small, frequent meals and plenty of nutritious snacks. Also, children who do not eat meat may not get enough iron. To help iron absorption, give foods or drinks containing vitamin C when you serve iron-rich foods. (Breakfast cereals and legumes are good sources of iron.)

From a distance

Keeping in touch with your toddler grandchild

If your grandchild lives near enough for you to see him regularly, keeping in touch is fairly easy. But today it is a rare child who has four grandparents within easy reach. And although modern transportation is fast and efficient, few people have the time and money to simply drop everything whenever they want to see their grandchildren.

When your grandchild is young, you will have to rely on his parents to help keep up the contact. But if they lead busy lives or your relationship with them is not good, communication may be difficult. If you feel you are losing touch with your grandchild, mention this to his parents and discuss ways in which the situation can be improved.

Try to do so without acrimony or getting upset. The parents may have no idea how

Almost all children love using the telephone from a very early age. If you can think of ways to make your calls extra special for your grandchild, so much the better. You could, for example, sing him a nursery rhyme or get your dog to bark a greeting. On special occasions, consider reading him a short story.

you feel or they may have problems you are unaware of. Be prepared to be the one who makes the greater effort to keep in touch, especially when your grandchild is young.

Fortunately, new means of communication make keeping in touch easier than it was a generation ago. Communication will of course become much easier as your grandchild grows older and is able to write, telephone, or visit by himself (see pp. 108–109 and 122–23).

Telephoning

Talking on the telephone is one of the easiest and quickest ways to maintain contact with your grandchild. As soon as he is old enough, set aside a regular time each week or month when you make a special telephone call to your grandchild only, rather than including him as part of a family call.

Check with his parents about what day and time are best so that your calls are not at an inconvenient hour and do not conflict with bedtime. If you usually call at a regular time and know that you cannot make this one day, tell your grandchild or his parents in advance, to avoid disappointing him.

Don't be surprised, however, if your grandchild does not seem to respond to you when you talk. You cannot see each other, but he may well be nodding his head as he listens or simply not have enough words in his vocabulary to answer you fully. He is also likely to hold things up to the telephone for you to see—and it may take all your ingenuity to figure out what he is holding!

Video and tape recording

If you don't own a camcorder, consider renting one from time to time (see pp. 36–37). Include a special message for your grandchild on a video you are sending to your family or make one especially for him.

Many young children have good memories, and certainly by two and a half or three, your grandchild may remember a visit to your house. Show yourself doing something he particularly liked while he was with you—such as baking his favorite cake or visiting the park and feeding the ducks, or show him how "his" flowers are progressing in the garden.

If he has never seen your home, make him a video tour of your house and yard, showing him the room where he will sleep if he comes to visit. And ask his parents to reciprocate by sending you an occasional video of him too.

Make audiocassettes regularly, and be sure to send a special message for his birthday or for a festive occasion, such as Christmas. Tell him what you have been doing, or what you will do when he comes to stay with you or you visit him. If you are confident, record some songs for him. Ask if he can sing or talk into a tape for you to listen to as well.

Making pictures

If his parents have not been regularly sending photographs since he was a baby, ask them to resume now. Except for holidays and vacations, busy parents tend to take fewer pictures as their children grow, but encourage them to send a duplicate set of prints each time they complete a roll of film. Send him photographs of yourself and of your house and pets if you have any. Make a special photograph album of all family members, including your parents, to share with him as he gets older.

If you and his parents have access to a fax machine, send drawings and short letters and stories regularly. Ask his parents to fax you something he has done at

When you live far away, little gifts can make you seem more real to your grandchild. Vacation souvenirs are an obvious choice, but you can also send such simple, everyday items as a small drawing book and some thick crayons or a barrette.

preschool or nursery school each week. (This has the advantage that your grandchild keeps the original: some children can be very proprietary about their work.)

Send postcards addressed especially to your grandchild. Don't restrict yourself to vacation locations (although these will make a fascinating record for him when he is a little older), but include also pictures of the area where you live.

STORIES

All children love stories and from toddlerhood up respond to simple tales recounted with expression. Stories calm fractious children for a nap or bedtime and can relieve the monotony of a car journey for a short time. You can buy cassettes of well-loved children's stories, often with an accompanying book. But it is more personal—and more special for your grandchild—to record one or two favorites from a book of fairytales or other stories yourself.

Keep the stories short for the very young; you can begin to increase their complexity or record a chapter at a time when your grandchild is older. Send these tapes regularly.

If you enjoy storytelling (see pp. 94–95), you might record stories you have composed, personalizing them to your grandchild and including any special objects he likes to play with at your house.

CHAPTER FOUR

Preschoolers
3 to 5 years

In her preschool years, your grandchild begins to learn many of the socialization and independence skills she will need for the rest of her life. These are fascinating years, and experiencing the novelty of the world through her eyes can give you indescribable pleasure. Gradually, she will start to move away from her immediate family of parents and siblings in preparation for preschool or kindergarten. You can help in this transitional period by introducing her to new surroundings and experiences.

Because your grandchild is interested in everything around her and everything you do, the time you spend together can be tremendously rewarding. She will ask endless questions and be willing to learn anything you can teach her. This time can be as precious to you as your own child's preschool years. But now you probably have more time, more patience, and perhaps a more relaxed approach to child rearing. You also have the chance to do all those things you wish you had done with your own child but somehow never got around to!

What preschoolers like doing
Choosing games and activities to fill a young child's day

Children of three and four are constantly busy. They play, as they did when they were younger, but now their play is more considered and organized. Through play of all kinds, young children begin to develop the essential skills they will need in the real world; the rehearsal for life has begun in earnest.

Your job when your grandchild is with you is to provide her with the materials she needs to fuel her creative, imaginative, and physical abilities; then stand back and watch her take off.

Creative play

All young children love to draw and paint, and the ability to create recognizable pictures develops gradually as they get older. By the age of four, your grandchild will be able to draw people with bodies, heads, and the right number of limbs, for example. Art materials of all kinds are essential. She needs pencils, crayons, felt-tip pens (buy nontoxic, washable ones in case she decides to draw on the wallpaper), nontoxic, washable paints, large brushes, and plenty of paper, preferably in different colors. When she draws a picture for you, always praise it. If you don't recognize what it is, suggest she tell you about it rather than asking "What's that?"

Making collages is also popular. Save catalogs and brochures with lots of pictures for her to cut out and paste onto sheets of paper. She may do some snipping with blunt, child-size scissors, but it's unlikely she will be able to follow a straight line. If she gets frustrated, encourage her to tear out the picture carefully instead.

Your grandchild will be proud if the pictures she has created for you are displayed on your bulletin board or a cabinet door or stuck with a magnet to the refrigerator when she comes to call. An even better idea is to keep a record of her artistic development by saving her drawings and paintings and storing them in a special loose-leaf folder. You will enjoy looking at them together, and she will be encouraged to make more special pictures for you.

You may recall from when you were bringing up your own children how things you had previously regarded as junk suddenly became valuable playthings. Save cereal and egg boxes,

Babies often discard a new toy in favor of the box it came in, but by the time your grandchild is three, a box has even more play potential. Don't throw away the cartons in which new household appliances are delivered. In no time at all she will convert them into a house, car, store, spaceship, boat, castle, or countless other things.

spools and shoe boxes, scraps of yarn and plastic drinking straws so that when your grandchild comes she has a wealth of things to sort, cut, glue, and assemble. It is fascinating to see what a young child can create out of the most unlikely material.

Imaginative play

Three- and four-year-olds are beginning to sort out the difference between the world of the imagination and the real world. One way they do this is through role play—taking on a different persona in order to find out how it feels to be mother, father, teacher, doctor, nurse, or any of the other people they meet in their daily life. The particularly satisfying part of "let's pretend" for your grandchild is that she has control over the actions of the adult person she has become, rather than having the adult organize her, as in real life.

A large selection of dress-up clothes is a wonderful way to keep a child of this age occupied for hours. Your grandchild will be used to ready-made outfits from nursery school (although if you are handy with a sewing machine, you can make costumes more or less on demand). But it's just as much fun for her to dress up in your old petticoat, nightgown, vest or hat.

With a bead necklace and an adult-size purse or briefcase for props, a little girl can instantly become "mommy." She will copy her parent's mannerisms and tone of voice and be very, very serious. It can be highly amusing to see your own adult child through the eyes of the next generation, but be sure to laugh with, rather than at, your grandchild. You may also learn a few things about your family's life that you weren't aware of.

Of course, dressing up at this age is also about fantasy play, pretending to be the people your grandchild knows through nursery rhymes, television programs, and her books. Curtains, especially those in heavy fabrics such as velvet, make wonderful cloaks for a pretend king or queen (old

Face painting gives you a chance to practice creating a "picture" in a new medium, but it can also be a valuable prop in fantasy play, helping you to become cats in the backyard, tigers in the jungle, or clowns at the circus.

bath towels are a good substitute). An old lace curtain can transform your granddaughter into a princess (or a bride). Add belts, necklaces, earrings, combs, discarded eyeglasses—preferably with the lenses removed—and a tiara or crown. Scarves and any other strips of material, the flimsier and shinier the better, are also useful additions to the dress-up box.

Dressing up should be as entertaining an activity for boys as it is for girls. There's no need to become anxious if your little grandson wants to wear a satin nightgown or to deck himself in ropes of beads. Like their sisters, little boys enjoy the tactile experiences of satin and velvet. With play of this sort, you are laying the foundations for later drama sessions, when children can act out favorite fairy tales and nursery rhymes. Don't force this, but be ready to follow your grandchild's lead when the time comes.

Finally, dressing up is even more fun if you can provide a full-length mirror so that fashionable creations can be examined from every angle. And if you have one with folding side panels, so much the better.

What preschoolers like doing

The right setting

Satisfactory role play requires an appropriate setting—"mommies and daddies" is invariably played in a "home corner," for example, but this can be simply a rug or cushions in the corner of the room. Ready-made play furniture can be too realistic, thereby restricting its uses and curtailing your grandchild's chance for imaginative play. Playhouses are attractive and have their place, but your grandchild will manage just as well with a sheet or bedspread stretched over two dining chairs. This also makes a great den or tent.

Playing store is another favorite game, largely because shopping is one of your grandchild's everyday experiences. A board balanced on two chairs makes an excellent counter. You will also need items to sell, a bag, and some money; use small coins,

Play structures do not need to be particularly high for children to practice their physical skills. The most important factor is that a piece of equipment offer plenty of opportunity to develop different skills, such as climbing, swinging, and balancing.

foreign currency left over from a vacation, or make your own coins from cardboard circles covered with foil. Encourage your grandchild to make her own bills, and add a toy cash register for authenticity.

The easiest store to re-create is a supermarket stocked with cans and boxes from your pantry, but it is possible to "sell" almost anything. You will probably be expected to play both customer and storekeeper in turn to prolong the game.

There is great learning potential in playing restaurant or office. For a restaurant you'll need a table and chairs—preferably child-size—some play food, and a pad on which to scribble orders. Plan the menus and set the table. Then, along with the teddy bears and dolls, take your place and give your grandchild your order. Again, be prepared to reverse roles.

An office can be brought to life with old calendars, check stubs, forms, and brochures. And, of course, a toy telephone is a must.

Being helpful

Preschoolers are naturally helpful and happy to do household tasks that adults label chores. Remove any small or valuable knickknacks, then give your grandchild a dustcloth and let her get to work. She will happily sweep the floor, help you hang out the washing, and sort the dry laundry. She may enjoy setting the table, which will also help her counting skills. When you go to the supermarket, let her select goods and put them in the cart for you. This might slow your progress but it will give her pleasure. Small responsibilities such as these help to build self-esteem.

Outdoor play

If you have a backyard—and especially if you have several grandchildren—you may want to buy equipment to help them expend some of their physical energy when they come to see you. When considering a

Playing store is more than great role play. It also helps your grandchild to develop early math skills through counting coins, making change, and handing you—and any other customers—the right number of items.

Outdoor play in summer is incomplete without a wading pool or a sandbox. An inflatable wading pool is easy to store when it is not in use; if you provide a sandbox in your yard, keep it covered between play sessions so that it isn't used by squirrels, cats, birds, or raccoons. Scoops, rakes, buckets, and other equipment can be stored inside.

Keep hoops and a jump rope or two with which to devise an obstacle course. A large cardboard box makes an ideal prop; open-ended on its side, it makes a great tunnel to crawl through or hide in.

Talking

Above all, preschoolers love talking, and as a grandparent, you may have more time to listen and more patience to answer her seemingly endless questions than anyone else. Don't become unnecessarily alarmed if she gives some vivid details about what mommy and daddy do at home—make allowances for a lively imagination.

piece of equipment, look for an activity center with a climbing frame, a slide, bars to swing on, and a tunnel to crawl through.

It is natural to feel alarmed as you watch your grandchild scale the equipment, but children gain confidence by being allowed to test their abilities. Praise her enthusiasm, rather than worrying about potential hazards. If she is reluctant to climb and slide, don't force her. Children do vary enormously in the ages at which they acquire physical skills.

You may prefer equipment that can be packed away when your grandchild is not with you. If so, look for something that can be assembled easily. Since repeated erecting and dismantling may make bolts and screws loose, make a thorough inspection each time the equipment is used.

If you are a skilled carpenter, a treehouse is a good idea for older preschoolers as long as you have a suitable tree on which to build. A low platform may be more suitable than one high in the branches in case your grandchild is reluctant to climb down (or wants you to climb up with her). Add a safety rail and some kind of cover, such as a tarpaulin, and your grandchild will have hours of fun tucked away inside, whatever the weather outside.

HANDY TIPS

- Store felt-tip pens in jars with lids to keep them from drying out.

- Use a kitchen flatware tray to store art supplies and keep them separate.

- Clear a low shelf in one of your kitchen cabinets for a collection of empty boxes and cans so your grandchild has easy access to supplies for playing store.

- Your grandchild will need an apron to protect her clothes from paint and glue. An old shirt worn back to front is a good alternative to purchased coveralls.

- Plastic stackable crates are ideal for storing playthings in the garage, shed, or attic when they are not needed.

Toys for preschoolers

Choosing gifts that complement your grandchild's developing skills

Preschool children can make excellent use of homemade items (see pp. 76–79), so there is no need to buy lots of toys and games for when your grandchild comes to play—or to stay—at your house. There will be times, however, when you want to buy something special—for a birthday or Christmas gift, or as a particular gift to mark an extended stay. And if two or more children are coming to visit, you may need to increase your toy collection so that you have enough variety to keep them interested.

Before buying any toy, but especially for a preschooler, check the recommended age range on the box. If you find something that is technically "too old," but you think your grandchild will love it, be guided by your instincts. Some children develop skills in certain areas much more quickly than others. If you are planning to buy an expensive item, ask her parents if it is appropriate and what she has already. Near or exact duplications are a sure recipe for tears, particularly on a special occasion, such as a birthday.

The chart opposite gives ideas for toys suitable for three- to five-year-olds and indicates their developmental value. Keep an open mind when choosing gifts—some boys enjoy pushing toys and animals around in doll carriages, and girls can be as adept with construction kits as their brothers.

TYPE OF TOY

Creative
These toys and materials allow children to express themselves. Many also encourage manipulative skills.

Manipulative
These toys let children practice moving their hands. Many also encourage spatial awareness.

Imaginative
These are props that allow children to be someone else for a time.

Outdoor
This is a self-evident category, but don't forget that some indoor equipment can be taken outside—use bath toys in the wading pool, for example, and plastic kitchen cups and strainers in the sandbox.

Technological
This category covers everything from toys that encourage simple math and spelling games to interactive computer games.

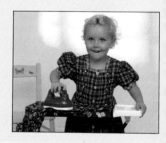

TOY CHOICES

IMPORTANCE

Crayons, felt-tip pens, paint box and brushes, chalks, easel, coloring books, pads of different-colored paper or rolls of paper for the easel; modeling clay; face paints; musical instruments—tambourines, drums, castanets, xylophones.

Children can explore various media and figure out the differences between them. These toys will also help their observational skills: observation is a key skill in learning to read.

Construction sets of all kinds (many offer opportunity for expansion as children get older); beads and strings for threading; sewing cards; jigsaw puzzles with large pieces; miniature tool kits.

Without the ability to manipulate small objects, everyday life would be almost impossible. Manipulative skills are vital for most daily tasks, from holding a pencil to fastening a button.

Tea sets; miniature household equipment, such as ironing board and iron, dustpan and brush; baby doll, crib, doll's house and furniture; cash register, play groceries; dress-up clothes—doctor's and nurse's uniforms plus toy first-aid kit, hats and helmets (firefighter, police officer); toy camera, binoculars, telephone.

Pretending to be somebody different is the first step in learning how others feel. Until she can do this, a child has no concept of why hurting someone else is so bad, nor can she relate to characters in stories, such as sharing Goldilocks' surprise when the bears find her.

Miniature tools, wheelbarrow; jump ropes, hoops, balls; sandbox, pails, shovel; wading pool and water-play equipment—containers, scoops, and water wheels; swing, activity center; tricycle, scooter, roller skates.

Outdoors, children can use their boundless energy and make more mess and noise than most of us can cope with indoors. Most outdoor equipment also encourages physical skills—running, climbing, balancing.

There is a wealth of preschool programs on the market—some excellent, others indifferent. If you are not up-to-date on new software, check magazine reviews or ask in computer stores, and learn alongside your grandchild.

Learning how new technology works is an important part of primary education; familiarity with a keyboard and mouse is useful; computer games help children to learn prereading skills, counting, and problem solving.

Then and now:

Preschool education

A three-year-old may seem young to spend time in a learning environment. But preschool education is extremely valuable in developing children's social and intellectual skills.

THEN

Like school, preschool groups were once more formal, with all children engaged in the same "learning" activities (above); today more emphasis is placed on play and self-motivation (above right).

If you believe that a young child's place is in the home with her mother or another caregiver until she is legally required to go to kindergarten, you may feel a few pangs on hearing that your three- or four-year-old grandchild is to start attending preschool or nursery school. Particularly if your own children stayed at home with you, with plenty of activities to occupy them and lots of visits from friends, you may feel that a more structured environment is unnecessary for your grandchild. It may help you to know, therefore, that preschool education has been thoroughly evaluated over the last few decades, and it is now widely accepted that almost all children benefit from attending preschool or a nursery for at least a few hours a day.

One long-term study in Michigan, for example, followed more than 100 children. Half experienced a high-quality preschool program, and half stayed at home. The results were published in 1993: those children who had participated in the preschool program did better at school, needed less remedial teaching, stayed at school longer, and were more likely to go on to higher education.

As in other studies, this concentrated on children from poor families who, it was believed, did not get enough stimulation at home, so the preschools took over part of the parental role. Such studies largely ignored those children at the other end of the social spectrum, whose parents could afford the fees of fashionable private establishments, and those children who came between these extremes—the majority—who stayed home until they were of school age. The playgroup movement, started in Britain in the 1960s, gave more children the advantages of preschool, and the idea has spread through most of the developed world: preschool education is now available to most families.

The idea that preschools might usurp the parents' role is no longer commonly held. Far from supplanting parents, preschool

NOW

teachers and other staff work in partnership with parents—always the child's first educators—so that they are informed about and involved in their children's progress at all times.

The preschool experience

Preschools and nurseries give children the opportunity to develop self-reliance and to learn to cooperate with adults and with children of their own age. They offer equipment, toys, and games that may not be available at home and plenty of space to play—an important factor for those who live in crowded conditions. Some preschool experience also makes the transition from home to school easier. The prime objective is not to teach reading, writing, and early math—although a child who wants to develop these skills will not be held back—but to provide the groundwork so that these skills become easier to learn once a child starts school.

If your grandchild attends a day-care center, she may also be receiving some preschool education, perhaps spending part of her day engaged in a variety of structured activities. But she should still have time for free play and naps, as if she were at home.

PRESCHOOL EDUCATORS

Friedrich Froebel

Although he died in 1852, many of the ideas of Froebel, the German educational philosospher who established the first kindergarten ("children's garden") are still in use today. Froebel believed that play was a serious, significant activity for young children and in 1826 wrote "The focus of play at this age is the core of the whole future."

Maria Montessori

The first Montessori nursery, the Casa dei Bambini ("children's house"), opened in 1907 for children living in the industrial areas of Rome. Montessori believed she could compensate for the experiences children missed by not living in the country or in a house with a backyard. She emphasized the child's interest in the process of doing rather than in the finished product and believed that children should be taught to do tasks for themselves. The equipment she developed—such as "dressing frames" to help children learn how to fasten buttons and tie laces—is still widely used today. She also placed great value on everyday skills, such as setting the table and looking after plants and animals, and believed that children should learn self-discipline as early as possible.

Rudolf Steiner

Steiner founded his first school in 1919 in Stuttgart, Germany, for the children of workers in the Waldorf Astoria cigarette factory. In such schools children between the ages of 4 and 18 are grouped according to mental rather than actual age. The youngest children are encouraged to act spontaneously, and emphasis is placed on developing the artistic and spiritual sides of their nature as well as intellectual and practical skills.

David Weikart

Weikart, an American, developed the High Scope curriculum in the 1980s. This is based on the belief that children learn best when they are given a choice of what they do. Children participate in a plan-do-review sequence in which they are expected to see each task through, then discuss with a teacher what they have achieved. This method encourages decision-making at an early age to develop the child's self-confidence.

When a sibling comes along

Your special role in making a firstborn child secure

It is often difficult for grown-ups to understand the depth of children's feelings on hearing that they are to have a brother or sister. Consider the situation in adult terms: a man who has been happily married for several years announces that he is bringing a new wife into the house. He assures his first wife that it will make no difference to their relationship, and he will continue to love her as much as ever. Rare is the wife who would be happy with such reassurances. A child feels much the same. She finds it difficult to believe that she won't be displaced in her parents' affections by the new arrival.

Jealousy of a new baby is normal; very few children show no negative reactions at all. But there is a great deal you can do to alleviate possible problems by helping her parents to prepare your grandchild for the new baby and by being a friend and ally in the weeks after the birth.

The pregnancy

One mistake people often make is to talk about the impending birth too soon. Children under five have little concept of time and become impatient if they are told what is going to happen eight or nine months before the event. Discuss with the parents when it is reasonable to start talking about the new arrival. It is often best to wait until the baby is becoming physically evident, although even then young children do not necessarily notice that mom is looking different.

Refrain from talking about the baby as a new playmate; your grandchild will be bitterly disappointed when the tiny bundle can't immediately join in her games. Find out from the parents the terms in which they have described what is happening and answer questions as honestly as possible. The days of fobbing children off with stories about storks are long gone. There are a number of good books that can help children understand how a baby grows in the womb (see pp. 210–11).

Avoid talking about difficulties with the pregnancy, however minor, within earshot of your grandchild. Children can misinterpret what is said, and, unable to fully understand the implications of problems, they may become unnecessarily anxious. As the date of delivery gets nearer, and perhaps her mother gets increasingly tired and uncomfortable, take your

A baby doll may help to get your grandchild used to the idea of a new baby in the house. It can also help you prepare her for the fact that babies are not able to play the moment they arrive, but spend most of the time asleep.

grandchild shopping for items for the new baby. Even a three-year-old can help choose something to wear and a special "welcome to the family" gift for the baby. If you can, make it a treat for her, too, by having lunch out or going to see a movie.

After the birth

Once the baby has been born, in addition to helping with the extra chores, put your relationship with the baby on hold for a few weeks in order to spend as much time as possible with your elder grandchild, giving her the attention she may feel is lacking from her parents. While her mother is in the hospital and in the first few days after the birth, it may be best for your grandchild to remain at home. If she comes to stay with you, she may feel more rejected or worry about what is happening in her absence; on the other hand, staying at your house may make her feel especially grown up, so play the situation by ear.

It may help if you are on hand when your grandchild first meets her new brother or sister. The baby should be lying in a crib or in the arms of another person, so the mother is free to give the older child a cuddle. At a time when most presents will be for the mother and new arrival, this is a good occasion to give your firstborn grandchild a gift of her own.

If you live close by and her parents are willing, be available for a few days so you can be on hand to give the older child your full attention. A new mother may find it difficult to be sure that your grandchild's bathtime is not cut short and that a bedtime story is uninterrupted by the baby's crying, for example. If it is not feasible for you to be around in the evening, help with another part of the daily routine—getting the child to preschool in the morning, for example, going with her to the park, or snuggling together to watch a favorite TV program.

However sensitively you and her parents handle this period, be prepared for some difficult behavior. Jealousy of a new baby is

Expect your grandchild to have mixed reactions toward his new sibling. A child of three or four has no way of knowing what to expect and cannot understand that you and his parents can love the new baby without loving him less.

likely to arise whatever your grandchild's age. Older children are often more difficult than younger ones, simply because they have had their parents to themselves for so much longer and thus have greater cause to resent the disruption to their routines.

You may experience some rejection. Despite your efforts, there will be times when only her parents' attention is good enough. If she regresses from toilet training for a while, offer to help with extra laundry. Go along with her wishes if she wants a bottle or feeding cup—it is understandable for her to think a baby's life is more appealing than hers at the moment. Help correct this misconception by emphasizing all the things she can do and the activities you can share which the baby can't. Arrange a couple of "grown-up" excursions to reinforce this.

When a sibling doesn't come along

Being positive about the prospect of having only one grandchild

It is not unusual today for people to choose to have only one child. If your adult child and his or her partner have made this decision, you will have to learn to live with it, however much you want more grandchildren. Although it is acceptable in some cultures for grandparents to pressure their children to enlarge the family, if your grandchild's parents do not talk openly about their plans for a second baby, it is generally wise to resist the temptation to ask whether they plan to have one.

There are many reasons why couples decide to restrict the size of their family. Some wish to have the experience of being parents, but accept that the necessity of a career break or prohibitive childcare costs make having more than one child unworkable. Despite the apparent ease with which a first child is often conceived, some couples can develop medical problems that make having a second child difficult. And, while most of us abhor the idea of the state imposing limits on family size, many people do limit their family to a single child because of concerns about overpopulation. Whatever the reason, throughout the Western world the one-child family is becoming more common.

If you have had several children yourself, you may find it particularly sad that one has chosen not to replicate his or her own childhood. Don't look for implied criticism of the way you raised your family, but accept that your child wants something different. Eldest daughters of large families, in particular, may feel that they have done enough mothering already and may not wish to have several children of their own.

If your only grandchild is a daughter, her parents may feel under pressure to produce a boy—in some cultures, the birth of a male child is welcomed more enthusiastically than that of a female. You, too, may feel that a family is incomplete without a "son and heir" or someone to continue the family

In her preschool years, one of the most important things you can do for a grandchild with no siblings is to broaden her social circle and give her a wider experience of people. Since only children are used to playing alone, they may have difficulty in relating to others and learning how to share. By helping this way you can play a pivotal role in preparing your grandchild for the later demands of school.

Without an older sibling to show him how it is done, an only child may happily spend time working things out for himself. Join in his games if he asks you to, but be prepared for him to amuse himself for quite long periods.

name. In these days of equality, however, many women choose to keep—and give their children—their family name.

If you suspect that there is a medical reason why another child has not appeared, don't pry. The parents are most likely desperately upset that they seem unable to conceive a longed-for second child. If it is your daughter who is having fertility problems, she may confide in you anyway when she feels the time is right, and you can offer her love and support then. If your relationship with your daughter-in-law is less open, she may feel embarrassed to discuss such matters with you. It is important to respect her wish for privacy. Equally important, don't always assume that it is the woman who is having problems—and accept the fact that your son or son-in-law is even less likely to want to discuss a fertility problem with you.

Your special role

However disappointed you feel, be positive about the advantages an only child has. Your only grandchild will never have to compete for her parents' attention or feel that she has any rival for their love. She will never experience the feelings of rejection and jealousy, however unfounded, when a little brother or sister comes along. Only children, along with firstborns, tend to be high achievers at school and work, demonstrating strong leadership skills. Used to playing alone, they are likely to be more self-sufficient and inventive, qualities that stand them in good stead in later life. They also tend to relate well to grown-ups, since they live in a family of adults.

Your only grandchild may, however, be self-centered, find it difficult to share, and experience an enduring sense of loneliness.

She may also be hindered by her parents' reluctance to accept her independence, or pushed into behaving like a little adult before she is ready. Only children can also make enormous demands on their parents: an only child expects to have constant attention, with the result that parents have little time to be alone together. Parents, in turn, can make too many demands on an only child, investing all their hopes and aspirations in her.

As a grandparent, you can take positive action to counteract some of this pressure. Because your grandchild's immediate family is limited, contact with other relatives becomes very important. Cousins, particularly those of a similar age, can be extra-special to an only child and are an excellent substitute for brothers and sisters.

If you have several grandchildren, you may be able to arrange social events for all of them. If cousins are not available, invite a neighbor's child when your grandchild comes to visit or team up with another grandparent for play dates and excursions. Whatever you plan, her parents will probably be delighted if you take your grandchild off their hands for a while and allow them time to themselves.

Shared skills: cooking
Introducing your grandchild to preparing food

It is surprising how much a preschool child can do in the kitchen—under your supervision, of course—and how many new skills she can acquire in the process. To begin with, you are laying one of the foundations for independent living as a young adult. In addition, the measuring involved in cooking is a good introduction to math, and the way in which heat transforms basic ingredients into different shapes and textures foreshadows later experiments in science.

Working together in the kitchen also offers an opportunity to discuss what constitutes healthy food and the importance of thinking carefully about what we eat. And, perhaps even more valuable, giving your grandchild small responsibilities will boost her self-confidence. It is for these reasons that cooking is a favorite activity in preschool and kindergarten.

Allow plenty of time for your cooking sessions so that you both feel relaxed. If your grandchild takes a long time to complete a task, resist the temptation of taking over or hurrying her along. And leave time at the end of any session for her to help you to wash the dishes and clean up, leaving the kitchen in perfect order. You may even be able to instill a habit that will last a lifetime.

What to make
There are a lot of simple dishes that you and your grandchild can make together. Anything that involves cookie dough is bound to delight her. At first, she may treat it like play dough, so make the point that if the cookie dough is to become something edible, it needs special handling. Children as young as three love rolling it out—buy your grandchild a small rolling pin and plenty of cutters of all shapes and sizes. An

Clean hands that are not too hot and sticky are important when you are making cookie dough. Encourage your grandchild to wash and dry them frequently. Once you have rolled the dough out to your satisfaction, cut it into any shape you like and add flavorings and toppings.

As an alternative to cookie dough, try bread dough, which even very young children can knead, divide, and shape.

Spending time in the kitchen does not necessarily have to mean cooking at every session. Preparing foods and decorations that are an integral part of a holiday—such as the pumpkin at Halloween—is another activity that you can share with your grandchild.

older child can make jam tarts almost all by herself, although you should put them into the oven and take them out, and warn her not to take a bite while the jelly is hot.

For special occasions, you can roll out and shape marzipan. If you have some small cutters and different food colorings, you can produce exciting-looking candy that makes an ideal gift for your grandchild to share with her parents and friends.

Preparing her own food
Children take great pleasure in making their own desserts. Powdered instant puddings are a good choice. Or cut up some fresh fruit for your grandchild to mix with plain yogurt or ice cream. Put some rainbow sprinkles on top for a special treat.

Making Jell-O is a satisfying occupation as long as it is you who pours the hot liquid into the molds. Traffic-light Jell-O is very popular. Make green gelatin and pour it into a large mold. When it has set, add orange gelatin, then repeat with red. Try to make all the layers the same thickness.

Your grandchild can also play an important part in cake-making sessions. She can sift flour, whisk eggs, and mix ingredients (do the final whisk yourself to make sure everything is evenly blended). She will also love frosting the cake once it is baked and adding other finishing touches.

Fostering good food habits
A child who is reluctant to eat vegetables or salads may attack them with relish if she has helped prepare them. Something as simple as popping the peas out of the pod may encourage her to eat them, especially if she has only tried frozen ones before.

Preparing a basic salad—washing and tearing lettuce and arranging tomatoes, cucumber, and hard-boiled eggs—is also within your grandchild's capabilities. She can also scrape potatoes and carrots for you to chop into small pieces to make soup.

Another idea that helps to encourage healthy eating is to let her scoop out the insides of baked potatoes and mix them with tuna, cottage cheese, or scrambled eggs, then return the fillings to their skins. Allowing her to arrange the food on plates may also make her more willing to eat the finished results enthusiastically.

Regional specialties
Spending time in the kitchen with your grandchild also gives you the opportunity to introduce her to your culture's culinary specialties. It is a sad fact that convenience foods have meant the loss of many traditional ways of cooking and national staple dishes. You can begin to familiarize your grandchild with the special vegetables and fruits essential to ethnic meals or let her sniff and taste the spices and herbs she may not encounter in her everyday eating. By passing on this culinary knowledge to your grandchild, you may be helping to restore enthusiasm for traditional dishes.

Pacing yourself
Having a positive attitude toward physical limitations

If you found the physical demands your grandchild made as a baby and toddler too much to cope with, be reassured that older children do not require the concentrated care that younger ones need.

If you became a grandparent later in life and have less stamina than you once did, or have a disability or chronic illness, you can still do lots of things with your grandchild when the two of you spend time together. Although you may be unable to take your grandchild to the playground or kick a ball around with her in the backyard, you still have much to offer. You can give time and interest—both of which are invaluable.

It is important that you be aware of your limitations and be prepared to admit when you feel tired. Call a halt and admit when you need to take a break. Even young children are capable of understanding that you are not as energetic as they are or that you have to rest. They will probably be kind and sympathetic. Your grandchild may ask questions about your health, particularly if you are in a wheelchair or have to spend a lot of time in bed. Be as honest as possible without making her unduly anxious. A close relationship with a disabled or elderly person may make her a more tolerant and caring adult.

Remember, too, that time with a child does not have to mean endless physical activity. With a little thought and planning, you can provide your grandchild with lots of stimulating activities you both enjoy.

Quiet activities
Reading together is obviously one of the most accessible activities if your problem is mobility, but if your sight is not good, invest in a cassette player and start collecting tapes of children's stories and

Being outdoors with your grandchild does not have to put undue physical strain on you. Depending on the time of year, suggest he hunt for pine cones, acorns, or walnuts and bring them to show you. See if he can find the first flower in spring (he must not pick it, but should call you to come and look at it), or how many different leaves he can pick up from the ground.

rhymes. Don't play the stories straight through, but stop the tape every so often to discuss what is happening and give her time to ask questions, as you would if you were looking at a book together. If you are playing a selection of songs and rhymes, make sure you join in. Even better, sing together and record yourselves—children love hearing a recording of their own voice.

You can also use a cassette player to introduce your grandchild to some of your favorite music. Ask her to tell you how the music makes her feel, to enhance her understanding. You can extend this by drawing happy, sad, angry, and worried faces and asking her to point out which one best suits the mood of the music.

Perennial favorites

The memory game Put, say, six to eight different items on a tray—household objects are fine. Ask your grandchild to look carefully, then cover them with a cloth and see how many she can remember.

This can be extended by asking her to turn her back while you remove something. She then has to look again and decide what is missing. She will enjoy it if you play as well, even if you have to pretend that you have forgotten what was there. Being able to memorize is an important prereading skill, so this game is not only fun but also aids learning.

Make a feely bag Hide lots of different unbreakable objects in a fabric bag—a pillowcase will do—and let her feel them and try to guess what each shape is.

Board and card games By the age of three, most children can manage a simple card or board game, although their concentration varies. Don't expect a preschooler to spend more than 20 minutes playing this type of game. Old favorites—Snap, Old Maid, Go Fish, for example—that have entertained

generations of children work well with young children, so you don't need to spend money on apparently more sophisticated modern options. It is, however, worth buying good-quality games with thick cards and bright, clear illustrations that will stand repeated use.

Jigsaws The age guide on a jigsaw puzzle is approximate, so ascertain for yourself which level of difficulty is appropriate for your grandchild. Jigsaw puzzles are valuable for developing manipulative skills, but as many children loathe them as love them. Be guided by your grandchild's response.

Letting off steam

Of course small children can't be expected to sit still for long periods, and your grandchild will sometimes feel the need to let off steam. This should not be a problem, since there are physical games you can play while sitting in your armchair.

A ball of crumpled newspaper is a good substitute for the real thing and is less of a threat to the knickknacks. Make several, place an empty basket in a strategic position, and see how many you can get in while sitting together on the couch. Move the basket farther away, or ask her to do it, as her skill improves.

Alternatively, line up some empty plastic bottles on the floor and see how many you can knock down by rolling a foam rubber ball along the floor. Put your grandchild in charge of going to stand them up again.

When she tires of these games and still has energy to spare, bring out the cassette player and tapes again and play Statues. Explain that she can dance, skip, and jump as much as she wants, but she must freeze as soon as you turn the music off—a game that enables her to let off steam and you to keep her exuberance under control.

Books for young children

Choosing and reading books with your preschool grandchild

Preschool children need access to books of all kinds—stories, poetry, and nonfiction titles that explain the world around them. You have probably been sharing cloth and board books with your grandchild since her babyhood, but at around the age of three or four, children learn that books are both a means of communication and a way to extend their knowledge and imagination. In addition to encouraging your grandchild to want to read, a good storybook can help to develop social, personal, and language skills.

Books for the young traditionally combine pictures—which should enhance a story and be full of detail to encourage observational skills—with minimal text. Your grandchild will also enjoy alphabet books, picture word books, and those that involve some counting. Novelty books, such as those with pop-up pictures, lift-up flaps, pull-down tabs, or buttons that produce a sound when pressed, have lots of appeal because they involve anticipation and participation. Their drawback is that they are easily damaged and have to be handled with care.

Don't avoid stories that deal with subjects like starting school, illness, a new baby in the family, bullying, or even death. Buy or borrow these books from the library at appropriate times—they can be useful in helping a child to talk about any anxieties she may have.

Choose a book you like so that you can communicate your enthusiasm to your grandchild. Make sure it is appropriate to her age, too: it is easy for adults to get carried away by beautiful illustrations.

Reading with your grandchild

Always choose somewhere comfortable to share a book together. Most children prefer to sit on your lap or snuggle up close to you. Show your grandchild how to hold the book properly and to turn the pages in the correct order. Follow the sentences with your finger sometimes so that she learns which way language reads. Put some expression into your voice, or adopt a tone for each character. If she stops you while you are reading and wants to take over, let her. A young child can learn a favorite story by heart and want to feel grown up by "reading" it to you.

When a story is too long or complicated, she may fidget or be obviously uninterested. Put the book away for the time being and bring it out again in a few months' time. Resist the temptation to introduce a new book if your grandchild insists on

If you are reading to more than one child, make sure they are in close contact with you and can see the book clearly. Be prepared for even more discussion of the story than with only one child.

Novelty books get children interested in looking at and enjoying books; storybooks with colorful pictures are still popular choices, especially before bedtime.

an old favorite. The familiarity that you may find boring on the umpteenth repetition gives your grandchild a wonderful feeling of security—she will even enjoy reciting parts of the story that she knows by heart as you read. A favorite book is almost an alternative to a security blanket. If you have kept some of your own child's books, introduce them, too. They may look old-fashioned and tattered, but your grandchild will love having a book her parent enjoyed, and you will like the sense of continuity that reading it brings.

Sharing books and stories with your grandchild can be one of the most pleasurable activities of your times together. By supplying her with books, you are giving the tools that will encourage her to become a reader herself. And if she sees her family enjoying books—and other reading material, such as newspapers and magazines—she, too, is likely to develop a lifelong love of reading.

HOW TO CHOOSE A BOOK

Ask yourself the following questions before you select a book for your grandchild:

• Does it have an attractive overall appearance? A dull-looking book will not inspire a child to examine it more closely.

• Read a few pages. Does it seem well written?

• Are the illustrations clear and detailed?

• Are the story and the language used appropriate for her age?

• Will your grandchild be able to sympathize with or relate to the characters?

• Does it reflect the world she lives in or teach about other lifestyles and cultures?

• Does it offer positive images? Are the people depicted from a variety of cultures? Are the characters stereotyped—are the girls and women shown in passive roles, for example, while the boys and men are active?

• Does the story involve lots of repetition? Children love familiarity and the sense of control given by knowing what comes next.

Storytelling

Maintaining and reviving the oral tradition

Telling stories to your grandchild, as opposed to reading a story, will enthrall her and offers more intimacy than almost any other shared activity. If you hold her close to you as you talk, there is nothing to disturb your concentration—not even the turning of a page. This can be particularly soothing when she is tired or fractious, since telling your own stories allows you to adapt themes and storylines to suit the mood or the moment. It is also entirely personal—nobody else will ever tell your grandchild the tale you tell in the way you tell it.

Storytelling may come easily to you, particularly if you are from a culture with a strong oral tradition and can easily recall the tales you were told by your parents and grandparents. Nevertheless, your own child may have shown little interest in this time-honored skill: competition from television has often been unbeatable. There are signs, however, that this is changing as more people of all ages become disillusioned with

the passive nature of watching television and seek a leisure pursuit that allows them to interact with other people and to share experiences. Storytelling groups are becoming more popular, and a professional group may visit your grandchild's school at some time.

Don't feel that you need special talent to enchant your grandchild with your stories. You do not need great acting skills or special fluency, although it does help if you can attempt a few different "voices"—perhaps a gruff one for the bad guys or a high one for the princess or heroine.

Old favorites

If you don't have a specific cultural oral tradition on which to draw, think of the numerous fairy tales we all know by heart. Generations of children

When you tell a story, sit close and turn a prop around and around so that your grandchild can see it from all angles and appreciate its pivotal role in the story. If you are not using props, maintain eye contact so that you can gauge if the pace is flagging. A high level of skill is not necessary; more important is your enthusiasm for the tale you are weaving.

have enjoyed stories like "The Three Bears," "Cinderella," and "Little Red Riding Hood" and will continue to demand them. These stories are valuable because they involve basic concepts of good and evil and frequently present simple moral dilemmas that you can go on to discuss with your grandchild.

The great advantage of telling—as opposed to reading—a well-loved fairy tale is that you can adapt the story to suit your grandchild, omitting sections she might find frightening, changing the ending, or giving one of the characters her name to make it extra-interesting. These stories can develop with your grandchild's participation. Encourage her to think of different endings to traditional tales. What would have happened to Cinderella if Prince Charming hadn't found the slipper?

Small children also love to hear stories about your childhood and about when their own parents were young. These can be the simplest accounts of a vacation trip or a memorable birthday party. Such tales may well pass into your family's folklore and be handed down to your great-grandchildren some day.

Helping the story along

If you find it difficult to conjure up stories from memory or imagination, you can always use props. Stories about your own child's early years are easy to evoke by getting out the photograph album and talking about the people in the pictures and what they are doing. But other visual material can also stimulate stories. A book of famous works of art, for example, can prompt a conversation about the people featured and lead to your making up stories about them

and what they were doing before they were frozen in time by the artist. Choose paintings that appeal to you but can also be understood by a young child, such as landscapes, portraits, or still lifes of familiar objects.

If you prefer three-dimensional props, choose a couple of objects and weave a story around them. Keep the objects and stories simple to begin with—a shell may evoke a story about a girl finding it on the seashore and the magical sounds she hears inside it, for example—and make them more complicated as you gain confidence.

You could also consider using dolls or puppets as aids to your imagination. Ready-made puppets, although the result of someone else's imagination, can be useful. Choose hand or finger puppets—those on strings look appealing but are almost impossible to manipulate unless you are a skilled puppeteer. Finger puppets are easy to make at home, but there are other simple ways to create characters. Drawing faces on plain paper plates and taping a drinking straw or thin stick to the back gives your grandchild several puppets with which to act out a story as you tell it. She will also enjoy coloring the faces.

Don't feel self-conscious about acting out stories, it's a skill that is easily acquired and a young child is invariably an appreciative audience. You can have a lot of fun stretching your imagination this way and if you lose your direction at any point, you'll have a ready prompter on hand.

When to intervene

Identifying and reacting to signs of neglect or abuse

There will inevitably be times when you disagree with the way in which your grandchild is being brought up. You may think that her parents are too lax about table manners or too strict about bedtime. It is usually better to bite your tongue and accept that the parents have the right to set their own family agenda.

More serious, however, are situations that make you suspect that they are being overly harsh with the child. Perhaps they are physically cold with her, pushing her away when she wants a cuddle. Or they might seem to expect too much of her and be unreasonably irritated by aspects of her behavior. You might notice bruising or sores that can't be explained. Any of these observations could indicate that your grandchild is being emotionally or physically abused.

Even more unpalatable is the suspicion that your grandchild is being sexually abused, a term that covers inappropriate fondling and kissing through to full-scale penetration of her body, or being pressured or coerced into touching and fondling an adult in a sexual manner.

You would not be the first grandparent to find yourself in this situation. It is a sad fact that most abuse is carried out by someone known to the child, despite the emphasis we place on the danger of strangers. It also happens in families from all cultural and social backgrounds.

If you suspect that your grandchild is being neglected or abused, you cannot ignore it. Your first approach must be to inform her parents. If they are the culprits, they will no doubt deny responsibility, but if someone else is the perpetrator, you will have alerted them. If they cannot explain to your satisfaction what you have seen or heard, try enlisting the help of the other grandparents. They will be as concerned as you are, and you may be able to resolve the situation.

If the signs of neglect or abuse have become apparent since the birth of a new baby, it is possible that your

If your grandchild is being abused, you can help by being her ally. Abuse often thrives on secrecy, with the result that she may not tell you directly what is happening—she may be too young even to put into words what is going on. But her behavior and the way she reacts when she is with you may be enough to arouse, or confirm, your suspicions.

CASE HISTORY

My daughter Diane and three-year-old granddaughter, Louise, live a long way away and I don't see them often, so I was delighted when Louise came to stay while her mother was taking a course. She seemed a bright, if quiet, little girl. But one thing worried me: she had extensive bruising on her back, so bad that she flinched when I tried to dry her. And she was vague when I asked how it had happened.

I could hardly bear to think about it, but wondered if Diane had been hitting Louise. Her marriage had recently broken up, and she was stressed. She had taken on a full-time job and had had to find someone to care for Louise—I knew that she had been delighted when a neighbor who was also a professional sitter had agreed to look after her.

When Diane arrived to pick up Louise, I asked about the bruising. Diane said that the injuries had happened at the sitter's—another child had punched Louise. The sitter had promised that it wouldn't happen again. I was uneasy that such bullying appeared to be tolerated, and I sensed that Diane felt the same, but when I tried to push her further, she became angry and told me that I had no idea how difficult it was to find child-care. Being able to leave Louise a few doors away made things easy.

I knew that Diane had been too busy to do a great deal of research into child-care in her area and offered to return with her for a week or so and see if together we could find somewhere more suitable. To my relief, Diane agreed. I had a lovely time visiting daycare centers with Louise and was delighted when there was a place for her where the staff had been particularly friendly and taken a real interest in Louise. It cost more than the sitter, but I offered to pay a small sum into Diane's bank account every month to cover the difference, and Diane accepted. Louise has settled down well, and Diane is delighted with her progress.

We didn't challenge the sitter, which we regret—a few months ago she was charged with assaulting a little boy in her care.

If a normally outgoing child suddenly becomes withdrawn, she may have experienced some trauma. Ask her parents if they can explain her changed behavior.

daughter or daughter-in-law is suffering from postnatal depression; encourage her as strongly as you can to seek medical advice. If the parents have financial or marital problems and you suspect they might be taking out their frustration on their child, you may help by offering to babysit or have your grandchild to stay with you for a short time while they sort out their difficulties.

If you cannot resolve the problem in these ways, report your fears to your grandchild's doctor or the police—her health and happiness must be paramount.

The warning signs

Of neglect Dirty hair; unwashed clothes; dull skin lacking in luster; noticeable weight loss; body odor.

Of abuse Unexplained bruising and sores on her body.

Of sexual abuse Soreness around her genitals; refusal to let you wash and dry those parts of her body; precocious or inappropriate sexual behavior, like insisting on mouth-to-mouth kissing, or trying to put her tongue in your mouth when you kiss her.

CHAPTER FIVE

The Younger Schoolchild
5 to 8 years

In the years between five and eight, your grandchild takes one of the most significant steps of his life: he begins his formal education. School opens many doors for young children, broadening their view of the world, their social skills, and intellectual abilities almost beyond recognition in a few short months. If you are not in close contact with your grandchild, you may be surprised at how quickly his understanding of the world matures.

During these years your grandchild will become a fluent reader, be able to write you a legible, well-constructed story, and be able to do simple math. He will also have a host of questions about subjects of which your knowledge may be rusty or nonexistent. Equally important, he will become more independent—deciding when he wants to come to see you, for how long, and what he would like to do while he is with you.

Sharing the discoveries of these years with your grandchild can make this a hugely satisfying period in your relationship.

What 5- to 8-year-olds like doing

Fun games and activities for your young grandchild

School helps to strengthen children's concentration skills, with the result that once absorbed in an activity, your grandchild is likely to be happy with it for some time. This increased concentration means that you can make familiar games more difficult and means you can introduce some new ones as well. School will open his eyes to the world around him, building on his interest in everyday things, so that he will have information to share with you on every aspect of his world. In fact, simply talking with you is one of the activities your grandchild is likely to enjoy most.

Indoor activities

Five- to eight-year-olds retain their love of the familiar and like to watch a favorite video again and again. They will enjoy it even more if you are there to watch, too. Watching does not have to be passive (which is parents' major complaint about TV). Talk about the scenes you like (see if they differ from your grandchild's preferred sequences). Freeze-frame once or twice—not too often or he will get annoyed—and ask your grandchild to tell you why a character behaved in a certain way (to show you are as involved as he is). If you want to make the occasion special, pretend you are at the movies, make some popcorn and serve bottles or cartons of juice with straws.

As they practice writing and drawing, children make innumerable lists and write endless stories. When your grandchild comes to stay, provide plenty of paper and pens. Although writing is an individual activity,

Gardening instills in children a respect for the natural world, fosters a love of beauty, introduces the concept of life cycles, and makes them aware of the changing seasons.

he is likely to ask for lots of help with spelling. It's tempting to provide answers all the time, but at school some kinds of work are done without the use of dictionaries or teacher input, relying instead on educated guessing. You can do this by sounding out a word for your grandchild, or asking him how he thinks it should be spelled before you give him the answer.

The love of books you fostered in his earlier years will pay dividends now. He may want to show off his reading skill, which is a good idea, but he may get tired or bored if he has to read a long story. A way around this is for you to read one page and him the next. A trip to the library or bookstore to choose a book—perhaps to pick one to leave at your house for future trips—will also give him pleasure.

Now is a wonderful time to introduce your grandchild to some old-fashioned games. Some five- and six-year-olds can master checkers with a patient partner; Go Fish is still a popular card game; and word games, such as Scrabble for Juniors,

By this age, many children have the patience and dexterity to enjoy playing with model trains, helping to make station buildings, and choosing figures to complete a realistic scene.

are fun for all. Some children also like Monopoly Junior, Sorry, and Parchessi. If he didn't like them when he was younger, your grandchild may not start to like jigsaw puzzles now. But for those children who take to them, puzzles now provide great family fun. Dominoes is also entertaining.

Finally, children in this age group are constantly busy making or doing things. Many of the gift suggestions for craft kits on pp. 102–103 are not costly; they can even be improvised and your grandchild will love them.

The great outdoors

Playgrounds with rope ladders and tire swings come into their own at this age. Children have learned a little caution, so your grandchild is unlikely to be at the top of a rope ladder before you can stop him. Swings and slides are still fun for those at the younger end of the age group. In the park your grandchild will continue to enjoy activities from his preschool years, such as collecting leaves and pine cones. Introduce him to such

games as bowling (use a plastic beach set). Miniature golf is also good outdoor fun for family members of all ages.

Model-making is very popular with five- to eight-year-olds. If you have plenty of space, model airplanes are a good choice; and if you are a model-train enthusiast, this is the age when your grandchild is likely to become interested, if he is going to do so. It is a good idea to keep an eye out for local events, or local societies with a junior branch whose meetings you could attend.

During the early school years, children become very interested in the growth of living things, making gardening an ideal activity. If you don't have a yard, buy some quick-growing herbs that your grandchild can plant in a small planter. Or choose some indoor bulbs and help him plant them in time for a table display at Christmas, or whenever else your family gets together. If you have a yard, and your grandchild is a frequent visitor (or accepts help from you in his absence), give him a small plot that is his alone.

Look through books on flowers together to find suitable plants that will grow in your area. To avoid disappointment, suggest that he select the colors and leave the choice of varieties to you.

It's natural to want to let children win at board games, since they get so much pleasure from it. But remind them that there can be only one winner each time, and encourage a love of playing the game for its own sake, not simply in order to win.

Gifts for 5- to 8-year-olds

Birthdays, Christmas, and spur-of-the-moment purchases

Children develop rapidly once they start school, and their interests and ideas change under the burgeoning influence of their peers. This can be difficult if you are a long-distance grandparent; a child who is quite immature on one visit may seem very grown up on the next. All these factors can make choosing appropriate gifts tricky.

It helps if you keep in contact through letters and phone calls. That way, you will learn what he has that is new and what he has given his friends for their birthdays (often a good indicator of what he might like for himself). You will also keep up-to-date with his developing interests and hobbies.

You may, unwittingly, tend to err on the side of caution, keen to buy gifts that last. Obviously some "useful" presents (additions to construction sets, for example, or collectibles such as stamps, coins, dolls, or minerals) are a good idea, but give your grandchild toys (including stuffed animals)

Christmas and birthdays are still magical for five- to eight-year-olds. But over-excitement can easily lead to tears if your grandchild considers a gift too babyish. Choose according to personality, not the age on the box.

and fun items, too. There is no point buying something indestructible if he not going to play with it or get any fun from it. Try to see the world through his eyes when choosing a gift.

Large purchases

Always check with your grandchild's parents first to ensure that the gift you are considering is acceptable. You may see nothing wrong with buying a seven-year-old a TV for his room, for example, but his parents may have serious reservations. Suitable items in this category include a computer or audio equipment; a bicycle; sports equipment; and toys for the yard.

Origami is an ancient art, worth sharing with your grandchild. You can buy a simple how-to kit that will provide everything you need including instructions. Alternatively, borrow a book from the library and buy a selection of paper. Your grandchild might like to fold place settings for a special family meal.

CRAFT GIFTS AND KITS

These are the ages at which manual dexterity improves by leaps and bounds—which is why children's handwriting becomes increasingly legible. In many ways this gives enormous scope when you are considering "things to do" gifts.

Paper
Kits that enable you to make things from paper, such as flowers or buildings; stencil sets; blocks of different-colored papers; kits to make paper itself.

Jewelry
Sets of beads from which to create necklaces and bracelets; kits for making barrettes and badges; hair-braiding kits.

Models
Children who loved play dough when younger will like modeling clay. Some kinds air-dry; others need baking in the oven. Some make such items as refrigerator magnets, brooches, or barrettes. Preformed kits to make items like dinosaurs, boats, cars, and planes are also popular.

Wool and fabric
Simple tapestry pictures; learn-to-knit kits; making finger puppets (this may not involve sewing, as many can be glued together); friendship bracelets; small weaving loom; kit for making clothespin dolls.

Art
Water-soluble crayons, which come in packages with a paintbrush (they can be used as colored pencils, but when brushed with a wet paintbrush they react like watercolor); a beginner's watercolor set; felt-tip markers; glitter pens; sand art (packs of colored sands that stick onto precut designs).

Videos, books, and tapes
Much-heralded new video releases are obvious gifts for children in this age group, but they are usually acquired fairly quickly so check with his parents in advance. Older stories, although apparently less in demand, may prove as popular in the long run.

By this age, children are able to take care of books, which makes hardcover editions a more special gift. As well as perennial favorites, many of which are regularly reissued with new illustrations, you could also consider simple, easy-to-read stories with lively illustrations that children can read alone; and longer tales, perhaps with chapters, for an adult to read over several nights at bedtime.

Story tapes are useful on car trips and can be a good introduction to classic children's literature, which is too difficult for five- to eight-year-olds to read alone.

Music tapes make good gifts too. Children this young may enjoy listening to music channels on the radio, and some CDs or cassettes that are "theirs" can be special.

TV power
At this stage TV advertising ceases to be of passing interest and becomes a trigger for a constant cry of "I want." Parents suffer more from this than you will, but if you ask your grandchild what he would like as a present, you may get an answer that you don't understand (unless you watch children's TV too) or a request that you are unwilling to honor. Keep a sense of proportion. What to you is an ugly piece of plastic may give your grandchild hours of imaginative play. But don't compromise your principles. If you are worried about the effect of toy weapons, for example, or physically "perfect" dolls, don't buy them.

Excursions with 5- to 8-year-olds

Special days out with your young grandchild

You have several advantages over parents when planning excursions with your grandchildren. You can take them places during school vacations, when their parents may be working; you can probably devote more time—both to choosing a suitable destination and visiting it—and you may get concessionary entrance fees because of your age.

Choosing a destination

Try to think of something that will be out of the ordinary for your grandchild. All children like theme parks, for example, but they may have been several times with their parents or friends already. And while movies are always popular, they may go regularly enough that this does not seem special. Live action, however, is different— ice shows, children's theater, puppets, and magicians are all treats.

Most children love animals. Some are happy to join in any activity available— holding, feeding, and being photographed with exhibits (below). Others prefer to watch from a distance (right).

Plan ahead, and to avoid disappointment, don't mention it to your grandchild until you have the tickets.

The natural world

Most city children like farms; check whether there is anything of special interest—such as sheep shearing, baby lambs, or new chicks that a child can hold. A child who has not been around animals much may be wary of having a lamb or kid eating out of his hand, so proceed cautiously. And no matter how interesting you find the animals, be prepared for him to spend time in a playground area, if there is one.

Many zoos no longer keep large animals in cages; however they may have safari rides or fenced areas where the animals can be viewed. Or you could go to a national or safari park. Check how far you may need to walk: five- or six-year-olds tire easily. If you have to stay in your car, make sure your binoculars are suitable for a child; yours may be too heavy for him to hold for long. A child who likes animals may also like a nature trail.

Aquariums are worth a visit. You may be surprised that many children do not choose to watch the tropical fish, although they are fascinated by those that have unusual coloring. They prefer "scary" creatures such as sharks and unusual ones such as octopuses.

Museums and collections

The days of stuffy museums patroled by humorless curators are long gone. Most museums today are friendly, child-oriented places. The scope is

endless—science and technology, natural history, transportation, clothes, toys. Ask what your grandchild is doing at school and choose a place that complements or expands his current activities. If you are not sure whether something is appropriate, call the museum, give your grandchild's age and interests, and ask for advice.

Check in advance what subject areas the museum covers and whether it has any literature that might help you decide what to look at—a trail to spot different animals or certain clothes in the collection, for example, or puzzles and quizzes relating to it. If the collection is large, pick a few areas that you know will be of interest, and leave some time to return to something that really appeals. Expect the unexpected: he is

MAKING IT PERSONAL

Your grandchildren are likely to be captivated by anything to do with you, so if you played a sport when you were younger, one of them might like to go with you to a sporting collection or hall of fame; if you worked in the automobile industry, he may be interested in a museum or collection devoted to cars or motorcycles, for example; if you were an engineer, a collection of model trains may spark enthusiasm.

Five- and six-year-olds don't really have much concept of the past, so your grand-child may be unable to differentiate the recent past (when you were his father's age, say) from 100 years ago. Nor do most children now study history chronologically. If you are visiting something to do with your past, be prepared for misunderstandings over exactly how long ago it all happened.

Trips for all the children in the family tend to be less successful as they get older and their interests begin to differ. It is often best to arrange an excursion for one child at a time. If you want to take two or more of your grandchildren, take those of a similar age rather than brothers or sisters, unless they are very close. Both younger and older children will get bored.

likely to glance over what you think he will find fascinating and spend a long time on something you find mundane. Particularly with science, technology, and transportation, opt for areas of the collection that are "hands-on"—children like to be able to touch and to discover that pressing a certain lever releases a spring or sounds a horn.

Include art galleries on your "to visit" list, but again, choose with care. A room in which there are paintings of children or animals may be appealing, as will one in which most of the exhibits are colorful. But many five- to eight-year-olds don't have the concentration or artistic appreciation to gain an enormous amount from art collections: be prepared to keep the visit short.

Places of interest

Historic houses tend to be of little interest to young children unless there is something specific that has inherent child appeal, such as a good collection of old toys. Castles and forts, however, can fire their imaginations, especially if you are able to explain how they worked. Reconstructed or model communities can also be fascinating. Your grandchild is likely to be most interested in the bathroom arrangements and where the food was cooked, but it is worth trying to get him to think about the differences between what he is seeing and what he is used to—such as how small living spaces were, and the fact that there was no TV.

Finally, ships appeal to many children. Again the eating, bathroom, and sleeping arrangements are likely to hold their attention for the longest, but they may be interested in where the food was stored, the rigging, and in guns or cannons on deck.

Then and now:

Attitudes about discipline

For generations it was thought that the best way to discipline children was with physical punishment. Attitudes are now radically different. Spanking is widely disapproved, and parents can be prosecuted for using undue force against their children.

THEN

Many parents today do not physically punish their children, preferring to find other ways to deal with unacceptable behavior. The best that can be said for spanking is that it sometimes (temporarily) shocks a child into doing what you want.

But the arguments against it are far more persuasive. Spanking (whether with hand, belt, or stick) reinforces the view that might is right. And it raises the question of how much violence is acceptable: when do you know that you have hit hard enough? If you spank in the anger of the moment, you risk injuring a child; if you wait until you have cooled off, the punishment is unrelated to the crime, and in fact seems even more callous.

Spanking does little good. Children who are physically punished for a misdemeanor remember their anger and resentment at the pain inflicted, instead of the nature of the offense that caused the punishment. Briefly explaining why behavior is unacceptable is more likely to lead to acceptable behavior in the future.

It is hard, when the media appear to back the perception that standards of behavior are declining, not to voice the opinion that "I was spanked and it didn't do me any harm." In individual cases, this may be true. But parents who physically abuse their children are overwhelmingly those who were severely physically punished themselves.

Setting standards

Children are impulsive and can be thoughtless time and again. They also do things that they know they shouldn't, for a number of reasons—to get attention, because they are bored, or because they simply feel like it. Every parent learns that disciplining a child is sometimes necessary.

Discipline teaches children the meaning of right and wrong. It helps them to learn self-control, teaches respect for others' feelings, helps them cope with the real world, and keeps them safe. Children respond to limits, but the limits must be reasonable, and there should not be too many of them.

NOW

Humiliating a child who disrupts others is no longer judged an acceptable approach to school discipline (far left). At home, as well as at school, giving a child time to cool off and consider the reasons for your disappointment at her behavior is likely to be more productive in the long run.

Discipline should be consistent. The children who grow up with fewer problems are those who come from homes where discipline is consistent. If your grandchild stays with you, it is important to learn from his parents in advance where they set the limits and what behavior they accept. It is vital not to go against their wishes, simply because the child is with you.

At school

When you and perhaps even your children were in school, discipline might have included standing in a corner or outside the principal's office. More serious offenses might have been physically punished either by the class teacher or the principal. That is now against the law in many jurisdictions.

Most schools have a code of behavior, which is explained in appropriate terms to pupils. Teachers rely on a consensus among parents, pupils, and teachers to maintain acceptable standards. For persistent code violations, schools have the right to exclude a pupil for one or more days. The final sanction is expulsion.

ALTERNATIVES TO SPANKING

These are the most common ways in which parents show disapproval of their children's behavior. Your grandchild may behave better when he is with you than at home, but if you need to discipline him, find out in advance what his parents do. All these methods have merits and drawbacks.

- **Time-outs**
These can be used from toddlerhood onward. The idea is that you pick a place where the child who has misbehaved sits for a short, specified period of time. This gives him an opportunity to consider his actions. Time-outs don't work for some children, who go to their room and have a relaxing time reading or playing. But for a child who dislikes being away from other family members, a short period in his room is a punishment. And sending him to his room even for a few minutes gives everyone time to cool off.

- **Loss of privileges**
This includes such measures as withholding pocket money, canceling specific trips or excursions, and banning favorite TV programs or computer time. These can work, but it is important to consider the feelings of others too. Canceling a visit from a friend punishes the friend too, and calling off a trip to the movies deprives other members of the family who would have enjoyed it.

- **Tasks**
This is a way of appropriating otherwise free time that would be spent in enjoyable pursuits. The problems are that children then associate tasks that you might expect of them—washing dishes, raking leaves—with punishment, and there is a time lag between the offense and the punishment.

Don't withhold affection as a punishment: disapprove of your grandchild's behavior, not of him.

When grandchildren come to stay
Providing a happy and trouble-free visit

Having grandchildren to stay is a thrilling experience, for you and for them. But it can also be a worrying time. Will they miss their parents? What will you do if one is sick? How can you make sure they have enough sleep? If they are familiar with your home and have slept there with or without their parents almost from birth, staying alone or extending a stay is unlikely to cause problems. But if your grandchildren have not spent the night before, there are some factors to consider.

Calling the parents
Establish with your child the circumstances under which he or she wants to be called back to your house, but be guided by your instincts. If your grandchild is staying by himself and becomes genuinely distressed, you must call his parents. If you have more than one child staying, peer pressure may help the one who is homesick to settle down, but don't let the situation escalate so that you have three unhappy children instead of one.

Don't put yourself in the position of being unable to get hold of the parents for more than a few hours until you have had several trial runs, gradually increasing the time the children spend with you. If the proposed first visit to you is an extended stay while the parents are away, you may prefer to refuse, rather than run the risk of having inconsolable children for several days.

Saying no
Some people find it difficult to say no to anyone, and it is doubly hard to say no to a loved grandchild. But most children need boundaries and respect those who set them.
• If you genuinely can't agree to a request, say no calmly. You don't have to give a reason; in fact, doing so may embroil you in an argument. Simple reasons that don't invite a reply—"It's too late." "Nobody plays football indoors here"—are best.
• If he shouts or cries, let him. You are probably getting a milder version of how he manifests annoyance at home. When his

Most five- to eight-year-olds view sleeping away from home without their parents as a sign that they are "grown up" and may look forward for weeks to the day their parents leave them at your house. After a couple of short trips, staying with you can become an integral part of some of their school vacations and an ideal opportunity to catch up on what you have all been doing.

EMERGENCIES CHECKLIST

• Keep a first-aid box on hand, and make sure that supplies are replenished regularly.

• Attend a first-aid course or study an illustrated book on first aid. You may be confident about dealing with splinters and cuts, but it is essential to know how to react in a life-threatening emergency—a child losing consciousness, suffering acute burns, or severe bleeding, for example. Prompt action could save your grandchild's life.

• Adapt the home and backyard safety procedures on pages 66–69 to suit the ages of the children, but err on the side of caution.

• If a child is ill at your house, be guided by your instincts. Remember that childhood illnesses come on very quickly. Monitor his temperature; if it is over 101°F (38.3°C), call the doctor. If in doubt, call the doctor and the child's parents.

• If you are unable to reach a doctor, call an ambulance, and give details of your grand-child's age and symptoms.

anger has passed, hug him and remind him that you love him, but don't change your mind over the issue that caused the problem.
• If he still won't accept your decision, leave the room for a short time so that he has a chance to reassess the situation and you are not tempted to give in.
• When you return, change the subject, suggest something else to play, or talk about what to do tomorrow. Don't mention the disagreement again.

Bedtime

Talk through in advance what you might expect at bedtime—some children protest vehemently at the thought of going to bed but settle down once they are actually there. Agree with their mother or father in front of the children what time they should go to bed. Take into account that they might be excited at the thought of staying at your house and be prepared to be a little flexible, but don't override parents' wishes.

In the half hour or so before they go to bed, make sure children are calm and relaxed, rather than running around getting overexcited. A suitable book, a short video or television program, or a quiet game with you may calm them down. When it is time for bed, turn the television off—even if you are going to watch it later—so that they don't have the excuse that they might be missing something.

Check whether the children have a set bedtime routine, but again be prepared to be flexible. If you are telling rather than reading a story, for example, they may want you to tell another. Once you have finished, however, tuck them under the covers, say goodnight, and leave the room. Find out in advance whether they are used to a night light, or leave a light on in the hall so they can find the bathroom or you during the night.

If a child gets out of bed, take him straight back. Settle him down, perhaps sit with him for a short while, but be firm. It is past bedtime, and he should be asleep. Requests for food or drink—or a wish to go to the bathroom again—are likely to be delaying tactics. Let him go to the bathroom once and bring him a drink of water in case he is genuinely thirsty, but refuse subsequent requests. Leave the room, and say that you will be back in 10 minutes to check on him. Make sure that you return after the set time.

A child who sleepwalks may worry you but is unlikely to come to any harm. Don't wake him if you can avoid it, but gently guide him back to bed.

If a child wets his bed, don't make a fuss. Change his pajamas and the bed as quickly and quietly as you can and settle him back down to sleep.

Making your home a haven

Providing a welcome environment for your young visitor

When your grandchildren come to stay, they leave familiar toys and games behind and enter an adult environment. It is important, therefore, that there be some child-centered areas in your house and some toys that they can remember from one visit to the next.

A room of their own

If you have the space, it is a good idea for children to have their own room at your house. It isn't necessary to decorate it especially for children—they will outgrow it too quickly—but try to make it light and bright. Hang some pictures on the wall and choose lights and bedcovers that will appeal to them. Make sure that there is at least one drawer for each child to put clothes in and somewhere to hang things.

If your guest room is shared, put away the adult trappings before your grandchildren arrive. Keep some children's books to replace the adult ones on the shelves, and swap some of the pictures on the wall for ones more suitable for children. Don't worry too much about furniture, but put away any knickknacks and make sure that there are no sharp corners or other hazards on furniture.

Keep a small toy chest especially for your grandchildren. Remember that variety is important: if you have only what they have at home, there is less point in coming to play at your house. Some sort of construction set, plenty of paper and crayons or felt-tips, with perhaps some small dolls or cars, and something to play with outdoors, such as a ball, will be enough for a visit of a couple of days. If they are to stay longer, make sure they bring favorites from home.

If more than one set of children play with toys, some breakage is inevitable. One way to minimize potential distress is to buy one small

Staying with you often gives your grandchild an opportunity to be younger than her years and indulge in favorite games and pastimes from her preschool days. If you have a box of dress-up clothes—especially if they belonged to you or to her mother— you and your young grandchild will have hours of fun.

What to play

If you have not been around children since your own were young, you may be tempted to try to organize an activity for every minute they are with you. Some children are indeed very keen on company and will happily talk to you for hours. Most children in this age group, however, are happy playing alone for some of the time, and tire easily if they never have a quiet moment to themselves to sit with a book or watch a video.

Organize some games and join in their play when they ask you to (or offer to if you think they would like it), but don't be afraid to include your grandchildren in some of your daily activities, such as shopping or setting the table. Arrange one or two outings over the course of their stay, and if they complain that they are bored, be ready to improvise—go to the park, bake some cookies, or make glove puppets out of old socks, buttons, and scraps of yarn.

Your home is perhaps the only place where your grandchild can enjoy old-fashioned games. You may find yourself involved in endless games of Chutes and Ladders, for example.

new toy or game each time a child comes to stay. In this way, all the children have the excitement of opening something new before they realize that a former favorite is no longer there. Children also find toys that their parents owned fascinating, so if you managed to hold on to some of those, produce them as a special treat.

Telling tales

If the house in which you live is also the one in which your son or daughter grew up, your grandchild is likely to be captivated by stories of his or her parent's young life there. Don't limit your tales to particular exploits—the time he climbed the tree in the yard and couldn't get down, for example—but include his habits too, such as where he kept his toys, where his favorite hiding places were, and how his room was arranged. If you have photographs or even old movies of your child, so much the better.

CASE HISTORY

As soon as we saw the house, I knew which room was going to be the one I set aside for the "babies." It was lovely and light, and just across the landing from the bathroom. I didn't decorate it to appeal to children, but I had a patchwork quilt that my mother had made and a lovely throw a friend had brought back from a trip, and they immediately gave the room some color.

I still had a few of my own toys, including a very bald dog and a rag doll that my grandmother made when I was born. I also had quite a few of my daughter's toys that she had long forgotten—a tea set, some building blocks, and a couple of cuddly toys.

I've always liked children's books and already had quite a collection, but once my daughter had children, I started adding to it, so now there is a whole bookcase full of things to read that are special to Granny's house. Every so often, I buy something new to take account of the fact that they are growing, but usually the children can't wait to get up to "their" room and find all "their" toys when they come to stay.

Family vacations

Special days and weeks with your children and grandchildren

Spending a week or two with your grandchildren and their parents is an appealing prospect and obviously stands the best chance of being successful if you know that you can live together amicably—if you often spend weekends at each other's homes, for example. It is a good idea to have this sort of dry run before you embark on a costly trip.

Another factor that contributes to success is recognizing that you all have different needs. A vacation on which you are all expected to do the same thing is less likely to work than one on which you please yourselves, going off in ones and twos when you feel like it and gathering as a family at other times.

On whose terms?

If your child has asked you to join his family's vacation, check in advance what your role is going to be. If you suspect—or know—that you are being asked to serve as babysitters, agree to go only if you are prepared to act in this capacity. Of course you would be happy to sit once or twice if the parents want an evening out, but you may want a vacation for yourselves, too. If you have been asked as a convenient sitter, don't assume that your own child's motives are altruistic and those of his or her partner are selfish: daughters and sons can be as self-interested as in-laws at these times.

Areas of conflict

Even the best relationships can start to crack once you are all under the same roof. There are three potential minefields in a family vacation—who does what, who pays for what, and arguments about the children.

If your family is doing its own cooking, discuss in advance who will do which chores. It is obviously unfair for one person to do all the cooking or cleaning. Although it may seem rather formal, it is probably worth compiling a list of the major chores (include over-fives—they can help wash and dry dishes). Otherwise, the most house-proud—you—will do more than a fair share. If you think that you are being expected to do too much, say so calmly. Don't wait until you feel resentful or allow

A week or two away from the normal routine in beautiful or interesting surroundings can be idyllic. Make sure it works for everyone by discussing areas of potential conflict in advance.

If you are clear about the ground rules, special family occasions such as Thanksgiving and Christmas can be wonderfully happy days that your grandchildren will remember for years.

yourself to be a martyr. If the worst happens and you have a major disagreement, keep it between the adults—don't let it spill over and ruin your grandchildren's vacation.

Discuss the financial arrangements well in advance. Also check expectations: if the family intends to eat out each evening, do you want to go along? How much will that cost? If you can't afford to do as they do, say so. Conversely, if you are considerably better off than they are, don't insist on treating at every turn. Simply offer to take them all out for a meal, for example, or perhaps take the children somewhere special.

When they are on an exciting vacation, even the best-behaved children can lose all control. Discipline, however, is a matter for their parents. If you are in charge, follow the parents' guidelines; giving children two sets of rules to live up to is not fair.

Family holidays

Large clan gatherings at Christmas and Thanksgiving can be occasions to treasure, particularly if you don't live close to other members of your family. On the other hand, such holidays can be very stressful. Because they know each other so well, family members often speak to and treat one another in ways they would never dream of doing with their friends.

If you are the host

• Usually you will be in charge of menu planning, so it is up to you to decide how much you want others to do. You may want to ask for suggestions or contributions of particular dishes from different members of the family. Think in advance about who you will allow to help you in the kitchen on the day, what exactly you will ask them to do, and for how long.

• Do you think there will be conflicts over the children's behavior? If this is a potential problem, discuss with the parents what you expect. Try to be flexible in your standards— it's unrealistic to expect excited children to sit at the table until everyone has finished eating, for example—but be sure to tell parents that you will intervene if they don't when you feel that a child's behavior is getting out of hand.

If you are a guest

• Offer to help, but if your offer is refused, don't interfere. If what annoys you—empty glasses left unwashed, children's toys all over the floor—does not bother the hosts, let well enough alone. Don't assume they haven't seen them: they have and are genuinely unconcerned.

• If you consider that the behavior of one of the children is unacceptable but his parents say nothing, keep quiet. Have a word with his parents later if you must, but be prepared for nothing to be done.

• Don't compare the occasion—favorably or otherwise—with a previous year's. This is unfair to your hosts. Again, be wary of the tendency to praise all your son or daughter does at the expense of your daughter-in-law or son-in-law.

• Don't offer advice on any aspect of the food or other arrangements. Be considerate, complimentary, open-minded. Your host's way of making cranberry sauce is likely to be as good as yours. And refrain from making remarks of the "I always made my own pies rather than buying them from the bakery" kind.

Shared skills: swimming

Keeping your grandchild safe in the water

Public schools generally do not offer swimming as a routine part of the curriculum. Consequently, your grandchild must depend on his family to teach him this useful and fun skill. If you can swim and are fairly fit—or if you think that you would benefit from the exercise— this is a job that you might well consider taking on.

Many parents do not have the time (and may not have the skill) to devote to sports coaching of any sort. And in many cases, children are reluctant to accept their parents as teachers. You, however, can probably devote time to the activity, may well have greater reserves of patience than his parents, and are very possibly a more acceptable teacher to your grandchild.

If he is not used to the swimming pool, go a few times before you start teaching. The sounds and smells of the pool will be unfamiliar to him, and he needs to be prepared to be splashed, for other swimmers to make waves, for his hair to be wet, and for his head to go under water. Encourage him to hold his nose and submerge his head. He may also need time to adjust to your new role as his instructor.

Mastering the art

Making lessons too long and tiring is likely to be counterproductive. Short, frequent sessions are the best way to learn. Leave time to play before and after your lesson and have a drink and snack afterward, perhaps while you watch other swimmers.

The steps that follow cover the basics that should be mastered. It is worthwhile to contact your local pool or a national swimming association for advice on the best ways to teach a child (or read a book on the subject). Remember that what works with one child may not work for another. And be patient— some children learn quickly; others take many months to become proficient. A

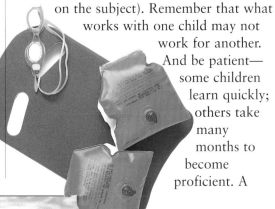

It is sensible to have one adult to look after each child at this age. By turning a trip to the pool into a family occasion, you can keep an eye on children with different levels of expertise. You will probably find that you enjoy the exercise too.

Knowing she has something to keep her afloat increases your grandchild's confidence in the water. Make sure it is safety approved. An inflatable ring will still be fun to play with when she can swim.

SAFETY CHECKLIST

• Use approved water wings or another flotation aid, but remember that these are only aids; they are no substitute for your presence.

• Make sure at least one of the pool staff is trained in resuscitation; if you can, learn these techniques yourself.

• Ignore people who say that children are natural swimmers and advocate throwing them into the water. In such a situation, some children do not panic and manage to stay afloat, but many are put off swimming for years by such an experience. Proper coaching at the child's pace is the best approach.

• Don't take your eyes off your grandchild, even when he is starting to swim alone. Older children move fast, and a quiet area of the pool one minute can be a frightening place for someone small the next.

• Sooner or later your grandchild will feel confident that he can manage without flotation aids. Let him try, but stand close and be ready to pull him out gently and without panic if he doesn't stay above water.

child who is having fun is likely to master this skill more easily than one who finds it a chore. So make sure your grandchild keeps up other sports and activities, too. He will soon become bored if he has no other outlets for his energy and enthusiasm.

Use a flotation aid that your grandchild finds comfortable; water wings are the most popular. Start by supporting him while he floats so that he gets used to the feeling of not having his feet on the bottom of the pool. Next, try to get him to move through the water with his feet off the bottom. This is more difficult than it sounds. You may find it helps to hold his hands and "pull" him along as he paddles with his feet. Show him how to kick his feet.

When he can do this, let go of one arm, then the other. Encourage him to paddle his hands, while keeping up the movement with his feet. Work toward a good overarm movement. Gradually increase the distance he paddles. The easiest way to do this is for him to start at the side of the pool and swim to you; you, of course, are standing farther and farther away as his confidence steadily grows.

The next step is to reduce his reliance on the water wings. Either gradually decrease the air in them or encourage him to try for longer and longer periods without them.

Nonswimming grandparents
If you can't swim yourself, you might consider enrolling both yourself and your grandchild in learn-how-to-swim courses.

Usually courses for adults and children are taught separately. Or you can offer to take your grandchild to and from the lessons. Courses are often oversubscribed on weekends, so if you are free during the week when his parents are not, you will be doing them a favor.

If you can't swim, you may have to rule out trips to the pool unless a swimming parent comes too. Although the water is shallow in children's pools, and you may never be out of your depth, you must be able to cope in an emergency. But once your grandchild is older and can swim confidently, you could invite one of his friends along and watch them, initially from the poolside, then from the spectators' gallery. Make sure that you do watch; your grandchild will expect you to notice everything he does.

Shared skills: handicrafts

Teaching your grandchild to sew and knit

In the past most girls, in particular, learned to knit and sew out of economic necessity. It was cheaper to knit sweaters than to buy them; a dress that could be let out or rehemmed might last another summer; darning socks gave them a few more weeks of life.

Higher living standards and a shift toward a more disposable society mean that these skills are no longer so crucial, and it has become easy to forget the many benefits of learning to knit and sew. Both skills build on children's manual dexterity: manipulating knitting needles or a needle and thread are completely different from manipulating a pencil or modeling clay. They give children the satisfaction of producing something, whether a finished tapestry to frame as a gift, or a scarf to keep a doll or teddy bear warm in winter. And they offer a means of expressing individuality. (Two children who start off with the same pattern and color yarn will still produce individual pieces of knitwear.)

If you are a knitter or are skilled in needlecraft, it may be second nature to you to pass these skills on to your grandchildren, boys as well as girls. (Traditional fishermen's sweaters were produced by men, and among many of the world's renowned knitters there are men as well as women.)

A child who has grown up seeing you occupied with either of these crafts is more likely to be eager to try and may ask for your help. Don't rule yourself out if these crafts are not your special hobby. As long as you know the basics and would like to pass them on, can remember some of the frustration involved in learning, and have plenty of patience, your grandchild will find you are a good teacher.

Once she has mastered the basics—casting on, binding off, knit, purl, and perhaps increasing and decreasing—the scope for knitting projects is enormous. If she is enthusiastic and her reading skills are up to it, look for simple patterns—something for a baby, for example—and help her to understand them, too.

Where to start

Set aside a time when you are not likely to be interrupted. It is often easier, with knitting in particular, to sit your grandchild in your lap so that you can help him position his hands correctly. But if he is too big or reluctant, sit next to him.

You can buy starter kits for knitting, embroidery, and needlepoint. Aimed at children, these are ideal if you are unsure what size needles to use, for example, or don't know what your grandchild might be able to achieve without getting bored. But these are not essential. If you have a full sewing basket or knitting bag, you are almost sure to have something suitable for a beginner. Short, thick knitting needles are easier for children to handle. For sewing, the opposite is true: the bigger the needle, the better. Bright threads and yarns are more popular than somber colors.

What to knit

Scarves for teddy bears and dolls are easy items to start with. You can knit a whole scarf in one color or teach him how to join colors in stripes. An older child in the five-to-eight age group may be able to knit a scarf for himself, as long as he really wants to try. Knitted squares and diamonds can be sewn together (you may have to do this) to make blankets for a doll or toy stroller.

A child who shows a real interest can probably manage mittens. Use a circular needle and be prepared to do the shaping yourself if problems arise. There are also many patterns for knitted soft toys.

What to sew

Needlepoint pictures are a good place to start. Choose one that is appropriate for his age and that will make a picture he likes. Alternatively, try a simple stenciled embroidery design that can be filled using only one or two different stitches.

Curtains or bedcovers for a doll's house are easy for beginners. A simple skirt or a dress for a large doll are also good projects

You may have to offer to sew on badges earned for sporting ability, even after your grandchild is proficient with a needle. The fine stitches needed require greater control than many eight-year-olds can manage.

for beginners. And for older children a drawstring purse can hold anything from small pieces of jewelry to dolls' clothes, depending on size (make this extra-special by helping to glue on beads or sequins, or applying an iron-on appliqué design).

Tips for success

Do:
• Be prepared for mistakes: dropped stitches, knotted thread, crinkled backgrounds
• Give help when he asks for it
• Resist the temptation to take over or do a few rows, or a bit of sky, to "make it grow" unless he specifically asks you to.

Don't:
• Criticize his choice of project
• Suggest a long-term project. He will be bored by the slow progress
• Give up too easily. If he doesn't like knitting, try crochet. If needlepoint doesn't appeal, suggest patchwork or appliqué
• Press if he really isn't happy. Put it all away for a few months until his hand control has improved, then try again.

Common dilemma: Am I jealous?

When the other grandparents seem to have it all

A good relationship with your grandchild's other grandparents can prevent awkward situations from developing into problems. If they are your friends, it is often easier to remember that they are not trying to upstage you. They are simply acting in what they believe to be your grandchild's best interests—as you are.

I t is a common occurrence: you buy your grandchild a book you are sure he will enjoy, only to find that his other grandparents have bought a bicycle. You take him to the movies for a treat; his other grandparents spend a couple of days at a theme park with him. You see your grandchild for a couple of weekends a year, but the other grandparents are frequent visitors. How you cope with such inequalities can make all the difference between happy and uncomfortable family relationships.

Financial concerns

If differences in your financial situations bother you, talk to your child. He or she may be unaware of your feelings. A word to his or her partner, who can mention the matter to the other grandparents, may make you more comfortable. They may simply be unaware that their generosity is embarrassing you or making you feel awkward. It is important to remember,

however, that all grandparents want the best for their grandchildren and to some people that includes material things. If they can afford it, why shouldn't they give now? It is a persuasive argument.

Also bear in mind past circumstances. Age may be a factor: perhaps you helped your child and his or her partner when they were setting up their home, when the in-laws were still paying college fees for younger children. Now that you are retired and they are still working, it is their turn to give. This does not mean that your contribution was or is any less valuable.

Your grandchild's perspective

Children tend to take things at face value. Just as some grandparents are more active than others (see pp. 90–91), so one set may take them on different sorts of excursions and offer different kinds of gifts. Five- and six-year-olds also have a limited concept of the value of gifts—if they consider the issue

CASE HISTORY

My granddaughter's other grandparents were overgenerous to her—to my mind—right from the start. One of the first things they did was pay to have her professionally photographed when she was a few weeks old. They are lovely photographs but at the time I rather resented it. And so it went on: they took the whole family on vacation every year and bought our granddaughter expensive presents. I tried not to be uncharitable, but Charlotte didn't play with many of the things they bought—the toys needed more manipulative hands than hers, or the batteries kept running out, or they took too long to set up and she got bored waiting to play. I talked to my daughter, but her attitude was "They can afford it, where's the harm?"

Matters came to a head one Christmas when we all shared a beach house. We'd bought Charlotte a kite. Her other grandparents bought a rocking horse, which of course bowled Charlotte over. She'd have eaten her meals sitting on it if we'd let her. But a day later, she was bored with Black Beauty. The sun came out, and my husband took Charlotte down to the beach to fly her kite. They were gone for hours and came back exhausted, but with very rosy cheeks.

The night before we left, I heard my daughter and Charlotte talking in the next room. My daughter asked what she had liked most about the vacation. Charlotte replied with no hesitation: "Flying my kite with Granddad. I like that Granddad." I realized how foolish I had been all these years—it was the time we spent with her that she valued, and I should have been doing the same.

at all. For this reason, a gift that costs a little will be as welcome as one that costs a lot if it is something your grandchild wants. It costs nothing to listen to him before deciding on the perfect present.

A lot depends on his parents' attitude. If they treat all gifts the same—to be received with thanks—your grandchild is likely to as well. The same goes for excursions: if your grandchild looks forward to a day with you, where you go and what you do are less important than your company. Besides, he is unlikely in any case to know who pays for what. He knows that he always goes to the beach with his other grandparents for a week, not that they foot the bill.

It is also a truism that money doesn't buy affection. Your grandchild loves you for who you are, not the material things you give him. In later life he is as likely to remember an afternoon when you took him on a picnic as he is that he had the best seats at a children's play every year at Christmas time or went to a theme park before anyone else in his class.

Give what you can. If this is time rather than money, don't undervalue yourself. Time itself is a priceless commodity. Your grandchild may be just as happy, even happier, to have your undivided attention.

Time constraints

If you are grandparenting at a distance and the others live nearby—or have a large house that makes extended stays more practical—don't waste time and energy bemoaning your situation. Make the most of the time you spend with your grandchild and find other ways of being close. You may discover that you know as much about what he is doing from a scheduled weekly phone call as the grandparents who see him a couple of times a week. He may be less likely to interrupt his routine—playing with friends, going to sports practice, and so on—for their more frequent visits.

Understanding the jargon
Computers and computer technology

Computers are a fact of life for your grandchild. He may have one at home and may even have used one in kindergarten. Now that he is at school, he will be more than familiar with how to switch one on, load a program, use the mouse, play a game or type a short story, and shut down when he has finished. And he may have a console that can be used with a TV or computer monitor for games at home, or a portable machine so that he can play games while traveling in the car or on the bus or train.

If you use a computer every day, you will probably consider this early introduction to new technology an excellent idea. If you are unfamiliar with computers, you may be baffled by his enthusiasm and the jargon.

Whatever you think of the desirability of your grandchild's sitting for long periods in front of a computer screen or battling against himself on a portable mini-games machine, it is worth making an effort to understand at least the basics of computers if you want to communicate with him. There are several ways in which you can keep up-to-date with developments.

• Hands-on experience

If your grandchild is more knowledgeable than you are, ask him to explain what he is doing. Although you might feel reluctant to admit your ignorance, he will be delighted to know something that you don't. But if you think that he will be too quick for you, and you prefer to grasp at least the basics in advance, enroll in a course. Or visit a computer show, and perhaps take your grandchild along to show you the ropes. (Phone in advance to check which days and times are likely to be the least busy.)

• Books and magazines

Some computer books are too technical for beginners; others are for absolute beginners and are fine. The problem with books, however, is that by the time they are produced, technology has moved on. Magazines can keep you up-to-date with what is happening, but some of them assume a basic knowledge. You may need to browse through several before you find one that meets your needs. Alternatively, see which magazines your grandchild is reading and start with them.

Some nonspecialist magazines aimed at younger readers have a review section of new games and programs for computers and consoles. Some newspapers have weekly computer columns or supplements that feature reviews of games and other software for children.

If you are considering a purchase—either for yourself or as a gift for your grandchild—ask around to find out which store or warehouse in your area is best. Pick a time when the clerks are not too busy and when an enthusiast can demonstrate exactly what a machine can do.

COMMON TERMS EXPLAINED

Byte The space occupied by a single character in a computer memory or on a disk. The amount of data that can be stored is usually measured in kilobytes, K (1,024 bytes); megabytes, MB (1,024 K); or gigabytes, GB (1,024 MB).

CD-ROM An optical disk read by laser that stores words, music, and animated pictures. A CD-ROM cannot be altered, so it is impossible to delete the material on the disk by mistake.

CPU The central processing unit (CPU) of a computer carries out the instructions given it by a program. The CPU is contained within the hard drive or the games console.

E-mail A method of sending messages electronically from one computer to another.

Format To prepare a disk so that information can be written onto it or read off it.

Game console A machine that plays a CD-ROM or cartridge containing a video game. Most consoles use the TV screen or a computer monitor (with an adequate graphics capability).

Hardware The pieces of the computer itself: the screen or monitor, hard drive, keyboard, mouse, and printer.

Interactive A program that allows you to control it by changing the story. Many games for young children are interactive, allowing them to get out of a haunted house, for example.

Mouse A plastic device connected to the computer by a cable, which sends information to the computer, allowing you to move around the screen, draw an image, or select a course of action from a menu.

Program A set of instructions that tells a computer how to do a particular task.

RAM This stands for "random access memory," and describes the temporary memory in which data and programs are stored while the computer is using them.

ROM Short for "read only memory", this is a permanent memory that stores data even if the computer is switched off.

Software The programs and instructions that allow you to use the computer to perform various tasks.

Virtual reality Technology that creates the illusion of a three-dimensional world in which you take part and influence the action.

• TV, video, and radio
Many children's TV and radio programs feature reviews of new games, often compiled by young players. These will give you some idea of what may be worth buying or renting to play with your grandchild. Some interactive CDs are previewed on videos that your grandchild may see. These are likely to be extensions of, or related to, feature film releases.

Buying software
Some computer games have a short life, but others are played over and over again, so it is worth asking your grandchild what he would like before you buy. Games usually work with one make of computer or game console (although some are produced in different formats), so check compatibility.

Depending on your grandchild's interests, consider some of the more enduring games you know, many of which have now been produced for computer. Simple games like hangman (for younger children) and solitaire exist for computer, as does chess (for older children in this age range). You can also play tennis, golf, or soccer on screen. Try a special game shop, computer store, or a large toy store.

The educational CD-ROMs make good gifts, but ask your grandchild or his parents which ones he uses at school (some children like to have them at home too; others prefer something different). Many bookstores have good multimedia departments, where you may be able to try out a CD-ROM you are considering. The choice here is sometimes limited to reference rather than fun titles.

From a distance

Keeping in touch with a schoolchild who lives far away

It gets easier to be a long-distance grandparent as children get older. You can encourage parents to keep sending you photographs and videos, but your grandchild himself is now better able to take the initiative and keep you in touch with what is happening in his life.

The telephone

Although you can communicate by phone with your grandchild as soon as he can talk, "conversations" are largely one-way. Over the years, as your grandchild's vocabulary and understanding of language improve, and his horizons broaden, he will be able to communicate more. A child of five has a vocabulary of 3,000 to 5,000 words, and you can expect to have fairly lengthy conversations with him.

Let him tell you what he has been doing. Even if you know something exciting has happened, allow him to fill you in on the more mundane parts of his week (they are interesting to him) before you ask. Be aware of the family's routine—which days he has sports practice, or friends around, and what time the family usually eats dinner—so that when you call, you do so at a time when he is not playing or having storytime and he is able to talk. Or encourage him to ask permission to call you once in a while. If cost is a problem, keep the conversation reasonably short.

Writing and drawing

As they move through their first couple of years at school, children's ability to write improves, and many happily spend time practicing their handwriting, either by writing stories about themselves or others, or by spelling out words. Encourage your grandchild to send you examples of his writing—stories, accounts of his favorite book or video, or simply lists of his friends or activities. Until his writing is proficient, he might like to complement these pieces with drawings or paintings.

A child can record the details of a day at school on a disposable camera, giving you an ideal insight into your grandchild's daily life.

Try to avoid "one-way traffic"; write letters to him. Keep them short and simple to begin with, and gradually increase the length and the complexity of the words you use. Telling him what you have been

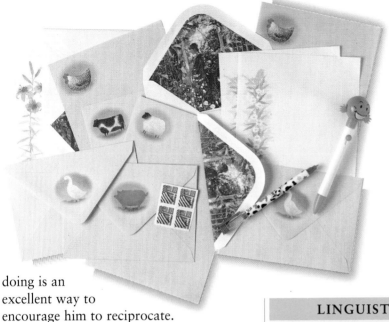

You can encourage your grandchild to write letters by sending him stationery and pens, and perhaps—if you live in the same country—adding a few stamps so that it is easy for him to mail you a letter as soon as it is finished.

doing is an excellent way to encourage him to reciprocate.

New technological developments have made it possible to write a letter on a computer and send it at the touch of a button to another computer (this is more expensive than conventional mail, but cheaper than a telephone call). If you and your grandchild have access to computers, investigate the possibilities of e-mail.

Recording daily life

If your grandchild has a cassette recorder, send him cassettes on which to record his activities or make up stories for you. Again, this need not be one-sided: tell him what you have been doing on tape, too.

If you want visual reminders of important occasions—or even simple daily routines—send him a disposable camera every so often. You can make specific requests, like asking him to take it to school, if his teacher agrees—it could be a good activity for the end of the term—or let him decide what to photograph. Expect a few shots of the sky or ground until he is competent with the camera. It's unfair to ask him to document his own birthday party, since he'll be too busy enjoying it, but he could take pictures when friends come to play, on a day out, or of his pets or the yard. Keep his photographs in a separate album or box so that when he comes to stay he can look through them with you.

LINGUISTIC BARRIERS

When grandparents and their grandchildren speak different languages, communication obviously becomes more difficult. There are two common situations in which such problems arise. First, your child has moved to another country, settled with a native of that country, and is bringing up your grandchildren to speak his or her partner's mother tongue.

Alternatively, you all live in America, and although your grandchildren's first language is English, yours is not. In this scenario, problems usually surface only if your grandchildren don't live nearby. If you see them regularly, it is easy to talk in more than one tongue: children brought up bilingually from birth rarely have difficulties telling their two languages apart. If you live at a distance, however, when the telephone might be the obvious way to stay in touch, it is harder to keep the lines of communication open.

First, try not to criticize your child or feel resentful that he or she no longer uses your native tongue and has not passed it on to your grandchildren. While it is under-standable that you want to keep your cultural heritage alive, you must appreciate the importance of your grandchildren being secure in their environment and feeling comfortable with their peers.

If talking on the telephone is difficult, keep in touch with photographs and videos. Write short, obvious greetings and notes such as "Happy Birthday," or "Good luck with your exam" in your language. And—with their parents' permission—send stories or songs in your language so your grandchildren do not grow up unaware of their heritage.

CHAPTER SIX

The Older Schoolchild
8 to 12 years

This is likely to be one of the most rewarding and enjoyable stages in your grandchild's life. She has learned to walk and run, hold the tiniest bead and catch the largest ball, can communicate clearly, and has grasped the fundamental differences between right and wrong. Although she is on the road to independence, with her own ideas about who she is and what she likes, she nevertheless retains much of her childish enthusiasm and innocence.

Now is the time to enjoy taking your grandchild on excursions, choosing gifts for her, showing her skills that will stay with her forever, talking and, more important, listening to what she is interested in and what she has found out about life. A child's developing mental capacities are thought to be most active at this pre-puberty stage. Your grandchild will be articulate, appreciative, and challenging. Whatever you do and say to her now, she will remember in the future. This is the beginning of her real friendship with you.

What 8- to 12-year-olds like doing

Making the most of your grandchild's unbridled new enthusiasms

Between the ages of 8 and 12, children acquire strong views on how they want to spend their leisure time. They may play games their parents have never played, become passionate about subjects of which the adults around them are more or less ignorant, or take up a new hobby simply because their friends are interested in it. Such steps are part of the child's growing independence. As a grandparent, you can support and enjoy the untrammeled enthusiasm with which children of this age approach new interests.

You can encourage and share in your grandchild's newly discovered activity when her interest might otherwise dwindle due to lack of parental involvement. You may remember from your own parenting—and constantly witness now—that there can be days, even weeks, when all that parents can cope with are the basic necessities of childrearing, work, and housekeeping. But if you live close by, you can participate in your grandchild's chosen pastime and make the most of this rewarding phase of her life.

Sports

You can introduce a grandchild who shows an avid interest in sports to games she may never have considered before. If basketball is her current enthusiasm, taking her along to watch professional games will stimulate her interest, but consider spending time on other sports as well. Your local library or community center should be able to provide information on sports instruction classes. You may be lucky enough to find some that allow you both to play.

Make your role one of learning as well as teaching and encouraging. It will give your grandchild immense pleasure if she can teach you in addition to receiving knowledge from you. Learning how to play a sport together is an experience both of you will long remember, and it will bring an extra closeness to your relationship.

Before you offer to enroll your grandchild in a course, consult her parents. They may have plans for her to take classes at another time, or for her to learn something different. In most cases, the parents will be delighted that you are willing to give your time to the child. It is equally important, before you get carried away by the idea of beginning yoga or scuba-diving classes together, that you know the child's true feelings on the subject.

If she is only trying to please you when she says she is happy for you both to take classes, hesitation or lack of eye contact when she is speaking may reveal her misgivings. Don't question her—that will make her feel uncomfortable. It is simpler

Young muscles are easily strained. With high-impact sports such as tennis or badminton, make sure that the playing surface is suitable and include some gentle warm-up and cool-down exercises before and after every session.

Most weekend teams lack volunteers to fulfill every role, so don't let the fact that you can't play rule out your participation. Your grandchild's parents will be delighted if you can make sure that your grandchild gets to and from the field safely with all her gear.

to book a class for her to participate in by herself and to accompany her there and take an interest in how she gets along. Although children of this age usually still like adult participation, she may fear her friends would tease her if you were actually to take part.

If your grandchild is already involved in a team or group activity, extra adult help is almost sure to be welcome, whether in the form of coaching, setting up nets and posts, providing refreshments, or driving children to and from the field or to away games. At this level, involvement can be addictive, and after running along the sidelines for a few weeks, you will be amazed at how much fitter you feel. While support and encouragement are always valued by children, try not to become too loudly partisan. Remember that this is the age at which children are easily embarrassed by the adults around them.

If you are eager to pass on to your grandchild your skills in a chosen sport, consult your local bookstore or library to find out how it is taught to children. The trick is to make learning seem easy and fun. Imagine yourself in her shoes, and at her height and strength, and keep sessions short.

Skating, skateboarding, swimming, and bicycling are high on the list of physical pastimes for this age group. Although you may prefer not to skateboard, you could take your grandchild to some safe sites so that she can enjoy the activity herself. If cycling is her passion, you could take up this form of exercise yourself. Remember that adults need helmets, too.

Sedentary interests

Eight- to 12-year-olds enjoy indoor activities as well as outdoor ones. Computers are very popular, and at this age she will be a more-than-competent operator. This is an area in which your grandchild may have much to teach you, or you can consider taking a course for adult beginners at a college. You may be surprised at how easy it is to learn.

While it's hard to be too knowledgeable about computers these days, resist the temptation to tell your grandchild all you have learned; she will get great pleasure from passsing on to you a skill that she is justifiably proud of. Don't dismiss computer games out of hand: many encourage manual dexterity, quick thinking, and problem solving. If you enjoy chess, buy a computer chess program, since your grandchild may be more eager to play in this format than to sit at a traditional board.

When your grandchild tires of playing on the computer, you can suggest card games, board games, darts, anything you have played in the past or have always wanted to try. Children of this age love to learn new skills, and provided you teach gently and do not resort to over-competitiveness, your grandchild will become your most enthusiastic game partner.

Gifts for 8- to12-year-olds

Inventive presents for older children

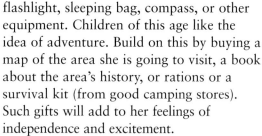

Buying presents for this age group does not necessarily involve a big expense: children genuinely appreciate presents that are unusual and surprising.

Along with her growing sense of independence, your grandchild will have ideas about what she would like to buy if she could afford it, so gifts of small amounts of money will be acceptable, as long as her parents don't object. Make these gifts irregular to ensure that your giving is not taken for granted. Also, if your grandchild makes a habit of telling you about something she wants but cannot afford, don't respond by opening your wallet immediately—you will start to appreciate each other less.

Most children enjoy the sense of power and independence that money in their hands gives. But if you want to give a gift certificate instead of money, check with your grandchild's parents to be sure that your choice is appropriate. A child with a passion for clothes will prefer a particular clothing store; a computer buff would be happier with the chance to buy new software.

Gifts are particularly appreciated when they add to a special event. If your grandchild is going camping or on an overnight school trip for the first time, you could buy a flashlight, sleeping bag, compass, or other equipment. Children of this age like the idea of adventure. Build on this by buying a map of the area she is going to visit, a book about the area's history, or rations or a survival kit (from good camping stores). Such gifts will add to her feelings of independence and excitement.

What you give can also trigger new interests. Many 8- to 12-year-olds love collecting. If your grandchild has started a collection of model cars or horses, for example, you can add to it, but if you listen to her conversation, you may discover other items she could collect. Children of this age collect anything from baseball caps to reproductions of Egyptian artifacts; any additions you provide are likely to prove a success. You may be surprised, on your next visit, to discover that one collection has been dropped in favor of a new one; passing enthusiasms are common.

If you live far away, gifts received in the mail will be some of the most exciting of all for your grandchild, especially if they are unexpected. Things that will add to her collections—books in a series, coins, stamps, badges—will all brighten a mundane day for her. And so will gifts that let her know you were thinking of her: a coin purse you saw while you were shopping, a headband, sunglasses, or a cap you know would suit her. It's not the expense of the items that makes them appealing, but the idea that she is always in your thoughts.

Pets awaken children's ability to look beyond themselves and care for creatures that are smaller and more vulnerable than they are. Knowing that an animal depends on him for survival will enhance your grandchild's sense of responsibility.

Roaring Twenties, in which case gather together some appropriate outfits and organize a photo session so that she can indulge her fantasies.

The important thing is to give graciously and in a spirit of generosity. Give what you feel your grandchild would like and not what you think she ought to have.

The purchase of a dog or cat requires parental approval. But if you can offer to care for the pet during vacations and live close enough to take the dog for walks when family members are busy or sick, you could give your grandchild the best present he will ever receive.

Ideas for collectibles abound: writing to pen pals could provide the basis for a stamp collection; an interest in a historical period could be enhanced by some coins. Keeping abreast of her current enthusiasms will give you the inspiration to find the perfect gift.

Special occasions

For birthdays and other special occasions, you may need to consult her parents to discover what is on your grandchild's wish list. Perhaps she can't decide between a personal stereo and skates. In that case, you can help her parents by offering to buy one of the items and, if necessary, sharing the cost with the other grandparents.

Children derive special pleasure from gifts they can keep and remember you by. This usually means jewelry, watches, and the like, but remember that at this age they are still quite young to care for valuable items. If you think that the loss of your gift would be really upsetting for you (and her), wait until your grandchild is a little older. The last thing you want to do is create guilt and stress over a gift you have given.

Children often can't think what they would like for their birthday other than the obvious big items they have asked their parents for. Be inventive. If your grandchild has expressed a desire to learn to ride a horse, consider signing her up for lessons. If this new hobby takes off, the gift-giving possibilities are nearly endless—hat, boots, books on horses, tickets to horse shows, and so on. Or perhaps she has developed a passionate interest in the Wild West or the

PRESENTS IN THE MAIL

If you live at a distance and want to find an appropriate gift that is also easy to mail, consider the following options:

• A subscription to your grandchild's favorite magazine.

• Membership at her local sports center or club.

• Adoption certificate for a whale or manatee (or any animal she loves that can be sponsored in this way).

• Newspaper clippings that contain humorous spelling errors or that describe funny incidents—made up into a book.

• Souvenirs from places you have visited without her, including postcards, little gifts, and interesting information.

• A formally laid out schedule of events planned for her next visit to you (be prepared to adhere to the plan).

• A collage or photo album of the places you have been together, the people you met, things she liked best.

Excursions with 8- to 12-year-olds

Exciting grown-up places for your special days together

Going on excursions with children 8- to 12-years old is a less stressful experience than with younger children, who need so much supervision, or older ones, who are far more difficult to please. This should be a time when you can both thoroughly enjoy yourselves and share some memorable experiences.

To get an idea of the type of places she would like to visit, listen to what she tells you during casual conversations. Almost all children of this age adore animals, but some are opposed to zoos on humane grounds. Children who seem to have a baseball mitt permanently glued to their hand will not necessarily enjoy being a spectator as much, though many will have a favorite team and relish the opportunity to see it play. Also, by this stage your grandchild may have visited the local aquarium so many times that she is less than enthusiastic about going again. Collect ideas for outings even when one isn't imminent. Check your nearest library; peruse local newspapers and entertainment listings to keep abreast of what is available.

If sports are a shared passion, going to watch a game together provides an obvious opportunity for an outing. Such excursions should be accompanied by a trip to her favorite pizza place or burger bar to give you time to talk about the game or answer any questions, particularly if you have chosen a sport that is new to her.

Trips to places that children may never have considered interesting are often unexpectedly successful. If her class is studying a particular historical topic, you could take her to a relevant museum or exhibition. Seeing the artifacts, paintings, or costumes for herself could help her with schoolwork and spark a desire for more excursions of this kind.

If you feel you have exhausted the possibilities of public transportation, think again. Vintage buses and steam trains remain very popular. Look for special excursions that can make the occasion more magical.

Science museums are often very hands-on, enabling children to see for themselves how things work, experiment with sound or visual effects, or observe the sky through a telescope. Trips to working windmills or water mills that still grind grain may help bring school lessons to life.

A picnic or outdoor twilight feast will appeal to a child at this age, and if she lives in a city, she will relish a trip to the countryside or seashore. You can give the day a flavor of adventure by marking a route on a road map and letting her direct the way. Or include a walk to a special point of interest, with plenty of rests and refreshment breaks along the way.

If your grandchild spends a great deal of time being transported by car, you could simply visit neighboring towns and areas by bus or train and allow her to lead the way in exploring when you get there. This sort of outing requires a preliminary visit by you alone to confirm that the area is safe and interesting, and that bus or train schedules suit your plans.

Abiding passions

Try to complement your grandchild's hobbies and pastimes. If she loves making model airplanes, be on the lookout for air shows. If horses are her passion, contact the relevant society to discover when point-to-point or dressage competitions take place. Don't be deterred if you have never been involved yourself or if you don't know where such events might take place. You may be surprised to learn how much your area offers.

If a big city with art galleries and historical sites is too far away to reach in a day, concentrate on local history. Again, contact with any appropriate groups might reveal that your town has a colorful past. You may find a walk or tour that could help your grandchild discover that there are no boring places, simply boring attitudes.

The importance of friends

Children often like to ask a friend to accompany them on outings. This is not because your grandchild finds your company boring, but because this is the age at which making friends becomes all-important. Accept how important these companions are to her. Communicate with the parents of the friend or make sure that your grandchild's parents have. Do not allow your grandchild to take sole charge of making the arrangements with friends who are to accompany you on an outing. You need to be clear about the time the friend is expected home, where she lives, and what the contact number is in case of an emergency.

The presence of an extra young person may make you more susceptible to coercion than normal. Make it clear that the rules you follow on outings must be adhered to, whoever comes along. Run through these with your grandchild and her friend before you venture out. That way, you can avoid misunderstandings or arguments about what is and is not allowed. Remember that children this age are prone to act differently when they are with friends than when you are with them by yourself.

Inexpensive options

It is important to organize some excursions that do not involve financial expense and treats. Picnics, walks, going on nature trails, exploring, observing the moon and stars from the seashore or a hilltop, and going to the library are low-cost options your grandchild might enjoy. You could even plan trips to visit relatives she may not often see with her parents and alternate these with the more "glamorous" outings.

Spectator sports come into their own with many children at this age. Younger children tend to be too overwhelmed by the noise and crowds to enjoy such trips. Choose seats with care; being able to follow the action easily is important to your grandchild's understanding and enjoyment of the game.

Then and now: Education

Successful education for children today involves a working partnership between teachers, parents, and pupils, in which all have a valuable contribution to make and different skills to share.

THEN

There is no doubt that educational theory and practice have changed a great deal since you were at school. Even your grandchild's parents are bound to comment on how different teaching methods and subject matter are from when they were pupils.

Broadly speaking, the biggest change that has taken place since you and your children were in school is that education is now more child centered. Large classrooms in which children are seated at fixed desks all facing the lecturing teacher at the front are no longer viewed as the best way to stimulate and teach children.

Today most subjects are approached through project work, and children may work cooperatively in small groups to discover facts and explore ideas, rather than be given information that they have to commit to memory. If you think back to learning a poem by rote, you may acknowledge that while you may still remember some of the lines of the poem, you probably did not understand or appreciate the language or feel inspired to try to write poetry yourself.

Present-day educators believe that the best way of understanding a subject is to experience it hands-on. You will probably notice that although your grandchild may not have as thorough a grasp of grammar

and syntax as you had at her age, her knowledge of some other subjects may be broader and more sophisticated than yours was. Her access to all sorts of information through television also means that she is probably much worldlier than you were at her age.

Relationships

Your grandchild's relationship with her teachers will differ from the ones you may remember. Although in almost all schools children still address their teachers by their last name, it is unlikely that your grandchild will feel the fear that you may recall in relation to some of your teachers. In retrospect, it is easy to make light of old schooldays and think that the ruling-through-fear approach was effective. But now most children experience far more humane and easygoing teaching methods, which are believed to lead to more effective learning. It is difficult to learn properly if you are scared of the person who is instructing you.

Physical punishment is absent from schools today. It may seem to you that this coincides with more difficult, badly behaved children, but long-term research indicates the opposite. When you tell your grandchildren about your schooldays, try not to voice too many criticisms of what is

NOW

In the past, education chiefly involved listening to a teacher impart information that had to be memorized and recalled (above left). Today the emphasis is on children exploring for themselves, discussing options, and sharing knowledge with their classmates (above).

happening now. Instead point out the positive aspects of your grandchild's school experience that differ from your own.

Parent participation

Another aspect of schooling today is that parents are expected to be actively involved; most educators believe that a child's education comes from a partnership between parents and teachers. The positive side of this is that your grandchild's parents should feel able to talk to people at the school when your grandchild is experiencing problems, and your grandchild will not feel that school is a world totally separate and alien from family life.

In addition, parents are encouraged to attend special assemblies, plays, and celebrations. This can produce added stress for working parents, and it is upsetting for your grandchild if her parents are always the ones who are absent from these events. This is an area where you can help out if you have time during school hours. Your presence will be much appreciated by the staff and your grandchild alike, whether you go to the short, one-on-one reading sessions or to watch your grandchild perform in a play or take part in a special project.

Private education

If you have not considered it before, as your grandchild approaches the age at which she changes from elementary school to junior high or high school, you may want to be more involved in her education, perhaps by paying for her to go to a private school. Obviously, this decision is one her parents must make, but if private education is a family tradition, they may appreciate a financial contribution from you.

If, however, you are happy to pay toward one grandchild's education, you need to consider whether you will be able to do the same for all your grandchildren. And the fact that you are providing funding doesn't mean that you can insist on which school is selected.

Don't push parents toward private education simply because you can afford to pay for it. But if they are concerned about which school their child will attend and are unable to afford the one that they think will be most suitable for her, offer to step in if you have the means. This will not give you the right to a greater say over your grandchild's future, and you should not use it as a means to gain power over your family. Remember, too, that the expenses involved in private education do not stop at tuition—there will be various fees, equipment, and all kinds of extras to pay for. Take these into account when budgeting and be sure you can afford them before you make any offers.

Shared skills: gifts for life

Introducing your grandchild to pastimes that have enriched your life

Young children often take up hobbies only to discard them in a matter of a weeks. But now that your grandchild is eight or nine years old, she is more likely to have the maturity to stick with something, even if it becomes difficult at times. Sharing some of the skills you have acquired can be a great way to spend time with her.

If your grandchild knows you go fishing regularly or hears you playing the piano, for example, she may ask you to take her with you on your next trip or teach her how to play. Alternatively, she may not consider it possible to do what you are doing, especially if you are a skillful musician or an avid fisherman.

It is up to you to build your grandchild's belief in her ability to learn what you have to teach her before you begin any instruction. Children love to hear stories about what adults were up to when they were young, and this is a good opportunity to relate how you first got involved in your hobby, the mistakes you made, and the setbacks you overcame. Keep your account lighthearted and, if possible, humorous, so as not to discourage her.

Before you begin to teach your grandchild to play an instrument, you will need to do some preparation of your own. She will need her own instrument, or at least easy access to one, probably yours. If you are planning to buy her a guitar or clarinet of her own, for example, avoid the impulse to invest in an expensive new instrument. However eager she may be initially, there is always the possibility that she will give up and your money will be wasted. Opt for a good secondhand instrument or investigate renting one until you see how she progresses. You can always graduate to something grander later.

If you are not sure how to teach a beginner, you may prefer to hire a professional teacher and support your grandchild's efforts between lessons. However, don't underestimate a child's willingness to learn from you. Even if you don't convey the information in exactly the same way as a professional tutor does, you have the closeness of a family relationship to help you. Your grandchild may find your methods a welcome change from formal instruction. You can lace your instruction

Learning to play an instrument is a skill that will enhance your grandchild's life. Move forward at her pace and resist the temptation to push her from one level to another, regardless of how proud you are of her achievements. Time to consolidate her skills and simply have fun with you are also important.

Fishing has many advantages. It's an outdoor activity that is not too strenuous, it's inexpensive for beginners, and the basics are easy to grasp.

Model-making can be rewarding. Don't restrict yourself to indoor models. Flying a plane or sailing a boat you have made is also great fun.

her to appreciate what is to be gained from sitting quietly for hours on end. But that does not mean she cannot enjoy shorter sessions with you, during which she can gradually become accustomed to what is required. Time begun in such companionable silence is conducive to intimate chats and shared confidences on the way home.

It is vital that your grandchild be suitably dressed and that you have enough refreshments with you for her not to view these occasions as wet, cold, and boring. Provide plenty of information about the birds you are watching or the fish you are catching. If your grandchild picks up your enthusiasm for the pastime, you will be able to equip her with binoculars, fishing tackle, or other items that will make her feel part of the whole experience.

Your skill in a more energetic pastime, such as horseback riding, may be the one your grandchild wants to share with you. If so, you will obviously have to make sure she'll be safe while she is learning. Sessions should be long enough for her to gain confidence, but not so long that she becomes overtired. Establish regular times for teaching—once or twice a week, say—so that she can enjoy rapid progress. If you vary the lessons with grooming and cleaning the stall, your grandchild will quickly grow used to being around horses without fearing them.

If none of these hobbies have attracted you over the years, you still have much to offer: a leisurely walk with time to talk and simply be in each other's company is one of the most wonderful gifts of all.

Finally, remember that in sharing any active skill you must make allowances for your grandchild's age so that she does not become physically or mentally overstrained.

with humor, go at a pace that suits you both, and take pride in any progress made, since it is a credit to both of you.

If you can't remember what you did when you first began to learn, consult some books on the subject before you start. If your grandchild is struggling to play a chord, don't take over and show her how easy it is. Respect her efforts and try to recall how difficult learning can be in the early stages. Never force a child to practice or persist with playing if she is tired or frustrated. The whole idea is to give her pleasure now and for the rest of her life.

Outdoor pursuits

If you share your love of bird-watching or fishing, you will also teach the importance of observation and immense patience. These are highly desirable, useful attributes in today's fast-moving and stressful world, but you should appreciate that your grandchild's youth predisposes her to movement and noise. It may take years for

Talking about death

Accepting that illness and death are part of our everyday lives

As you grow older, you may have to cope with an illness. And whether or not the illness is life-threatening, it will obviously affect your loved ones. Your grandchild, in particular, at this age is likely to feel many different and indeed confusing emotions in connection with what is happening to you.

Younger children find it difficult to comprehend illness or death, and adolescents may already have experienced it in their own or a friend's family, but 8- to 12-year-olds look to family relationships for stability and like to consider them everlasting. You can help your grandchild to accept the nature of life and death. You may also find that concentrating on readying your grandchild for the inevitable gives you the strength to come to terms with your own mortality.

Find times when both of you are relaxed and not tired to introduce this topic in a low-key way. Ideally, discussions should take place while you are still healthy, but if you are ill and not likely to recover fully, you need to give your grandchild reassurance. By this stage in her education, she will have looked at the life cycles of various small creatures, and at church and Sunday school she may have discussed life and death in a religious context. But when it comes to someone dear to her, she will need guidance to accept what is going to happen.

Try to talk about your illness in a matter-of-fact manner. You don't have to go into too much detail, but you can, at this stage, gently suggest that sometimes people don't make a recovery. If, despite the understated nature of your discussion, your grandchild becomes upset, don't rush to change the subject. Instead, acknowledge her feelings and try again on another occasion.

If you have a strong religious faith, you may not find it difficult to discuss death, but you need to be absolutely sure what her parents believe before you talk to your grandchild. To receive conflicting explanations from the adults around her would be confusing and distressing. Make it clear to your grandchild that she can ask questions whenever she likes. You will probably find that she has already been thinking quite deeply. There are some good books for this age range that deal with illness and death within the family, and if

A child's first experience of death may well be the loss of a pet. Accepting that all creatures die— because of an accident, illness, or old age—is the first step toward realizing that you are not always going to be there. Burying the pet in the backyard introduces the idea of burial and that there is a special place where memories of a loved one are particularly resonant.

you find it hard to begin your discussions, you could read one or two of these with her (see pp. 210–11).

If you are ill, you may worry that your grandchild will be frightened by visiting you. But remember that it is the unknown— things that children are not allowed to see but can only imagine—that creates the greatest fears. Keep an open mind about this. If your grandchild becomes distressed and her parents say she would rather not visit, accept her feelings and write to her instead (record a tape if you feel too tired to write).

Funerals

When your grandchild is talking to you about life and death, she may want to know about funerals. Most children of this age will not have attended any, and she may feel anxious about whether to attend yours when the time comes. Point out that many people will probably cry, but that it is good to be able to express grief.

If you are both strong enough, she may want to play a part in choosing some of the music and making sure that things will be as you want them to be. But whether or not her involvement is this detailed, make it clear that you are content with whatever she decides and that you do not expect her to attend if she would rather not.

Many children feel surprisingly strongly about attending funerals, and sometimes parents try to stop them to spare their grief. There has been a growing tendency in modern times to try to minimize the trappings of death, especially where children are concerned. But it should be acknowledged that children have intense feelings of grief when someone dies, and the funeral can often be as cathartic for them as it is for the adults.

Loving memories

While you obviously do not want to dwell on your own death, especially if you are at present fit and well, you will undoubtedly gain comfort from knowing that you will

Funerals give children the chance to say goodbye. This can be particularly important if they feel they didn't do so—if you die in a hospital, for example. Funerals also give an opportunity for all family members to gather together to remember you.

be fondly remembered and talked about. Your grandchild's memories of you will be a means of keeping you alive for her.

Make it easy for your grandchild to remember you happily. Arrange for some photographs to be taken of you together (without explaining your intentions) and give them to her. If you feel able to, write a letter describing some of your best outings together and moments you treasure. Place this with your lawyer or a relative to be given to your grandchild after your death.

Last, you may ease your grandchild's grief in advance if you can subtly convey to her some of the different emotions that people experience when a loved one dies. Children often feel total disbelief at their first experience of death. Disbelief can be followed by anger because you have left them and they miss you so much. These feelings may also be mixed with guilt because they didn't always behave as they know you wanted them to or they didn't come to see you as much as they could have. If you can tackle the difficult task of planting some understanding and acceptance in your grandchild's mind, you will have left her with the strength to remember you in the best possible way.

Then and now:

Personal freedom

As recently as a generation ago, on nice days, parents told their children to go out and play and helped them to feel independent by asking them to run errands. In today's world such freedoms may no longer be practical.

THEN

In recent years the freedom children enjoyed to come and go at will, play in the streets, and roam through fields without supervision has been severely curtailed. Some psychologists place the blame firmly on the increased number of cars on the roads: children are driven everywhere, so they do not develop the ability that previous generations had to judge situations and keep themselves safe. Furthermore, because everyone drives everywhere, the streets are not full of benign adults, as they once were, to whom a child in trouble could turn.

Other professionals blame the media. Events such as road accidents and assaults, which would previously have gone largely unnoticed in the wider community, now make headline news, producing panic among parents. The result is that your grandchild will not experience the freedoms your own children had at a similar age. Her parents' attitude toward her safety will be different from your own when you were parenting.

It is important to keep your attitude toward children's safety and personal freedom at this age in perspective. Before your grandchild went to school, she was too young to be permitted to wander off alone; when she reaches adolescence, it will be impossible to accompany her at all times. But 8- to 12-year-olds are in the middle. If your grandchild is to grow into an independent person who can make sensible, safe decisions, she must be allowed some freedom, but striking the right balance can be difficult.

You must know the rules her parents impose and stick to them when she comes to stay or when you sit for them. If you feel that they are being obsessively protective, or turning a blind eye to potential dangers, speak out tactfully. But in the meantime, don't go against her parents' wishes.

Eight- to 12-year-olds enjoy being treated as adults for much of the time and want to achieve a sense of self-sufficiency, but they also want security. The most popular books among this age group are those in which children of the same age have incredible adventures without adult supervision. These tales always end with the characters safe and sound. This says a lot about 8- to 12-year-olds' growing need for independence and security in equal measure. Support what your grandchild's

NOW

Fewer cars on the roads meant that city streets were once safe for children to play in (above left). Today heavy traffic and fear of strangers make most parents unwilling to allow their children to make even short journeys alone.

parents are doing and saying, help to alert her in a non-alarmist way to the potential hazards of the outside world, and allow her to make positive and successful forays into that world.

Some children are sensitive to the fears of adults and react adversely to media coverage of accidents to and crimes against children. If your grandchild refuses to do anything independently, discuss the matter with her parents; in severe cases professional help may be needed.

Noting the differences

When your grandchild comes to stay, check what her parents allow her to do alone, so that you do not give her freedoms that her parents consider inappropriate.
• **At the age of 8**
You went to the movies with a friend of the same age. If your grandchild asks to do the same, is there a safe way of making this happen that will be acceptable to all concerned? Is there a morning or early afternoon show that is properly supervised? Could you go with the children and sit apart from them but within their view?
• **At the age of 10**
You slept in the backyard in a tent in the summer. If your grandchild asks to do the same, can you make your yard secure? If not, would she accept your camping out with her? Would she sleep in the sunroom or the basement as an alternative?
• **At the age of 12**
You went by bus or train to meet friends in the nearest town. If your grandchild asks to do the same, would she accept a ride into town from you, so that you know she arrives safely and meets her friends? Could you accompany her on the bus or train and do something else while she is with her friends?

WHEN YOU ARE IN CHARGE

• Ask her parents how they would act in certain situations; contact them if you are unsure about allowing a solo trip your grandchild proposes.

• You can negotiate with your grandchild, but don't be coerced into allowing her to go somewhere or do something you are uncomfortable with.

• Before you allow a solo trip, ask your grandchild what she would do if she were approached by a stranger or had an accident or were asked for help. Encouraging her to visualize possible problems and talking over solutions with her is a good way to prepare her to face them. Don't overdramatize.

• Make sure your grandchild knows how to use a public telephone to call you or emergency services. Give her a phone card or enough coins to make the call.

• On joint excursions discuss possible risks and ways to minimize them. Remember that there are many more traffic accidents involving young people than there are assaults and abductions.

• Do not leave your grandchild in your house alone even if her parents do in theirs. She cannot be responsible for protecting your home.

Separation and divorce
Your special role when families are fractured

Apart from the death of a parent, the greatest upheaval a child may face is her parents' separation and/or divorce. There is no way of making this a painless experience for your grandchild. Your part in the proceedings has to be played with great delicacy and great understanding if you want to achieve what is best for her and for you.

Remaining neutral
You may find your emotions are in turmoil as you try to understand what has gone wrong. It is possible to feel that your son or daughter has been badly treated or disappointed and that his or her partner is behaving appallingly. To act in an overtly partisan manner, however, could ruin your chances of maintaining a close relationship with your grandchild in the future. That would be tragic for both of you. The child's interests must take precedence over what you would like to say to the adults involved.

At all costs, remain calm and appear impartial, stating from the outset that your main concern is for your grandchild's wellbeing. Do not be tempted to seek consolation through talking to other family members about the problem. When relationships turn sour, adults have to walk a tightrope to avoid being accused of taking sides and making matters worse. Keep telling yourself, even when you come under pressure to be partisan, that you must remain neutral for your grandchild's sake.

If you feel overwhelmed by what is happening—and it is common for grandparents to wonder if their own parenting skills are to blame for the failure of their children's marriages—talk to a professional counselor or phone an appropriate helpline so that you can discuss your worries in confidence.

One of the damaging aspects of relationship breakdowns for children is seeing the parents they love angry at each other. If you can shield your grandchild from some of the ugliness by offering temporary shelter while parents figure out their next step, you may help the situation.

Your grandchild's feelings
In the same way that you may hold yourself in some way culpable for your child's failure to sustain a happy marriage, your grandchild may think that the separation or divorce is her fault. She may have been the innocent pawn in a lot of arguments during the marriage and, as in so many cases, misunderstood the root of the trouble. It is usual for children in this situation to assume blame in an attempt to protect their parents from the burden. They would rather feel that they themselves are at fault than that their parents are imperfect, out of control, or willing to break up the family.

Without forcing discussions, you should be ready to listen for as long as your grandchild wants to talk about what has happened. That may help her to make sense of it. If she finds it hard to introduce the topic because she is so distressed, you should recognize the signs. Then give her a hug or a cuddle until she is ready to begin.

Your grandchild may well feel, as her parents start to make arrangements to live apart, that she too is being rejected. She may become insecure and revert to immature habits and behavior. If her parents' divorce involves her changing schools, homes, and possibly acquiring new step-siblings as well, she will have an immense amount to cope with. You may then be the one stable element in her life. Try to stifle your own feelings about what is going on and concentrate in a positive way on her feelings.

You can help your grandchild to cope with and accept all the adjustments she will have to make. You may well be the difference between her facing the future with total panic or feeling positive about it.

She may choose to focus on aspects of the problem that to you seem rather unimportant—what will happen to the family dog, for example. This is her way of trying to chip away at a dilemma that will for some time seem all-encompassing. You could set about relieving her anxiety by suggesting temporary or, where possible, permanent solutions to such problems. Always check that her parents will agree to anything you suggest before telling your grandchild. You might lend some help by agreeing to care for the family pets, for example, until everyone involved is permanently settled.

When emotions are running high, as they are in this situation, you may receive unexpected snubs when trying to help. Brace yourself to bear them in silence because, however resolute the adults involved may seem—and even if you can accept that their decision may be the right one—they are most certainly suffering, too.

CASE HISTORY

I always found my son's wife, Trudy, rather distant and cold, but made every effort to make her feel part of the family. And after my granddaughter, Laura, was born (she's eight now), we got along much better. Trudy was an only child and her mother was dead, so she seemed to turn to me for support and help with Laura. At the time my son seemed pleased, and we all spent a lot of time together.

It came as a complete shock when they separated, but my first thoughts were for Laura. I panicked at the idea that Trudy would take her away, and I would never see my granddaughter again. Imagine my surprise when my son told me that Trudy had agreed to his taking Laura when he relocated. He said it was the only way to become independent and get to know his daughter. He accused me of ganging up with Trudy against him and said I had turned his wife into a different person since Laura's birth. He needed to get away and start again.

That was six months ago, and I have only now received a letter from my son, including a recent photograph of Laura. She looks well. They intend to return soon, and I am trying to prepare myself for seeing my son and Laura. I feel bitter that he has blamed me for his marriage going wrong and deprived me of my granddaughter's company, but I do accept that somehow, in making a great effort to include Trudy in the family and to get to know Laura, I must without realizing it have excluded my son.

I intend to be very careful how I handle the situation, even though I'm desperate to see Laura.

Separation and divorce

If your time with your grandchild is more restricted after his parents' separation, you may feel reluctant to dilute it further by inviting a step-sibling to share in the activities and excursions you enjoy. But your acceptance of change will help your grandchild come to terms with the upheaval in his life.

Practical arrangements

Once you have negotiated all the emotional challenges created by separation and divorce, you still have to face up to the new arrangements that have been made.

You will, of course, have to respect the custody agreements that have been reached regarding your grandchild. If, for example, your son has access to your grandchild only on weekends, you will obviously be hoping that he will share some of this time with you, while appreciating that he will, at first anyway, probably want to have her to himself as much as possible. If you are lucky enough to have been able to maintain good relationships with both parents throughout their separation and divorce, you may be able to see your grandchild more frequently, as long as the parent with custody has not moved a long distance away.

Your child may have problems getting access to your grandchild. The parent with weekend only access may not have found a suitable new home, or may have moved in with a new partner, making the new home uncomfortable to the parent with custody. In these cases you could offer your home as neutral territory. The parents can meet there to transfer your grandchild to the other parent and discuss her welfare when necessary. This could help ease some of the discomfort your grandchild will feel during these meetings and give you some time with her.

If you are in the miserable position of having no access to your grandchild, make every effort to improve things. In the first instance, appeal to the parent with custody to allow you to spend time with your grandchild for the child's sake. If this has no effect, you could try appealing to your grandchild's other grandparents if you know they have access and you think they might be sympathetic to your plight. If this is not appropriate, try to find someone who is known and liked by all concerned and who can be relied upon to act in a neutral, sensitive way. If there simply isn't anyone who can help you among family and friends, contact the local social services agency to see if there is a family mediation unit through which contact between you and your grandchild might be reestablished.

If all informal mediation is to no avail, you have recourse under the law. Up until ten years ago, very few states recognized a grandparent's desire to visit the grandchild as a legal right. Although all states—with the exception of the District of Columbia—now have laws that allow grandparents to petition the courts for visitation rights, these rights are not enforceable in all cases. It is estimated that up to 50,000 cases are active at any one time. You also have the legal right to seek a contempt of court citation against parents who deny grandparents time with their grandchildren once visitation rights have been granted. The organizations listed under Useful addresses on pp. 210–211 can advise you on local legislation.

Seeking custody

If you believe that your grandchild would be better off living with you—either because the parent with custody is unable to care for her due to illness or has disappeared and left the child with you, or if you have been temporarily fostering your grandchild, or you strongly suspect that your grandchild is being abused or neglected—you may be able to apply through the juvenile courts for permission to seek custody. There are, however, no automatic circumstances under which this will be granted. Obviously your petition stands more chance of succeeding if your grandchild has already been living with you or if there are other exceptional circumstances.

In many states, a child whose parents cannot care for her is placed under state supervision, while parents have the opportunity to address the issues that prompted the state to act. The state can place the child with an appropriate adult (such as a grandparent) if the parent consents or if the court considers that the parent is unfit.

If your grandchild lives with you, but you do not have legal custody, you may have to pay not only for her support but also for her education. Financial assistance from the state or from Social Security may be available.

Your overall aim should be to reestablish for your grandchild the solid foundations that may have been severely shaken by her parents' divorce. In taking this on, bear in mind that the demands a child will make, in terms of your energy and time,

When emotions are running high, nobody behaves well. Apportioning blame when a relationship breaks down benefits no one. Your impartiality and fairness to all may help to relieve some of the tensions at this time, but be prepared to be caught in the crossfire.

will be considerably more than those of the normal grandparenting activities in which you have been involved.

Because you will be trying to repair the damage done by a family split, you should not shoulder the responsibility by yourself. It is vital that your grandchildren now experience some continuity in their lives. If there are other family members who can assist, call upon them. This will help conserve your strength for the months and years ahead. You will need every ounce you possess to complete this most demanding but rewarding job.

Some children view packing their belongings to move to a new home as an adventure, despite their need for stability when relationships break down. Be sure that you can carry out any offers of help or support you make. The last thing children of separated parents need is more uncertainty and broken promises.

Separation and divorce

Extended families

The initial repercussions of your child's divorce center around the care of your grandchild and any arrangements you are involved in making for her. But its impact does not stop there. Most couples who divorce remarry within a short time. One in three children in the United States will have divorced parents by the time he or she is 16, and about 50 percent of divorcees remarry in two to three years.

A grandchild whose parents remarry may have to face step-siblings becoming a part of her life, or one or both of her parents choosing to have more children, or both. If the new partner comes to the relationship with children of his or her own, you may be needed to counsel your grandchild into accepting and coping with the shifts in the family. In order to do this properly, you must first come to terms with the changes yourself.

A child who is brought into your family by the new partner may be feeling every bit as bewildered and unsure of herself as your own grandchild. You need to have enough love to go around, without making your own grandchild feel she is losing her special place in your affections.

If you have not taken to the new partner or have not been given the chance to do so, you might find it difficult to accept the child. However, it is to the detriment of your own grandchild and all your family relationships if you cannot stretch yourself a little further. If your step-grandchild has reached adolescence, be prepared for things to be a little more difficult than if she had met you earlier in her life. Having patience and striving to be tolerant and understanding will pay dividends in the end.

Adolescents often take their parents' divorce and subsequent remarriage a lot harder than younger children do. In addition to being forced to accept their parent's new relationship, they are also trying to cope with their own emerging adulthood. You could provide the steady influence that such a child needs; if you are able to do so, your grandchild will doubtless experience fewer problems in her own relationship with her step-sibling than she might otherwise.

Most children welcome or eventually warm to a new half-sibling. But an adolescent— above all one who has not accepted his parent's new relationship—can be ambivalent. Whatever your grandchild says, focus on the fact that the baby deserves all your love, and reassure the older child that his place in your heart is unaffected.

A new baby

If your son or daughter and new partner produce a new baby, in theory your emotions will be less complicated than with step-grandchildren because the baby is, after all, a "real" grandchild. In practice, you may not have fully accepted the new marital arrangements. Or you may be overwhelmed with anxieties about how the grandchild you know and love will cope with yet another new development in the family situation.

If you let your fears show, your grandchild will pick up on them and judge that there must really be something to worry about. An addition to the family is surely a positive thing, something to be welcomed. With luck, your grandchild, like most other children, will be delighted with the novelty of the new arrival, and you can allay any feelings of being left out by giving her lots of extra attention and time.

Parents who are still building their own relationship may seem to have time only for their new baby. If so, your task is to shield your grandchild from feelings of neglect. There are lots of good children's books on the subject of new arrivals and the mixed emotions they cause, so you could try reading some with your grandchild. You could also help to refocus the parents' attention on their older child by organizing family get-togethers that include other children. You could take the baby out so that the parents can spend some time with your other grandchild. Do not be afraid to tell them, tactfully, when you offer to look after the baby, that you think your grandchild is looking forward to spending some special time with them. They may simply not have noticed that they were leaving her out.

Fair shares

Once you have adjusted to the emotional changes that come with an extended family, you will need to make some practical readjustments. If you have put aside

The mixed emotions—fear, bewilderment, anger, betrayal, guilt, even relief—your grandchild feels toward her parents may spill over into her relationship with you. At this time you need all your love and patience to accept that any behavioral problems are temporary and that your easy rapport will return.

savings or bonds or set up a college plan for your first grandchild, you should extend these benefits to the new arrivals in your family. By being scrupulously fair in this way you will show everyone that you have accepted what has happened and give your children and grandchildren the best possible chances of making a success of their new relationships.

In addition to any financial provisions you may have made, you will also have to rethink how you spend your time with your grandchildren. If you normally take your grandchild out once a week, continue this exclusive arrangement for as long as she wants you to. Be sure to arrange a day for your step-grandchild to do something with you too. Also arrange to spend time with the new baby. At first, this may seem like a time-consuming and exhausting schedule of events, but eventually your first grandchild will probably suggest that her sibling come along on your excursions. When that happens, you will have the satisfaction of knowing that you did the right thing. One of the reasons she is better able to accept and enjoy her new family is the help you have given her.

CHAPTER SEVEN

The Young Adolescent
12 to 16 years

There will be times, even in the closest-knit families, when your adolescent grandchild's struggle for independence results in behavior that will test the patience of the most even-tempered parents. The fact that he is treading a well-worn path toward adulthood does not make the going easier, especially if he seems to be attacking everything your family stands for.

Your handling of such situations can make all the difference to their outcome. If you can listen when everyone else is exhausted, you may help to keep his relationship with his parents on a more even keel. Through sharing activities and skills, you will broaden his experience and give him resources to fall back on when life gets difficult. And by letting him know that you understand at least a part of his world and some of his concerns, you will keep the lines of communication open and build on the friendship you have always enjoyed.

Areas of conflict

Your special role in dealing with the ups and downs of adolescence

Few families escape completely the tempers and tantrums of early adolescence, a particularly sensitive time in your grandchild's growing years. If you live far away and see your grandchild infrequently, he may appear to be the polite, sweet-natured person you have always known, and you won't witness his more unattractive moments.

However, if you spend a lot of time with his family, the strain of being on his best behavior for you may be too much for him, and you too may be on the receiving end of his moods and angst. This will be as hurtful for you as it is for his parents. Try to talk calmly to him about what is bothering him: the younger he is, though, the more likely it is that he will listen to you and you will be able to influence him. At these times it is good to remember your own child's teens. Recall—silently—the moments when he was argumentative and moody, and tried your patience. Remember the fights about the length of his hair and what time he came home at night. And realize that you both survived!

The most challenging teenage behavior usually occurs between the ages of 11 and 15, the period of rapid growth and intense hormonal changes. Physically, your grandchild is almost an adult, capable of becoming a parent himself. Emotionally, he is still a child who tries to hide the fact, often by being moody and self-centered. It helps if all family members understand that he is reacting to a real—and perhaps deep-seated—fear of leaving the security of childhood for a less certain adulthood.

Making friends

Some areas of dispute seem to be common to most families with an adolescent in their midst. High on the list come his friends. In this transitional period your grandchild begins to seek security in a group of people his own age, and it is they who appear to exert the most influence over

Snacks at all hours of the day and night—with refrigerator door left ajar and juice cartons and leftovers not put away—may seem reasonable to most adolescents. But when your grandchild is at your house, you can insist that he and his friends clean up after themselves.

You and your granddaughter's parents may be horrified by dyed and gelled hair, eccentric clothes, and body piercing. But if you can accept that such fashions are part of growing up—and be willing to be seen having a good time in your grandchild's company—you may help her come to terms with her emerging adulthood.

him. For the most part peer pressure is positive: the group provides the comfort and companionship of a family at this time. Friends can offer mutual support because each one is experiencing similar conflicts.

Avoid criticizing his friends unless they are truly objectionable. Of course, if you or his parents suspect that someone is leading your grandchild into serious trouble, the friendship should be discouraged as firmly as possible without actually driving a headstrong teenager into defiance. But if the only opposition is the way a friend dresses or the fact that he is not as bright as your grandchild, leave well enough alone.

Encourage his parents to get to know his friends and invite them into their home, however unattractive they seem. Do this yourself if you live close by. They may be willing to meet at your house, and you may find that they are more pleasant than you imagined. Having a home where they are welcome limits the amount of time teenagers spend hanging out, often on street corners.

You should probably worry more if your grandchild appears to have no friends at all. If he has a fight with his parents, he has no one to call to get things off his chest and no one with whom to share stories about

his diabolical family and their unreasonable ways. Be sure your grandchild knows that you are always available to listen, even if he only wants to moan about his parents. If you don't live close by, encourage him to phone when he is lonely.

How he looks

The first signs of adolescent rebellion usually manifest themselves in a teenager's appearance. Your grandson may choose torn jeans and scruffy T-shirts, and your granddaughter may wear too much makeup and skirts that you think are too short. And at a time when you might expect them to be bold and flamboyant, both sexes dress from head to foot in black.

Adolescents also tend to experiment a lot with their hairstyle, since this is a quick and effective way of looking like a different person—which, of course, is what your grandchild now feels he is. Dyeing hair is popular, often in what you consider outrageous shades. Try to conceal your dismay or amusement; your grandchild is probably hoping to shock, so don't give him the satisfaction of reacting to his latest extravagance. Such crazes are usually short-lived and harmless.

▶

Areas of conflict

More difficult to accept is a teenager's urge to have some part of his body pierced. You can probably accept pierced ears even in your grandson, since it is now more common for boys to wear earrings too. But you may find it incomprehensible that he wants to wear a ring through his nose or have a stud in his navel.

This is only a matter of fashion, but he should know that once a hole has been pierced, it will not close completely again. Reminding him of this (his parents may simply have forbidden it, which will make him even more determined) may persuade him to delay having it done, and then he may give up the whole idea. If he goes ahead anyway, you don't have to like or admire it; but make sure he knows that it doesn't stop you from loving him.

Annoying habits

Teenagers tend to slump lethargically in front of the television. The amount of channel-surfing that goes on indicates their lack of absorption in any particular program. Your grandchild's parents may well decide to limit his television viewing if he is doing nothing else or if TV interferes with his schoolwork. Obviously, if you spend hours watching TV, you can't expect him not to do the same when he is with you. Suggest going to see a ballgame or a tennis match, going fishing, or whatever else might make him enthusiastic.

Sloppy bedrooms—unmade bed, dirty laundry scattered over the floor, unwashed glasses—can infuriate parents. The usual teenage response is that it is not worth making a fuss. He has more important things to worry about, such as the meaning of life or whether his friend's rock band will achieve worldwide fame. If his parents complain to you about this, console them

One day there is a lovable child, the next a surly, uncooperative monster who argues about everything, makes unreasonable demands, and sulks and slams doors when thwarted. Some parent-child conflict is inevitable in the teen years—try to support both sides.

with the fact that messy teens often become highly house-proud adults.

It may be difficult to lure a teenager out of bed in the morning. While it is true that excessive fatigue can be a sign of depression or drug abuse, teenagers do need to sleep more than younger children because of all the hormonal and physical changes taking place. As long as he is active and fit when awake, there is nothing to worry about. When he stays with you, don't hang around waiting to make his breakfast when he does emerge—leave that to him.

If you are worried about your grandchild's safety when she stays with you, set limits. If you go to bed early and are unwilling to let her stay out as late as her parents do, explain why. She may accept from you what she would call thoroughly unreasonable in her parents.

The state of his room at home may drive his parents to distraction, but this is less likely to be a problem for you, even if your grandchild has his own room at your house, simply because you can go in and clean up once he has gone home. You won't find month-old soft-drink cans if he stays only a few days.

Reasonable hours

If you are a witness to arguments between your grandchild and his parents over the hour at which he should return after a night out, don't remind your child in your grandchild's hearing of your own disagreements on this subject. These disputes are best solved by compromise. If parents insist that he come home by a reasonable time when he has to get up for school, but extend the curfew if he has a party or disco to go to, both sides should be happy.

Use your memories of parenting to advise his parents to get to know the parents of their teenager's friends. At least they may then learn where he is going, with whom, and what time he might be back.

Education

One of the most serious concerns parents have at this time is that their child appears to be dropping out of school, mentally if not physically. He seems to be doing less and less work, and endless arguments result from the fact that he won't sit down and do his homework or study for an important exam. Often this behavior is related to his fear of failing at school: he feels determined to reject school before it rejects him.

Sometimes this is caused by a lack of motivation, or social problems, or a temporary phase of teenage malaise. And some adolescents truly believe that they are too mature for school. In other cases the problem may be related to a particular subject and could be alleviated by arranging for a tutor or other extra help. Try to find out what the problem is; the ear of someone who is sympathetic, but less closely involved than his parents, is often just what is needed.

Encourage him to believe he can succeed by showing an interest in his schoolwork and making much of any academic success, however modest. Ask him about his plans for the future, and if you suspect that your grandchild would really be happier in a non-academic career, support him in whatever he chooses to do.

A safe haven

There will be times when your grandchild finds it easier to handle his anger and frustration if he is away from his immediate family. Knowing that he can use your house as a refuge when things get tough can be reassuring. His parents may also use you as a refuge when the fights and angst get to be too much for them.

Try not to take sides; you probably won't want to. In your special position you will have insight into both parent and child, which will help you to maintain a balanced viewpoint. It is this calm objectivity that is so valuable to all members of the family during these stressful times.

Gifts for 12- to 16-year-olds

Choosing an appropriate present for a young teenager

By the time children reach early adolescence, it is easier to give them gifts of money than to go out and buy them something you think they might like. Although 12- to 16-year-olds do appreciate receiving cash and take delight in being able to choose something for themselves, they also still enjoy the process of receiving a gift, unwrapping it, and discovering what's inside. Moreover, a gift you select yourself lets your grandchild know that you still think about what he might like.

FAIL-SAFE GIFT PLAN

• Season ticket to see his favorite sports team. This could also be a combined Christmas and birthday present because of the cost.

• Toiletries: aftershave (it doesn't matter that he doesn't shave yet), perfume, soaps, toilet kit filled with travel-size bottles (for sleepovers and trips), towels.

• A savings account for college.

• Gift certificate for a favorite hairdresser or barber, shoe store, or health club.

• Fan club membership of a best-loved group.

• A series of sessions at an ice rink, tennis court, gym, swimming pool, or ski slope.

• Materials for redecorating his room (as long as his parents have given permission).

• Set of hand weights, sports clothing, video workout.

• Bicycle, ice skates, in-line skates, skateboard. Ask his parents if there are favored brands to buy.

If you find you approach your grandchild's birthday every year without any good ideas of what to buy him, and don't want to ask him directly, look for clues about his interests in the preceding months. When you see him, listen carefully for any information that may help you to find him a special present when the time arrives. If he is enthusiastic about music, for example, you could purchase tickets for a concert near the time of his birthday; if he reveals an interest in car racing, you could arrange a trip to a go-kart track or lessons on a simulator, and so on.

Consider alternating gifts of money and surprise items. You can vary the way you give cash by pledging a set amount for each month from this birthday until the next or from Christmas the year-round. This may seem less exciting to him than receiving a larger sum, but it will be appreciated when he has splurged all the rest of his cash.

If your grandchild collects CDs or tapes, you could buy a gift certificate to be sure that you don't duplicate what is already in his collection. Subscriptions to favorite magazines give a lot of pleasure, and if your grandchild is concerned about endangered species, you could pay for him to adopt a whale or gorilla, for example. He will receive information on "his" animal and how the protection project is progressing.

Many young teens are adventurous about food. You could buy an appropriate cookbook, with a wok or pan and some interesting spices and starter ingredients. Consider a course in cooking, either at a school or on video. He will appreciate that you share his new interests and treat him with a little sophistication.

Ongoing gifts, such as subscriptions, are popular. And if you know which CD, computer game, or video is on his list, it will be a surefire hit. Sports equipment is a good choice, as is fitness gear. Many young teens are fitness-conscious. If you prefer to give money, add a purse or wallet.

In addition to catering to your grandchild's tastes, you could introduce him to some of yours. A teenager who scorns classic movies may be won over by the stormy romanticism of *Wuthering Heights*, for example, and this may spark a lifelong interest in old movies and prepare him for outings you both enjoy.

If he has always liked looking at your collection of stamps or coins, start him off with his own set. This is a gift you can add to, as long as his interest is genuine rather than stemming from a desire to please you.

Although 12- to 16-year-olds are fashion-conscious, buying clothes for them is a minefield. Ideas about what is acceptable are so well defined by the peer group that it is virtually impossible for an adult to get it right. A way around this is to plan a shopping trip together and stipulate an amount he can spend on clothes.

Gifts of an educational nature often seem unexciting, but if you can live with the initial lukewarm reception, you may find your grandchild expressing his appreciation later when he realizes the value of what you have given him. CD-ROMs, videos, books, and tapes may make all the difference when he is studying.

The thicker skin you developed when you were parenting may be useful now. Teens are hard to please and can be tactless about an unwanted present. Their greater maturity in many areas of life does not necessarily make them less fickle than when they were younger about longed-for gifts once they have had them a few weeks. If you find such fickleness in an older child upsetting, opt for money or gift certificates instead.

A computer game may bring your grandchild—and you—hours of fun, and educational CD-ROMs may help with his school work. You could also pay the membership fee for an Internet service.

Excursions with 12- to 16-year-olds

Broadening your grandchild's outlook on your trips with him

Now that your grandchild is an adolescent, there are lots of grown-up places to go with him. You might have loved sharing his enjoyment of zoos and theme parks, but you may find it a relief to introduce him to some more-adult pastimes—taking him to the theater, to a classical concert, to an art gallery, or even to a good restaurant. These interests will enrich his whole life if he has an unpressured introduction to them in his youth and has the opportunity to learn to appreciate them at his own pace.

You may be hesitant about suggesting such an excursion because he has an active social life of his own, and you may think that the last thing he wants is to be seen with you. However, he is more likely to agree with any plans you make than he is to comply with those of his parents. He may even convince himself that he is doing you a favor by accompanying you to a concert or the theater—which will make him feel grown up and good about himself.

Your grandchild may be antagonistic toward anything that smacks of culture, convinced that he is going to be bored, but you can overcome these prejudices in subtle, easygoing ways. A teenager who has shown no interest in serious theater may be more interested if the first production he sees is related to what he is studying at school and might help him to get better grades. Most plays come to life with professional actors in a way they never can

A visit to the ballet can be a magical experience. If you are unsure whether your grandchild will be happy to sit through an entire piece, choose a program featuring a selection of extracts for your first trip.

If you plan to attend an art exhibition (left), try to get hold of a catalog in advance so that you can both read about particular artists and the work on display before you go.

in a school production or when they are intoned in the classroom. Plays by popular authors such as Arthur Miller or Tennessee Williams, which may appear on the school curriculum, are often performed in local or municipal theaters. Your grandchild will be pleasantly surprised at how absorbing he finds the play, and he'll want to see others. Build on this initial interest by taking him to other plays or performances.

Music and art

If he listens to nothing but rock music, he may be reluctant to attend a classical concert. Make a deal with him: you will listen to a recording of his favorite band if he gives the classical composers a hearing. He may be surprised at how familiar some of the music is—a great deal is used as background music in films and television programs. If he becomes hooked, imagine the hours of pleasure you can spend together, going to concerts and listening to music on CDs and tapes. Take advantage of birthdays and other special occasions to buy him recordings of pieces that you have enjoyed together. You may discover that he is listening to Mozart rather than heavy metal on his stereo.

If going to art exhibitions is one of your favorite pastimes, suggest that he might like to go with you. Like the theater and classical music, art does not necessarily come into a young person's sphere of experience. A small exhibition by a single painter might be a good way to introduce him to the joys of viewing, rather than a gallery full of national treasures, which can be rather overwhelming.

An excursion with your grandchild might end with a meal in one of your favorite restaurants. It can be enormous fun giving a young person the chance to try new dishes, learn to manipulate chopsticks, or handle shellfish. Not only will he be proud of his new accomplishments, but he will also be acquiring social skills that will help him feel relaxed and confident in later life.

CASE HISTORY

We hardly ever ate out when I was a child, but once when I was about five we stayed with my grandparents, and the whole family went to a restaurant. My gran had a plate of what I was told were shellfish. While the rest of us ate turkey or steaks, she dismembered and peeled those shellfish of different sizes and ate them; some of them she just tipped into her mouth. I wanted to try them, so she slipped me a couple of things, which tasted delicious.

When I was 12 my grandparents moved nearer to us, and for my 13th birthday they offered to take me for a "grown-up" meal. I remembered the shellfish and said that was what I would like. They took me to a French restaurant and ordered a similar dish for me. There were some things I didn't like much, but most of it tasted wonderful.

After that I went out regularly with them and ate all sorts of things I had never tasted before. They took me to an Italian restaurant with candles in wine bottles on the tables, where I tasted pizza that bore no resemblance to those my friends and I ordered in. On another occasion we had sushi at a Japanese restaurant, and we all laughed as we tried to master chopsticks the first time we went to a Chinese restaurant.

I'll never forget the fun we had during those years. Thanks to my grandparents, I went away to college with a social confidence I wouldn't have had otherwise and was able to cook slightly unusual dishes that my friends loved. My gran's been dead for five years now, but I still think of her every time I go to a restaurant and try to guess what she would have chosen from the menu.

Then and now:

Sex and sexuality

Hasty experimentation and fears of pregnancy characterized relationships between the sexes as recently as two generations ago. Today's teenagers are more relaxed about sexuality.

THEN

Since the end of World War II, there has been an enormous shift in attitudes toward sexual behavior. Unless your parents were particularly open-minded, sex was almost certainly an unmentionable topic when you were growing up. Now it is discussed freely, and most children from the age of six or seven know something about the basic facts of life—not only about how a baby grows in mommy's tummy, but also how the "seed" gets there in the first place. You may find this openness embarrassing. But if you can remember the fear and ignorance that prevailed when you were young, perhaps you can understand the benefits of such frankness.

In the industrialized world, teenagers are physically ready for a sexual relationship and biologically capable of becoming parents long before society believes that they are emotionally prepared. Many teenagers no longer consider virginity to be a precious commodity; some view it as a burden to get rid of as soon as possible. The result is that although most countries set an age at which sexual intercourse is legal, many children experience it well before the legal age.

However, the perception that "everyone is doing it" is not true: there are still many young people who choose to wait to have sexual relationships until they feel ready for them. They also view decisions about sexual relationships as personal, rather than governed by the moral values imposed on them by previous generations or by religion. You may be able to take comfort from the fact that a majority of teenagers still say they believe lovemaking should take place in a stable, long-term relationship, although not necessarily one that is leading to marriage.

The rate of teenage pregnancies in some areas remains high, despite the fact that contraception is vastly improved and much more accessible than it was even a generation ago. Research has shown that teenage pregnancies are less likely when young people have the facts and are given access to family planning services. The old myth that knowledge inevitably leads to experimentation is not borne out by the evidence. The rate of teenage pregnancies in Holland, which has a liberal approach to teenage sexuality and excellent family planning services, is much lower than in other Western countries.

One factor that remains unchanged is that children still receive much of their information—or misinformation—from giggling groups in the school playground. Young people prefer this information to come primarily from their parents, with

NOW

teachers as a back-up. But many parents continue to opt out of this responsibility, despite the widespread discussion of sexual matters on television and in magazines and newspapers. The problem with sex as part of the curriculum is that school can convey the physical facts but is less effective in discussing the emotional implications of sexuality. Children need to understand how overwhelmingly strongly they can feel when aroused, and how much their emotions are tied in with physical drive.

Practical knowledge
Given that many young teens are sexually active, an important concern should be that they are informed enough to prevent conception. Many people of all ages find the concept of their parents' sexuality deeply embarrassing, so your grandchild may find it easier to talk to you than to them. If he feels he can discuss anything he likes with you and knows that it is in confidence, you may be able to give sensible advice that would be unacceptable coming from a parent. But do encourage him to talk to them, too.

The earlier teenagers become sexually active, the more important it is that they are properly informed. Despite health education efforts, some may still relate using a condom only to avoiding pregnancy. But all need to know that condoms are also important for the prevention of sexually transmitted diseases, including AIDS.

Contraception
Attitudes about sex and sexuality may cause heated exchanges between teenage children and their parents, and advising a young teen about contraception poses a dilemma for most adults. On one hand, there is reluctance to do anything that might appear to condone sexual activity; on the other, teenagers must be made aware of the need to take responsibility for their actions. If you know your grandchild is sexually active, encourage him to get professional advice on contraceptives. The most common are:

• **The Pill:** There is concern among health professionals that using the Pill before the menstrual cycle is well established can adversely affect fertility later. And long-term use has been linked with thrombosis and other problems. However, some parents and doctors think the advantages outweigh the risks if a young girl is sexually active.

• **Diaphragm:** Although a young girl could be fitted for a diaphragm, it's unlikely that this method will appeal to her or her partner. And because she is still growing, the diaphragm may not fit properly for long.

• **Condoms:** Unlike the Pill or a diaphragm, which provide protection only against pregnancy, condoms also protect against sexually transmitted diseases. The responsibility for carrying condoms should not be the boy's alone. A girl who goes out on a date knowing that she is likely to make love should take responsibility for her own protection.

Drug awareness
Understanding teenagers' interest in legal and illegal substances

Lots of adults drink and smoke—you may be one of them—but you would be horrified if someone suggested that you were a drug addict. Nevertheless, tobacco and alcohol are drugs and cause more widespread health and social problems than such illegal substances as marijuana or heroin. One difference is that alcohol and cigarettes are socially acceptable. It is important to bear this in mind when you are discussing drugs with your grandchild.

Smoking
Despite extensive health-education projects and the damage caused by smoking cigarettes (which young people might witness in their older relatives), young adolescents continue to take up smoking, with girls starting younger than boys. Teenagers know that over 80 percent of lung cancer cases are related to smoking, that smoking also causes bronchitis and other serious breathing difficulties, and that thousands of smokers die prematurely and in pain each year.

Smoking also makes the breath stale and discolors the teeth, and the smell of smoke lingers on clothes. Yet by the age of 15, nearly a third of adolescents have taken up the habit.

One reason children continue to find smoking so alluring is that they believe it makes them appear sophisticated. They are continually exposed to smoking (and drinking) if not at home, then in the street, in films, on television, and in advertising. Family example is also influential. Children who have two parents who smoke are three times more likely to take it up than the children of nonsmokers; those with older siblings who smoke are even more likely to be attracted to the idea. The positive news is that teenagers become much more aware of the risks associated with smoking as they grow older. The problem then is the difficulty of giving it up.

If you and other family members smoke, it is difficult to argue that your grandchild should not. The idea that you are setting a bad example may spur you to kick a lifelong habit. But if this is not your choice, the only thing you can do that is likely to have an impact is to emphasize to your grandchild the difficulties of giving up smoking once he starts. Telling him that nicotine is as addictive as heroin may get his attention. If you have never smoked and you disapprove, your grandchild may do it to defy you and his parents. That doesn't mean you have to allow him to smoke in your house.

The problem with alcohol is its ubiquity. If your grandchild often sees you enjoying a beer, cooking with wine, or drinking with each meal, he will believe that he can do so too. Aim for moderate social drinking when he is around.

WARNING SIGNS

Your grandchild may mask a developing alcohol problem for several months, simply because many of the symptoms, such as irritability, are so common among adolescents. If he is suffering from several of the symptoms listed below, however, he could be in trouble:
• mood changes
• irritability
• insomnia
• poor appetite or a craving for sweet things or eating enormous amounts between drinking bouts
• aggression
• loss of interest in hobbies and other pastimes
   If you suspect that his drinking is getting out of hand, tell his parents.

Young teens are constantly exposed to street drugs: in the playground, at parties, and in clubs and discos. Aim to give them the self-esteem to say no.

Alcohol

Alcohol abuse can cause a young person to harm himself and others. An easygoing, mild-mannered adolescent can become aggressive and violent under the influence of alcohol and may even find himself charged with a criminal offense.

You and the rest of the family can play an important part in teaching your grandchild sensible drinking habits, which is more effective than locking the liquor cabinet and warning him constantly about the dangers of alcohol. Forbidding a young teenager to have any alcohol at all may only make him even more curious and determined to try it.

The first alcoholic drinks tasted by most people tend to be given by parents or family at home—perhaps at a special family celebration meal—where young adults can experience the effects in a safe environment. A child who grows up accustomed to those around him drinking in moderation is more likely to develop sensible drinking habits when he is out with friends. Girls tend to receive less encouragement to drink—both at home

and socially—than boys, for whom there is still something of a macho element attached.

From about the age of 15 or 16, teenagers tend to drink with friends, and this is where problems can arise. Although laws govern the age at which young people can buy alcohol, many children openly flout them. There may be laziness or disregard on the part of the person selling the drinks, but it is also true that some teenagers look so mature that it does not occur to the vendor to ask for ID or to question their age.

When asked about the effects of alcohol, young people tend to emphasize the positive ones, such as feeling happy and relaxed and having a good time, rather than remembering the headaches, nausea, and hangovers that result from drinking too much. Although alcohol helps to relieve tension and aids relaxation, it does not offer any lasting solutions to problems or situations children may be having with family, friends, or schoolwork. Young people need to be made aware—through discussion, not angry rebuke—that overindulgence will, in the long run, add to their problems.

If your grandchild develops his social skills under the influence of alcohol, he may not learn how to behave without it. Those who drink heavily as teenagers are also more likely to use other drugs. A young person may develop a pattern of becoming inebriated with alcohol one evening and stoned on marijuana or even cocaine the next. You are likely to find this recklessness and disregard for his health and well-being most upsetting.

Drug awareness

Illegal drugs

Because illegal drugs may be outside your own experience, you may feel at a disadvantage when it comes to discussing them with your grandchild. Your own child might have occasionally smoked marijuana, but generally the use of illicit drugs was very low until the late 1960s. Today, a huge array of illicit drugs is available, and your grandchild may be tempted to experiment with a variety of substances. Older people often do not know enough to tackle this issue confidently. Since you may have to confront it at some point in your grandchild's adolescence, it is important to read and absorb as much information as you can.

All young teenagers need to be aware of the dangers of drugs. It is an alarming fact that children of only 13 and 14 years of age, and younger, may be exposed to drugs in the school playground. The reasons they try them are many and varied, but background and performance at school do not seem to be relevant factors. Peer pressure plays an enormous part—a child may take drugs to avoid being the odd one out. He may be tempted in an effort to escape from problems at home, or to dull the pain of failing an important exam or breaking up with a girlfriend. It may be simple curiosity, or he may be intrigued by

Drug use first became common among young people in the 1960s as one aspect of the new emphasis on personal freedom. Then, as now, marijuana was the most common street drug.

TELLING ALL

If you suspect that your grandchild is smoking, drinking excessively, or using illicit drugs, you must tell his parents. The chances are that you will only be confirming their own suspicions, but at least you can join forces at this particularly difficult time.

• Never offer your grandchild a cigarette.

• Encourage sensible drinking by setting an example.

• Be well informed about illicit drugs and their effects. A grandchild convinced of your ignorance may use drugs in your home.

• If you have charge of your grandchild and suspect alcohol or drug abuse, seek help immediately.

• Find out about counselors and community support groups for both him and his family.

the notion that some drugs can offer him insight into the meaning of life or the existence of God.

The effects

Once he has tried drugs, he may find it difficult to cope socially without the sense of euphoria or well-being they initially produce. If he becomes physically addicted, he may be unable to function normally without a fix, and attempts to give up the drugs may result in withdrawal symptoms— from sweats and cramps to sickness, fever, and a desperate craving for the substances he is trying to avoid.

If you find that your grandchild is in this position, make it clear that you will do everything you can to help him get well. Parents often find a child's drug problem difficult to deal with; you may be calmer and may also have more time to do some research and find appropriate professional help for your grandchild. Don't expect a speedy solution to his problem, but rest assured that your unconditional loving support will be an important part of the help he needs.

NAME	USAGE	EFFECTS AND HAZARDS
Cocaine/Crack Cocaine is a powerful stimulant, also known as coke or snow. Crack is cocaine that has been treated with chemicals to be absorbed faster. Both come as white powder.	Powder is sniffed (snorted) through a tube or dissolved in water and injected with a syringe. 	Creates a feeling of well-being, makes the user indifferent to pain and tiredness, and increases confidence. Users become dependent and tempted to increase dose and frequency; they often become nervous, excitable, and paranoid. Repeated sniffing damages the membranes lining the nose and the structure separating the nostrils. Smoking crack can cause various breathing problems and pains in the chest.

Ecstasy
White, brown, pink, or yellow tablets and capsules, also known as disco burgers, diamonds, New Yorkers, and rhubarb and custard.

Tablets or capsules taken by mouth.

The user experiences a "rush" followed by a feeling of calm and well-being; often gives a heightened perception of colors and sounds.
 Dangers include dehydration and heat stroke usually from prolonged nonstop dancing; water is necessary to combat the effects, but excessive water consumption can lead to medical complications and be fatal.

Heroin
An opiate also known as smack, junk, and skag. White powder often adulterated with other substances like talcum powder, so dose is unclear.

Injected, sniffed, or smoked.

Makes the user feel drowsy and content, although the first time he may feel nauseated and may vomit. Dependence develops quickly. There is also a danger of contracting HIV (the virus that causes AIDS) if needles are shared with other users.

LSD
A colorless, odorless, tasteless powder or solution; other names include acid, tabs, and trips.

Comes as tablets or capsules but usually supplied on small squares of blotting paper (tabs or trips) and taken orally.

Causes hallucinations for up to 12 hours. The brain is affected by the tiniest amount of the drug. A user can lose all sense of time and place, and sounds and colors can become confused.

Marijuana
Also known as cannabis, dope, hash, weed, and ganga, it can be bought as leaves, stalks, or seeds.

Usually smoked in a pipe or mixed with tobacco and rolled in a cigarette; can also be brewed into a drink or eaten.

Makes user talkative, cheerful, and relaxed, and increases the appetite. May cause feelings of paranoia if taken when depressed. Like nicotine, marijuana can cause lung cancer and breathing problems.

Solvents
Most common drug used by children aged 12 to 16. Involves sniffing chemical fumes in glues, aerosol sprays, nail polish remover, butane gas, and other household substances.

Sniffed, sometimes with a plastic bag over the head, until user feels high.

A user feels lightheaded and giddy, and may have hallucinations; death can occur from choking, vomiting, or suffocation. Long-term heavy use can damage the brain, liver, and kidneys. Damaged brain function can trigger long-term mental illness. Nightmarelike flashbacks can happen years later without warning. Although solvents are not usually addictive, a regular user can feel out of touch with the real world.

Understanding the jargon

Keeping up with current trends in music, film, clothes, and speech

It is likely that, for a variety of reasons, your grandchild's parents will be at best indifferent to and at worst actively dislike his taste in clothes, music, and film, and the way he speaks. You may remember your parents' disapproval of your generation's choices. Perhaps you took a stern parental role with your own children.

However, understanding the references your grandchild makes to the music he listens to and the films he sees—even if they are genres you would normally shun—shows him that you take his opinions

seriously on these and other matters. If you can be objective about what is currently popular, you may derive a lot of pleasure from seeing and listening to things you may not have considered. More important, you will let your grandchild know that you are open-minded enough to talk to, that it is only age that separates you, nothing more.

Popular culture and styles of dress and speech give adolescents a chance to express their separateness from the previous generation, and to identify with and be accepted by their peers. They are safe ways of rebelling. Listen to what your grandchild has to say but put forward your views too. Avoid becoming too judgmental about current styles and popular heroes, even if they seem sadly lacking to you—and avoid making comparisons with bygone trends. Your grandchild needs to feel that he is discovering something new that "belongs" to him. If you point out that a current favorite owes everything to John Lennon or that it's all been done a hundred times before, a sensitive adolescent may perceive it as a personal put-down.

Sharing his interests

Don't be obsessive about keeping up with your grandchild's chosen interests but do a little detective work. Teen magazines are a good source of information on current fads, trends, and heroes, and you will absorb a lot of new language as well. Many magazines are criticized for their explicit

You don't have to share all your grandchildren's interests—nor they yours—but if you look regularly in the "what's on" section of a local newspaper or magazine, you are sure to discover films, plays, concerts, or exhibitions that appeal to you all.

Popular culture changes fast and even some teenagers have trouble keeping up. It is more important to realize how central that culture is to your grandchild's life than to talk confidently about the latest releases.

nature and the fact that they are read by people younger than their professed target audience. Nevertheless, you can be sure that your grandchild will be familiar with everything discussed on their pages. You may feel shocked but remember that the writers are pandering to the young people's sophisticated ideas about themselves rather than truly reflecting their everyday lives.

Your grandchild is sure to watch a lot of videos, since they are a less expensive option than going to the movies. If his parents object because they often want to use the VCR themselves, consider inviting him to use yours if you live close by. Stipulate the maximum number of friends he may bring with him and reserve the right to know exactly what they plan to watch. Most parents are flexible about older children watching videos that are classified for a group one or two years above their actual age, but you should tread carefully. If in doubt, seek his parents' advice and/or ask to view the movie before he watches it.

As long as everyone acts consistently with regard to this kind of supervision, your grandchild will respect you for it, regardless of his protestations about what all his friends watch. Most young people see some unsuitable material from time to time, but that does not mean that they crave it or that it should be encouraged. Help your grandchild to resist unsuitable peer pressure by maintaining a levelheaded, open-minded attitude yourself.

Suggest to your grandchild that the two of you see some films together. Perhaps you could take him to the movies (there is

bound to be at least one film you both might enjoy), and gradually extend the films you go to so that they include those of your favorites you think he might appreciate.

Television is a more accessible medium and it is not difficult, when you have the time, to tune in to programs aimed at your grandchild's age group to discover what is popular and important now. You may be surprised at how central the issues of ecology and conservation are to young people today, and in what depth they are examined and discussed.

Playing computer games is an integral part of being a young teen. It may be hard to understand their appeal until you have played them yourself. Don't worry if you do not know how to play: your grandchild will be only too willing to have a convert. If you find you play for long periods every time you are together, try to compromise. Suggest a board or card game for a change and entice him outdoors occasionally, but don't denigrate his interest.

Teenage jargon

Perhaps the hardest part of understanding your grandchild at this stage is making sense of what he is talking about. Teenage jargon includes a new vocabulary about computers and electronic games, terms used in connection with music and dance, and language that bonds peers together. Remember that language constantly shifts and develops, and people use words and phrases to feel part of a chosen group. It's important to be able to understand what he is saying to you, but you will embarrass everyone if you start peppering your conversation with his terms. His desire to be different is a vital part of his life at these ages and you should not encroach on it.

Shared skills: crafts

Introducing your grandchild to practical skills and handicrafts

This is the age at which your grandchild may give the impression that he thinks you have nothing to teach him. His reaction is perhaps understandable at a time when everything about the adult world is new to him, and it takes some time to realize how much there is to learn. If you have skills you think are worth passing on, it's good to try to do so; sharing practical knowledge may make up for some of the closeness you feel you are losing due to his growing independence.

All children, but especially those at this stage, respond well to the hands-on approach rather than being lectured on the subject. Useful skills, such as woodwork, home decorating, and needlecraft, all lend themselves to this way of learning. To begin with, your grandchild may need the enticement of seeing you tackling a project of your own. Without placing pressure on him or letting him see it as a chore, enlist his assistance in a small way at first. If that goes well, then discuss a future project.

If you have redecorated your house recently, he may become inspired to paint or paper his room at home. There are three considerations to bear in mind if home decorating is the skill you are sharing. First, discuss your intentions with your grandchild's parents; they must be willing to let you and your grandchild take on this project in their home. Second, it is best to keep your advice and guidance low-key—as if you were helping an adult, not instructing a child—and this entails accepting results that may not be up to your own high standards. Last, be sure that you have the time to be present at each stage of the project and see it through to the end. Half-finished enterprises and unfulfilled promises are disappointing and frustrating for everyone, but especially so for children.

With an expensive project—such as redecorating a room—decide how much you are willing to contribute, then budget accordingly before you begin. Going to a few stores together and planning and pricing everything will allow your

Your grandchild may still be living with her parents' choice of decoration— which may be more appropriate for the child she was than the adult she is fast becoming. Your help in redecorating her haven is sure to be appreciated.

All of a sudden the child who wanted to hand you screws or hold your screwdriver or hammer is eager to learn some of the finer points of working with wood. Passing on traditional skills is a wonderful way to bring the two of you closer and a marvelous antidote to the frenzied pace of your grandchild's everyday life.

grandchild to grasp these basic concepts and prevent him from becoming too ambitious. Encourage him to buy good-quality materials and well-made tools that will last and can be used again and again, so that he views the skill he is acquiring as something he can develop and use later in life rather than as a one-shot lesson.

Start small

If you are sharing your love of carpentry with him, be patient. Discuss the idea that this is a long-term commitment, as it takes time to learn these skills. Start in a small way to avoid early frustration and disappointment. These skills may be part of his school curriculum, but students often have little choice as to what they make and frequently lose interest because the object they have created is of little relevance to them. You may start off, as with decorating, by encouraging your grandchild to assist you with one of your own projects, then progress to working on one of his ideas.

It may help to consult your local library for ideas about what can be made simply and also appeal to someone of this age. Forget such old standbys as pencil boxes, bookends, and small stools unless they are of an unusual design and your grandchild is genuinely eager to make them. Suggest that he make Christmas or birthday gifts

for his family—a spice rack for the cook, for example, or a rack to hold a music lover's CDs or tapes. Young people often have little or no money to spend on others, so this could be a satisfying solution for all concerned.

Other skills

You may have other skills that you had not realized would interest someone of your grandchild's age. Knitting has an old-fashioned image, but bright, bold knitwear is always in vogue, and your grandchild may jump at the idea of making something eye-catching for himself. The quality of yarns and availability of different textures and colors have improved dramatically over the years and are sure to interest a style-conscious adolescent. As you already know, knitting can be therapeutic. You could point out that it can be an antidote to pre-exam stress. If you are competent in this area, encourage your grandchild to design his own patterns: with your knowledge and his eye for fashion, you will make a winning team.

If you are skilled at sewing your own clothes, try to pass this on to your grandchild. Both boys and girls will benefit later from being able to sew on buttons, shorten pants, cover some old throw pillows, and even make curtains.

Shared skills: cooking

Fostering your grandchild's interest in choosing and preparing food

Cooking food for and with others is one of the most fulfilling things we do, enjoyable in itself and with a satisfying end result. Preparing a favorite dish for a friend, making Thanksgiving or Christmas dinner for the family, and baking a cake or some cookies for someone who is sick or upset all show we care. Such actions cement the undeniable connection between giving generously of our time and resources, and loving people.

The negative side of the busy lives we all lead is the lack of time and energy to cook on a regular basis for families and friends. Your grandchild will probably have a greater experience and knowledge of convenience and takeout foods than he does of home cooking and the pleasures of concocting special meals and treats. His parents may be pressed for time or simply lack the inclination to show him how important and rewarding this particular skill can be. If you decide to play the role of

Inviting his friends to sample a dish you have created together is probably the highest accolade your grandchild can give the skill you have shared with him.

master chef, you will find it a satisfying way of maintaining closeness, as well as having fun with your grandchild.

Children have enough formal teaching at school, so make the time your grandchild spends with you relaxing and fun. If you have never done much home baking or special cooking yourself but are keen to learn, now is a wonderful time to begin. Your grandchild will enjoy the experience of your learning step by step together just as much as he would enjoy your being the expert sharing your skills.

Whether you are a competent cook or not, begin your sessions with something that is sure to achieve results worth eating. Don't opt for a dish so simple that your grandchild will have done it when he was younger. But if despite your more exotic suggestions he wants to cook burgers, you can still make them special. Grind your own meat or experiment with meatless versions. Add herbs and spices to improve the bland taste he knows from burger chains and, for a real home-cooked touch, make your own French fries. If you are planning more than one session around this staple, consider making your own ketchup and relishes.

If, like many of his peers, your grandchild is vegetarian and you are not, choose recipes that you know he will eat and that you can make successfully. You may need to consult some books on the subject to make sure that your meal is nutritionally balanced. If you are genuinely interested, take the opportunity to ask him about his beliefs, but don't pressure him to eat anything he declines.

The art of cooking involves more than transforming ingredients into delicious meals: presentation is equally important in some cusines.

Adolescents often develop a desire to try different cuisines. This could be a worthwhile area to explore, since you can adapt and tailor tacos, curries, stir-fries, and so on to suit your individual palates. In your family you may have a strong ethnic cuisine, which perhaps his parents have not shared with him. Spend time leafing through recipe books and make a list of things you would both like to try. Once you are used to working together and become a competent team, you may want to invite the rest of the family to sample your efforts.

Baking bread can be highly satisfying if your grandchild has never tasted homemade loaves. Alternate these time-consuming recipes with some for making cakes and cookies that give quick results. If your grandchild is unsure of what to buy for family members or friends—or financially unable to afford a present—introduce him to the delights of homemade chocolates, toffee, and fudge. Attractively packaged, these make great gifts.

SHARING COOKING SKILLS

• If a recipe is not familiar to you, try it out before you involve your grandchild in the process.

• Have all the ingredients and utensils you will need ready before you begin working. This will allow you to start cooking right away.

• Alternate recipes he wants to try with surprises you think he will enjoy eating.

• Always leave enough time at the end of a session to sample what you have cooked.

• Do not comment during your cooking sessions (or at any other time) on his parents' cooking abilities, or the lack of them.

• Suggest that he start a notebook of the recipes you try together, adding comments and tips of your own which may help him. He may take it away to college with him.

Don't worry if things go wrong. Even the best chefs produce cakes that fall and soups that are unappetizing. But these efforts will be outnumbered by your successes. If you are not upset and can even laugh when the worst happens, your grandchild will learn to try again.

Shopping for new and unusual ingredients is half the fun of learning to cook international dishes. If you, too, are unused to such an array and unsure of what to buy, or feel overwhelmed with too many choices, ask for advice. Most gourmet shops will be pleased by your interest and give you helpful tips.

Allowances

How and when to offer financial help to your grandchild

Heated discussions over allowances seem to reach a peak at this stage in your grandchild's life. You may remember from your parenting days the problems this contentious issue caused; and you may also empathize with your grandchild because you know he is under peer pressure, as well as being lured by advertising, to buy expensive items and not to be different from everyone else. Because you can see both sides of the arguments—over the precise amount of money, whether or not it should be given in return for chores done or withheld as a punishment—you are in a position to help both your grandchild and his parents.

If you are aware that his parents have financial difficulties that are genuinely exacerbated by your grandchild's demands, you could, tactfully, offer to supplement the amount he receives. If his parents are set in their attitudes and concerned that their child is being unreasonable, you could offer a regular amount in return for chores done. But be sure that the tasks chosen are not beyond his abilities or too time-consuming.

If you live at a distance, check with his parents that the chores have been completed. If you live close by and he is doing chores for you, find something that is a real help to you so that he does not feel you are patronizing him. Window cleaning, car washing, and gardening are all useful jobs. But remember, if you contribute to your grandchild's allowance on a regular basis, you must operate with impeccable fairness: if you have other grandchildren, be prepared to give the same amount—with similar conditions attached—to them.

Young teens' allowances vary enormously. If you think your grandchild's parents are unrealistic in how little they give their child, you could casually mention the fact the next time you read a survey on the subject; these appear often in newspapers and magazines.

But if you can see that your grandchild's capacity to spend is limitless and that he shows no signs of saving anything or wanting to do anything with his money except spend it on himself, you may prefer to save a small weekly amount for him without telling him you are doing so. Then,

Gardening can be hard work, as every gardener knows. Asking your grandchild to rake leaves, mow grass, dig and plant beds, and carry out numerous other seasonal tasks—with your advice and participation—helps you and gives him the chance to supplement his allowance.

Young teenagers are under intense pressure to conform, and many of the latest "must haves" are expensive. If you want to help, consider offering half the cost of a pair of sneakers or new jeans; your grandchild should pay the rest with her own money.

when he has no money to buy gifts, you can introduce him to the pleasure of spending money on others. Make it clear that you saved the money for him so that he would not be embarrassed by his inability to buy a present for someone—though obviously you can do this only after he has admitted that he has no spending money.

Naturally, you must accept his parents' decision if they have made it clear that they do not want you to become involved in the allowance issue. Lavish time and attention on your grandchild instead of money, and help him make his allowance go further by showing him how to shop wisely, encouraging saving, and suggesting games and other recreation that do not involve expensive equipment. You can also, if you feel strongly on this matter, open a savings account in his name for when he becomes an adult. If you do, keep silent about it and do the same for all your grandchildren, or you may run the risk of family discord.

CASE HISTORY

*E*very time we visit our grandchildren, we notice that seven-year-old Andrew has more new toys. His mother says they are educational or they were bought because Andrew doesn't get an allowance yet. We are sure that his parents spend more on Andrew than they give 14-year-old Paul as an allowance, yet it is always Paul they argue with, usually over something he has asked for or that he can't afford. We have tended in the past to give Paul rather expensive birthday and Christmas gifts, when we have been sure that they were what he wanted, but his parents have asked us not to—they think we are spoiling him, and are concerned that he is growing up ignorant of the value of things. So, on recent visits although we have bought Paul the T-shirt he wanted and a new pair of sneakers, we have also been careful to buy something for Andrew, even though he has so much already.

Now we have decided to give Paul a small monthly amount to ease everybody's burden, and we've made it clear that we are putting exactly the same amount in savings for Andrew. We were surprised that there were no arguments over this, but we talked about how to word it before we made the offer. In the past we have tried to supplement Paul's allowance on occasion and been accused of undermining parental authority, but I think this time it was different because we took care to include Andrew and made it clear that Paul's allowance would stop if his parents said so.

The arrangement has been in effect for three months now, and there have definitely been fewer arguments in that household. Paul is making a real effort because he knows we have, and the extra amount we give him has brought him on a par with most of his friends.

Understanding the world

Helping your grandchild to make sense of his life and experiences

When you visit your adolescent grandchild's room, you may be overwhelmed by the amount of visual material that attests to her support of environmental and other causes. These causes range from large organizations acting on a global scale to local groups working on small, specific projects.

There are sure to be times when you may wonder what happened to the wide-eyed little child who looked to you for advice and information. You may ask yourself how he turned into this young person with such passionate views and highly charged emotions.

The next time you feel overwhelmed by your grandchild's opinions, remind yourself that this is what growing up is all about and be glad that he feels confident enough of your support to be using you as his sounding board. You should be far more concerned if he has nothing to say for himself and no ideas about the world in which he is about to make decisions.

Be prepared for him to accuse your generation and his parents' generation of making nothing but mistakes. This is his way of trying to make sense of the larger issues that confront him. It may help you to remember how angry or desperate you felt about causes before you gained enough maturity to cope with the often harsh realities of our world.

Politics

Whether they study politics as a subject in its own right or as part of a general-studies course, adolescents are frequently encouraged to discuss current global and local problems. As a result, politics is often a key issue for young teens.

There will, inevitably, be times when your grandchild reveals naiveté or impracticality in what he says. He will probably meet some adults (both in his own family and among the parents of his friends) who put him down because he is young and who use his age and lack of experience as weapons in discussions. Make sure that you are never among them. This is a crucial stage for your grandchild's self-confidence. Even if you disagree most strongly with everything he is saying, and can counter some of his ideas with solid argument, he deserves respect for his opinions and, obviously, has the right to express them.

Your grandchild is far more likely to take notice of your ideas if you have first listened to his without interruption. Treat him like an adult. If you fear that his politics may lead him into trouble, or that he is being influenced by an unsavory group, keep a close but unobtrusive eye on things—he may share what he is involved in with you rather than his parents—but take into account this age group's delight in exaggeration.

If you live at a distance, it's important to maintain telephone or written contact. If your grandchild has been accustomed to discussing issues with you, he is likely to talk about his enthusiasms, and you will have a picture of the depth of his interests and involvements. If anything he says gives you cause for concern, ask him about it, and explain why it concerns you.

Religion

One aspect of life that usually comes in for close scrutiny at this age is religion. If your family is devout, you may find that your grandchild chooses to rebel in some way. However offended you feel about this, it helps to recognize that questioning of assumptions shows intelligence and doesn't mean that he will be a permanent nonbeliever.

If his parents find this difficult to deal with, take some of the burden from them by listening to what your grandchild has to say. If you can't counter his arguments objectively—and if he is genuinely interested in discussion—you could enlist the help of the clergy. But applying pressure to bring him back to the family's way of thinking is a sure way to strengthen his resolve to be different.

By contrast, if your family is not committed to any faith, you may find that your grandchild suddenly becomes attached to one. This is often a way in which young people try to make sense of a difficult world, and as long as the group he has chosen does not seek to take him away from his family or alter the way in which he lives, there may be little to fear. But if your grandchild becomes involved with a sect or cult that you feel is an unwholesome influence, it is worth investigating—or at least discussing the matter with his parents—sooner rather than later.

A lively discussion centered around the issues of the day, using newspapers and magazines to support your views, helps your grandchild to understand the complexities of the adult world.

Understanding the world

Prejudices

It is common to find that your grandchild's views on race and prejudice are entirely different from yours. If he has experienced hostility from those of a particular racial group, he may have developed a less than liberal attitude. But gentle reasoning on your part—emphasizing that the characteristics of the individuals who have mistreated him cannot be attributed to an entire race—should help him to develop more tolerance. If, as is more likely, he has grown up among ethnic groups of which you have less experience and the prejudice is on your side, listen to him carefully.

Sex

A major interest for all adolescents is sex, and if you have always had a close relationship, your grandchild may want to talk to you rather than to his parents on this subject. Any personal information he shares with you should be treated in total confidence (unless his health or safety is in danger), even if you feel he is placing you in a difficult position with regard to his parents. If you are concerned that you are

In a religious group or sect, your grandchild may find the sense of belonging that he lacks in his school or social life. Listen sympathetically to his views, even if they are not ones you feel you can share.

betraying his parents' trust, tell your grandchild so in a way that does not make him turn from you completely.

He is more likely to talk about sex in a general way, and his attitudes are almost certain to differ from your own. Silently recall how many of us say we will never get married or have children and how many of us recant; and how our attitudes toward sex, marriage, and indeed life in general evolve and mature. Allow for his youth without being patronizing or revealing too much of your worldly wisdom. Be careful what you let slip about yourself. A risqué tale told to your grandchild could prove embarrassing if it spreads around your family. (See pages 156–57.)

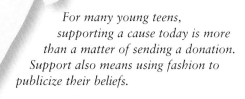

For many young teens, supporting a cause today is more than a matter of sending a donation. Support also means using fashion to publicize their beliefs.

A multitude of causes

Your grandchild is likely to espouse several different causes with a fervor bordering on the obsessive. Listen to his concerns and acknowledge their importance to him. While you do not have to accompany him on protest marches or write letters of support to various organizations (unless you want to), you should be pleased that he cares deeply about something in addition to himself. It is easier as we get older to turn our back on global problems with feelings of helplessness—we have, after all, witnessed so many. But it is important that your grandchild's energy and enthusiasm remain untainted by cynicism for as long as possible.

Even if you think his zeal could be better directed elsewhere, realize that he is learning to care in the broadest sense—good practice for when he has a family of his own. You might be bewildered by how often his concerns change, but this is simply a sign of how quickly his feelings and ideas develop. He is experiencing a tumult of emotions and ideas, which will calm down as he nears adulthood.

ARE YOU LISTENING?

Adolescence is one of the most exciting times of your grandchild's development. As he comes to terms with the adult world, he undoubtedly will have an opinion about everything. His youth and immaturity may make others hear only the strident and overbearing tone, not the content of what he is saying. If you are a good listener, you may find yourself drawn into some lively and interesting discussions.

• After a visit, make a list of what your grandchild said to you and recall any times when a conversation was begun but not finished. Write down what you told him of your concerns and life. If you discover that he has tried to tell you things that you didn't hear properly, or that you interrupted and finished the conversation, you need to think about approaching the conversation differently.

• Improve your listening skills. If you spend a lot of time alone you may have gotten out of the habit of listening.

• Develop the skill of "reflective listening." Rather than interject with helpful remarks or sympathetic words, simply feed back what your grandchild is saying in order to encourage him to say more:

Child: "I feel really angry with Mom."
Grandparent: "You're angry with your mom?"
Child: "She picks on me all the time."
Grandparent: "She's picking on you?"
Child: "She's annoyed about work and takes it out on me."

This may seem like a self-conscious mode of speaking but in fact your lack of reaction and interference encourages your grandchild to think about why his mother is annoyed and acknowledges that it is not his fault. By reflecting back enough of what is being said to let the speaker know you are listening, you can also give him the chance to think things through.

Comments designed to help like "Well, your mother has problems" or "You know what her temper is like" would not have encouraged your grandchild to pursue his line of thinking, but instead turned the attention away from the child, back toward you.

CHAPTER EIGHT

Into Adulthood
17 and up

As your grandchild grows to adulthood, your relationship will inevitably change. With the upheavals of adolescence behind her, she may be more relaxed about herself, have a more mature outlook on life, and be more responsive to you. On the other hand, you may find that the difference in age between you leads to some misunderstanding, or you might feel unable to come to terms with the way she lives if it conflicts with your own values. She may believe she cannot be as open with you as before. But with a little tolerance on both sides, your relationship can be as rewarding as ever.

Leaving school, finding work, and forming serious relationships are exciting, but daunting, prospects for a young adult. Your grandchild still needs your love and support, especially when the going gets tough. You can be there to sympathize if she fails an exam or breaks up with a boyfriend. You can offer financial or practical help when she is establishing a home of her own. And, most important, you can take pride in the capable, independent individual she has become—and take some of the credit.

Graduation rituals and gifts
Marking the transition from school to the adult world

Teenagers graduate from high school with a variety of feelings. Childhood is now truly behind them, and they will shortly have to learn to be self-reliant and responsible adults. Some can't wait for the day when they walk out of the school door for the last time. These are most likely to be children who have already assumed the outward appearance and habits of adulthood, and who have felt for some time that they were ready for the real world. Others may feel nervous about leaving the comparative safety of high school for the unknown of college or the workplace. How teenagers view this rite of passage also depends on how they have performed at school, whether they were academically successful and appear to have a glittering future ahead, or whether they feel they have not made the most of their opportunities and are entering a new world ill-equipped and with few qualifications.

However she feels about the future, your grandchild is likely to want to mark her graduation in some way. The traditional celebration is to go to a prom. The graduation prom may be the first grand occasion your grandchild has attended and her first real opportunity to dress up. If a fancy dress or evening gown is required and you are a competent dressmaker, you may be called upon to help out. You will both have fun poring over pattern books and fashion magazines and may be able to create something special and original for her big night. It's important that she look her best, and she and her friends will no doubt spend days, if not weeks, preparing for this occasion.

It would not be surprising if your idea of a formal outfit differed from your grandchild's. Formal, for your grandchild, may mean anything that isn't jeans and

Regardless of your grandchild's overall opinion of his schooldays, leaving school is a milestone in his life. In addition to the formal recognition of the occasion by his peers and teachers, his graduation from school to the world of work or college is an excellent opportunity to get the family together to wish him well in whatever he chooses to do next.

boots—and that applies to both sexes—so don't be disappointed if she opts for a stylish pants suit or slacks and a tunic instead. Your grandson may decide to rent a tuxedo for the occasion, but it could be an opportunity for him to buy a suit, which will also be useful for future interviews. Consider giving him the money to go shopping for suitable clothes. Don't offer to accompany him unless he asks you to, and don't insist that he have the most expensive suit in the store. If he is still growing, a suit will not last long. If he already has a suitable jacket and pants, suggest that he dress it up for the evening with a colorful vest or a silk tie.

If you want to contribute toward the costs of the prom, your other options are offering to pay for a limousine and driver for the evening, or a pre-prom dinner or for a party afterward.

Gift suggestions

You will probably want to mark your grandchild's high-school graduation with a gift. Of course, if she intends to go on to college and you helped her and her parents by funding a pre-graduation fact-finding trip to several possible colleges, or if you took her yourself to a number of campuses, then a token personal gift may be more appropriate now.

You could consider giving her a check when she leaves home. But if she is not particularly good at budgeting and is likely to spend all the money right away, you might decide to put a certain amount into her bank account each month. A grandchild who is starting work immediately will also be glad of financial help to help her buy clothes appropriate for her new life or to tide her over until her first paycheck arrives.

Grandparents often like to help with the cost of driving lessons or with the purchase of a car. A license is a handy qualification, and her own wheels may clinch your grandchild's first job. If you are considering buying her a car, check with her parents to make sure they agree that your grandchild is ready for the responsibility. Boys, in particular, need to be aware that a car is not something in which to prove to their friends how many risks they are prepared to take. Young people often forget, too, that the financial costs of owning a car go beyond the purchase price and that they need to set money aside for insurance and upkeep, as well as gas. A knowledge of auto maintenance is also likely to prove useful (see pp. 182–83).

A used car is ideal. Your grandchild may prefer a jalopy that she can individualize rather than a new model. This may mean respraying it shocking pink or decorating it with stickers. Secondhand cars do not need to be pristine, but they must be safe. Unless you are an expert yourself, get any car you are considering buying checked by a reputable mechanic.

Perhaps your grandchild is celebrating leaving school by taking her first vacation with friends instead of with the family. Once again, money is a welcome gift. Alternatively, she might be planning to travel more seriously, perhaps by taking a year off between school and college in order to see the world. You could offer to pay for an airline ticket or a season ticket on Amtrak or Interail, or consider buying a good backpack as a way of wishing her bon voyage.

Your grandchild's first thought as she leaves the inflexible routine of her schooldays behind her may be to see something of the world. She may want to travel before she becomes too involved in a career and forming lasting relationships.

Activities to share
Making the most of your adult grandchild's time with you

There is no reason why you and your grandchild should not continue to do things together now that she is grown up. But the fact that you may not see her as much as you would like makes it even more important that your times together be mutually fulfilling.

If you still have hobbies and interests in common, you will almost certainly continue to share them whenever possible. What could be better than striding across the golf course with your grandchild, putting on your walking boots in preparation for a hike through the hills with her, or going off to a ball game together? Especially if you introduced her to an activity in the first place, there is great satisfaction in knowing that it continues to enrich her life. You may, however, have to accept graciously the fact that your grandchild is now better at these activities than you are. But you can, at the same time, take a little of the credit for her achievements.

There are many grandparents who sparked a child's interest in an activity or spotted a particular talent.

With their encouragement, a child may have developed skills that now mean she is winning medals for athletics or has turned artistic leanings into a profession. The little granddaughter you taught to plant and weed may now be a landscape architect, while the small boy you taught carpentry may be making furniture for a living. Even if your grandchildren have not reached these pinnacles of achievement, the baker who makes celebration cakes for the family may welcome your advice from time to time, and a weekend athlete may like you to come and watch her run in a race.

Such developments can be even more satisfying if your own child showed no interest in your particular hobbies. Artistic skills and other talents often seem to skip a generation. There is a

Your grandchild may still value your help and advice—even if you think that by now you have taught her everything you know about dressmaking. There may be times when you are the only one who can get an outfit for a special occasion to look exactly right.

Teaching your grandchild to play golf—and continuing to play with him even when his handicap betters yours—is an ideal way to keep channels of communication open. It also gives you both some undemanding exercise in pleasant surroundings.

It may be that some interests you once shared have lapsed as your grandchild has grown older. Or perhaps poor health or reduced mobility has made your common passion for outdoor activities difficult for you to pursue. If so, invite her for a meal out every couple of months or so; try different restaurants and experiment with new foods. This will give you a regular opportunity to find out what is going on in her life, catch up on any developments in areas of mutual interest, and offer your help or advice.

great deal of enjoyment to be had in the role of onlooker, too—particularly if you have previously always been too active yourself to study the finer points of another's skill. Following your grandchild's progress may bring back happy memories of the fun you had at that age.

Now that your grandchild is a grown-up and your relationship is a more balanced, two-way affair, it may be her turn to introduce you to some new interests. It is sometimes difficult to admit that the younger generation may know more than you do, but in the area of new technology, this is often the case. If you would like to know more, ask your grandchild for information and try to keep up with developments together. Before you know it, you may be the owner of a computer and discovering a fascination with computer games or with surfing the Internet.

Similarly, if photography is a shared interest, you might extend this to videotaping. Once again, your grandchild may be the best person to introduce you to the intricacies of the camcorder. Soon you may both be filming family occasions.

KEEPING IN TOUCH

Now that your grandchild has left high school, and is away at college or working full-time, you are inevitably going to see less of her than you once did. You will miss her, but her absence doesn't mean that she has stopped caring about you; her life is now so full of new experiences and new friends that she undoubtedly finds it difficult to keep open the lines of communication. If she is far away, and you can afford it, you might suggest that you pay the train or airfare for her to visit you, but make the offer graciously, so that it doesn't seem like a bribe. Writing regularly is a good way to stay in touch, especially if—like many older people—you do not enjoy long telephone conversations. You will probably write much longer and more frequent letters than she does, and may have to be content with a quick postcard from her, but keep writing. She will be delighted to hear from you even if she doesn't reciprocate as often as she would like.

Then and now:

Fleeing the nest

Today's young adults often have the freedom to decide when to leave the parental home, but as before, it is a matter of financial expediency versus the yearning for independence.

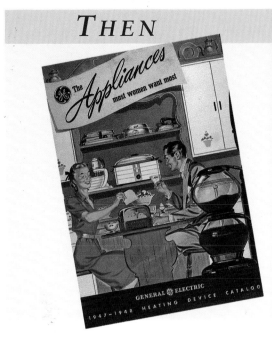

THEN

It is perfectly normal and healthy for your young adult grandchild to want to leave home. You may be part of the generation that left home only when they married, got a live-in job, or joined the armed forces. And if you did go from your parents' home to one of your own, you probably saved during your engagement in order to buy what you needed to make that new home comfortable. Or perhaps you married and lived with your parents while you saved long and hard for a place of your own.

In either case, you may find it strange that your grandchild prefers sharing a seedy apartment with a group of friends rather than remaining in her comfortable family home. She may even decide to live alone: single-person households are increasingly common today. Respect her need for independence and self-reliance; particularly if she has a number of siblings at home, she may be longing for time and space to herself.

If your grandchild is setting up a home, expect her to beg and borrow from you. Now is the time to clear the attic of some of the things you have been saving. Your granddaughter is unlikely to have been putting things away in preparation for the day she leaves home. Such forward planning is not characteristic of today's younger generation. Your grandchild will probably need everything—dishes, flatware, cooking utensils, even furniture. (What is provided in furnished apartments tends to be very basic.) Make sure that you really can live without the things you give away, even if you give them only on an extended-loan basis. And think about your other grandchildren. If you help one grandchild, are others going to ask for a similar gesture from you?

Stay-at-homes

Although you may have resented living at home when you reached your 20s or even 30s, the fact that many of your peers were doing the same probably made it less onerous than it might otherwise have been. Today, no matter how much they long to lead independent lives, many young people are forced by economic considerations to remain in their parents' home far longer than they expected. According to recent research, many young men in particular are still living at home with mom and dad and having everything done for them well into their 30s.

This can be a difficult situation for both your grandchild and her parents. Parents

NOW

Some years ago, advertising certainly supported the view that it was impossible to set up home satisfactorily without every modern appliance (far left). Today your grandchild is likely to be happy with a starter pack of the basic essentials (left), or even with odd bits and pieces from yard sales until she can afford something better.

remember the sense of relief you felt as you waved your last child off and got on with doing the things you had always wanted to do? A mother in particular may have embarked on a new career or resumed old interests, and may feel restricted by the return of her child. The same tensions that occur with a stay-at-home child may surface here.

In this situation the ideal solution is to adapt the house to provide separate living quarters for the adult child so that she can entertain friends. Extending the house may, in fact, be the only means of maintaining good family relations.

If the tension between your grandchild and her parents is growing, you may be able to intervene. Can you offer accommodations in your home? Some families find this an excellent compromise: if you are not in the best of health and do not leave the house much, it is good to have someone around on a daily basis, although it is important not to get too dependent on what will inevitably be a temporary arrangement. But it may allow you to stay in your own home for longer than might otherwise be possible. (If you expect your grandchild to help pay the household bills, or perform her share of the household chores, be sure to discuss it with her and the parents in advance.)

This situation is also a way of preserving the extended family network, which is so lacking today compared with even a generation ago. But take care not to pry into her life. Don't insist that she tell you where she is going and with whom every time she leaves the house. Respecting each other's privacy is essential if you are to live in harmony under the same roof.

can gain a great deal of satisfaction from watching their child establish herself as a separate entity. If she remains at home, it can be more difficult for them to accept that she is truly grown up, and she may feel that her parents unnecessarily interfere in her life. If this sounds familiar from your young adulthood, you will be sympathetic toward her plight, and you can use your own experience to reduce the tension between her and her parents.

Perhaps even more worrisome than an unwilling stay-at-home is the adult child who seems quite happy to remain with her parents, having her meals cooked, laundry done, and bedroom cleaned long after she might be expected to be living independently. With no experience of living alone, such children find life difficult when their parents are no longer around and they must belatedly fend for themselves.

Young people who have lived away from home may also find themselves forced back after college graduation or after a long-term relationship has ended. This can cause an uneasy situation with your grandchild's parents. They have probably become accustomed to having their home and lives to themselves again. Do you

Shared skills: practical competence

Helping your grandchild make the most of what she owns

It is a mistake to think that once your grandchild is grown up you have nothing more to offer her. Perhaps the most valuable skill she can continue to acquire from you is the ability to live life to the fullest, surmounting problems, getting along with the people around her, and being as contented and fulfilled as possible. Neither of you may be aware of it, but if you have had a long and close relationship, there will often be times when she draws on your experiences in order to deal with her own circumstances.

In particular, she may be lacking the very abilities she needs now that she is branching out on her own. The modern school curriculum often omits teaching children practical skills, and your grandchild may not become aware of her limitations until she tries to fix her car, maintain an apartment, or balance a checkbook. Unless she wants to pay someone every time she needs to change a fuse or do a routine service on her car, she needs to learn to do these things fast. This is where your help and advice can be of tremendous value.

Cars and motoring

If the first car she owns is rather old, it is likely to need a lot of maintenance. With your help she can learn how to do some basic servicing. Understanding the rudiments of the combustion engine may help her to resolve simple problems. You—and her parents—may worry less about the prospect of her breaking down on a lonely road if you know that she might be able to do something about it.

This is also the time to initiate her into the art of reading maps, if she doesn't already know how. Even teenagers who have studied geography extensively are often unable to make sense of a road map. Take her for drives and ask her to navigate. Make sure neither of you is on a tight schedule and if you get a bit lost, treat it as an adventure.

Home maintenance

Girls need to know as much about home maintenance as boys do. Your granddaughter may buy her own home, perhaps one in a state of disrepair, and have to pay people to knock down walls, rewire, and replumb. The grandchild with family members ready to take on these jobs for her is lucky indeed. But there is no reason why she should not do some of

Sharing your passion for repairing precision instruments, a skill requiring both patience and dexterity, can reap rewards in many areas of daily life.

Professional help is not needed for many routine tasks. If you pass on your knowledge of car maintenance, your grandchild will gain an invaluable skill: it is vital that she feels safe and confident in her own car.

the work herself with your help perhaps. You may find that you both develop such enormous enthusiasm for converting her rather unprepossessing basement apartment into something cheerful and special that in no time you are showing her how to plaster walls or lay a wooden floor.

Being able to spot the potential in the most unlikely pieces of furniture in a yard sale is also a talent worth passing on. It's amazing what can be done with secondhand furniture: pieces that might look decrepit can often be transformed by repairing, stripping, painting, or reupholstering. If you are a competent carpenter, your experience will again be valuable at this point in your grandchild's life. You may be enlisted to help build a set of kitchen cabinets or put up bookshelves. Don't take on all the work yourself. The only way to pass on practical skills like these is to give your pupil hands-on experience.

Gardening

This is also the time when she may begin to develop a genuine love of gardening. If you are already an enthusiastic gardener, you have probably been encouraging her to grow plants and flowers all her life. But now she may have her own yard, and who better to consult than you? You can show her how to sow or sod a lawn, lay a simple paved path, or—if she is ambitious—how to build and stock a small pond. Once again, you will be able to share the pleasure and satisfaction of transforming a bleak, neglected area into a thing of beauty.

Your grandchild will be delighted with all the tasks she has been able to accomplish with your help. Working together in this way will leave you both with some very happy memories.

CASE HISTORY

Everything I know about home repair my granddad taught me in the year I moved into my first home. The kitchen, in particular, was awful—small and dark with old cabinets on the wall, a tiny walk-in pantry and cracked linoleum on the floor. I had used all my savings to buy the place, so I had to do everything as cheaply as possible. Granddad offered to help me.

He showed me everything, starting with how to draw a scale plan. He moved his workbench in, then suggested we open the kitchen out into the pantry. I carried rubble away as he knocked down the wall, then he demonstrated how to make good the edges of the hole he had made and plaster its surface. He showed me how to install a large new window, which made an enormous difference in the light levels, and made me one wall cabinet. Then he lent me his tools and told me to copy his cabinet—and with his help, I did! Under his guidance I installed wall tiles and rented a sander to strip the lovely old floorboards he found buried under the floor covering. After all that, the painting was the easy part. My parents, who had been quite shocked at how much work needed to be done, couldn't believe the transformation.

When he died, my granddad left me his workbench and tools in his will. They are my most prized possessions.

Higher education

The choices facing your grandchild when she leaves high school

When you—and, indeed, your own children—graduated from high school, there were probably two paths available to young people. Those who had done well academically and who had the means went to college. Others looked for work, probably in their local area.

The situation facing your grandchild today is more complex. It is no longer only the high achievers and those who can afford the costs who go to college. Even those who find employment immediately probably spend some time in college-based training. There has been an enormous increase in the number of people remaining in school long after they are legally required to do so. It is argued that this is the result of the prolonged and worldwide recession, which has thrown people out of work and destroyed job opportunities. Many claim that young people go to college just to delay the need to search for work. It is certainly true that finding a first job, particularly straight from high school (but in many cases even after graduating from college or graduate school) is more difficult for the current generation than it ever was for you and perhaps for your children.

You may remember the days when entire communities were employed by just one or two local companies. All your friends and neighbors worked in the same place, whether on the factory floor or in a clerical or managerial position. Young people frequently followed in their parents' footsteps, and in some industries having a parent already employed in a certain area almost guaranteed the next generation a job. This gave young people a great sense of security, even if in some cases it may have limited their full potential.

Acquiring additional skills

The basic unskilled jobs that offered young people their first work experience and demanded whole armies of male and female employees have almost disappeared. Computer-driven machinery invariably does

Going to college is still an enormous and exciting step for young people. But today it is less likely to be a once-in-a-lifetime experience. College courses and retraining are becoming increasingly necessary in order for workers to keep pace with technological innovation and the demands of the marketplace.

such tasks today. Now employers are looking for skilled workers, and acquiring useful skills almost always requires some form of vocational education or training. Much of this training was once offered in apprenticeship programs in which a young person learned a trade step by step from experienced colleagues in the workplace, while perhaps studying part-time at college. Such apprenticeship programs still exist in some areas of employment—in catering or in the printing industry, for example—but they are much less common today.

As a result, there has been a huge increase in the choice of courses offered at college, and almost everyone can gain a diploma or other certificate of some kind. Although academic qualifications prove that she has successfully completed a course of higher education, they do not necessarily tell a prospective employer what that person might be capable of accomplishing in the workplace.

The main growth area in higher education has been in vocational courses, which train a young person for a particular job and are, therefore, more closely geared toward the needs of industry and commerce than traditional academic programs are.

Partly because technology is advancing so rapidly and partly because in the Western world in general jobs are becoming less secure, it is necessary for people to gain competence in more than one task. Many employers demand that each member of the work force be multiskilled. There are very few jobs that do not demand some knowledge of information technology: even doctors and nurses need to have basic computer skills. Computer graphic design, for example, is useful in many fields. In some areas, advanced degrees, such as a master's in business administration, are considered desirable and may in fact lead to a better job. The courses leading to a college degree are unlikely to equip your grandchild for all the demands that will be made on her during her career.

If a young adult opts for manual work, he may be able to learn his trade at a technical school, although it is still possible in some instances to be hired as an assistant and learn on the job.

Consider secretaries, for example. In the past they were trained in shorthand and typing at a commercial school. These skills meant that they could move easily from job to job—one typewriter was much like another—without further training. Now, to pursue such a career, your grandchild needs keyboard skills, as well as familiarity with a variety of computer software programs. And whenever she wants to change her job, she may first have to acquaint herself with several different computer programs.

Higher education is no longer for recent high-school graduates only. Many adults return to college or begin a new program in their late 20s or 30s, or even later, in order to extend or acquire the skills they need for the constantly changing world of work. Today more than 40 percent of all college students in the United States are over the age of 25. Throughout her life, your grandchild may dip in and out of education and vocational training in order to learn the work techniques that the modern world continues to demand of her.

The gay grandchild

Accepting your grandchild's sexual preferences

The revelation that your grandchild is gay may come as a complete shock to you, but if you have always been close to her, chances are you may have suspected it for some time. However you learn the truth, you may find that you have to battle with some turbulent emotions.

It isn't surprising that people in their middle and later years often find it difficult to accept the fact that a relative or friend is gay, since until recently this would have been considered shameful at best and would not have been discussed openly. In your youth sexual relationships between men were probably illegal and still are in certain jurisdictions. Support and lobbying groups, and the media to an extent, have removed much of the stigma from homosexuality. Nevertheless, discrimination on the grounds of sexual proclivities is still rife, and many people remain repelled by the idea of someone making love to another person of the same sex, believing it to be perverted and evil.

If this is how you feel, you need to be aware, first of all, that your grandchild cannot help being what she is. No one knows exactly why someone is gay, but there are many theories. The most prevalent focus on parent/child relationships and on genetic make-up.

Homosexuals constitute a large minority group throughout the world and are to be found in all walks of life.

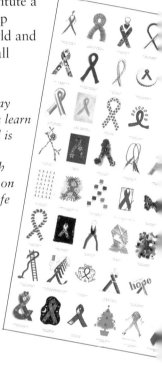

The fear of AIDS may haunt you when you learn that your grandchild is gay. But heightened awareness and health education programs on the importance of safe sex are having an impact on the prevalence of the disease among homosexuals.

Adolescent crushes on people of the same sex are common. But by the mid to late teens the feelings of being "different," which most gays say they remember experiencing from an early age, have usually coalesced into the certainty of their homosexuality. Your grandchild needs all your help as he comes to terms with his feelings at this time.

You should also realize that once your grandchild is in her late teens or early 20s, homosexuality is not a passing phase that she may grow out of. It is a physical and emotional orientation, and she will perceive any thoughts people may have of "curing" her of her sexuality as both disrespectful and inappropriate.

If your religion or culture condemns homosexuality, you may find it difficult not to reject your grandchild. But remember that she is never more in need of your love and support than when she is coming to terms with her own sexuality. The world can be a harsh place, particularly if her immediate family and friends are unsupportive. Her sexuality is only one part of her nature; she is still the same person with the same lovable characteristics that you have always known. If you feel the need to discuss honestly how you feel, there are support groups for the families of young homosexuals. It may help you to contact such a group and talk to other parents and grandparents who have faced—and come to terms with—the same situation.

Of course, accepting your grandchild's sexual orientation may be easier than welcoming her partner into your home when she establishes a steady relationship. Some people are embarrassed by open displays of affection between gay couples. If you would prefer that your grandchild not bring her partner with her when she visits, it is best to say so to avoid possible embarrassment. You will risk alienating her, but if your relationship is strong, she may be able to accept your feelings and adjust accordingly.

World AIDS Day

THE FACTS ABOUT AIDS

Among the most common misconceptions about AIDS is that it is inextricably linked with homosexuality. Despite awareness campaigns in the media, this and other myths prevail. If you are unsure of the facts, these notes will help.

• The World Health Organization estimates that 18 million adults and 1.5 million children have been infected with HIV since the beginning of the world epidemic in the 1970s. Of these, 4.5 million have developed AIDS.

• AIDS has been called a gay plague, and in the United States, the United Kingdom, and northern Europe, the most serious impact has been felt by the homosexual community. However, in the non-industrialized world, HIV is most often transmitted by heterosexual intercourse. In parts of the United States, Scotland, and southern Europe, sharing needles for injecting drugs is the most common way to contract the infection.

• HIV is a virus that attacks the body's immune system. At first, a person with HIV may feel completely well and have no symptoms. In time, he or she may develop rare illnesses and cancers because of this weakened immune system. When that happens, the person is said to have AIDS.

• To become infected with HIV, a sufficient amount of it must enter the bloodstream. The body fluids capable of containing enough HIV to infect someone else are blood, semen, vaginal fluids, and breast milk. Other body fluids, including saliva, sweat, and urine, may not contain enough virus to infect another person.

• It is possible to become infected with HIV through transfusions of blood that contained the virus. In most Western countries, blood and donor organs are screened for the virus, but in some countries infection rates through blood transfusion are still significant.

• A mother infected with HIV can pass the virus to her baby during breastfeeding.

• Although there is no cure for AIDS, many people with AIDS have lived in relatively good health for several years. New drugs are constantly being developed, and there are grounds for hoping that a cure may be found.

Changed relationships

Treating your grandchild as your peer

As your grandchild moves into adulthood, your relationship will inevitably change, but it will be no less valuable. The fact that she now has her own social life may mean that you both have to make adjustments if you are to keep in contact. She will not necessarily accompany her parents each time they come to see you and may have trouble finding time or perhaps the fare to visit you on her own. She may be unwilling to cancel a date if you arrive at her parents' house unexpectedly. A telephone call to plan a visit can help you to coordinate your schedules.

Accepting that your grandchild is grown up can be even more difficult than accepting your own child as an independent adult. The number of decades between you make her still seem very young in your eyes, and you probably can't help feeling protective.

But a relationship that has always been strong stands every chance of continuing to remain strong.

Your grandchild's opinions and beliefs are now being formed by her own experiences and other social contacts, rather than primarily deriving from her family. But she knows that you are there for her, and she may seek your advice when she has problems. She may, indeed, feel freer to talk to you than she does to her parents because she wants them to be confident that she can manage on her own. Perhaps she finds it much easier to admit mistakes to you than to her immediate family: she may worry that they will say "I told you so," but she will feel confident that you will not.

While it is probably true that your grandchild's lifestyle is very different from

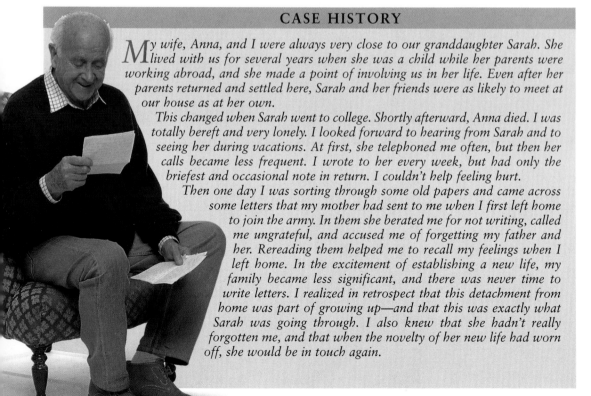

CASE HISTORY

My wife, Anna, and I were always very close to our granddaughter Sarah. She lived with us for several years when she was a child while her parents were working abroad, and she made a point of involving us in her life. Even after her parents returned and settled here, Sarah and her friends were as likely to meet at our house as at her own.

This changed when Sarah went to college. Shortly afterward, Anna died. I was totally bereft and very lonely. I looked forward to hearing from Sarah and to seeing her during vacations. At first, she telephoned me often, but then her calls became less frequent. I wrote to her every week, but had only the briefest and occasional note in return. I couldn't help feeling hurt.

Then one day I was sorting through some old papers and came across some letters that my mother had sent to me when I first left home to join the army. In them she berated me for not writing, called me ungrateful, and accused me of forgetting my father and her. Rereading them helped me to recall my feelings when I left home. In the excitement of establishing a new life, my family became less significant, and there was never time to write letters. I realized in retrospect that this detachment from home was part of growing up—and that this was exactly what Sarah was going through. I also knew that she hadn't really forgotten me, and that when the novelty of her new life had worn off, she would be in touch again.

Shopping trips with your grandchild take on an entirely new aspect now that you no longer have to worry about losing her in the shopping mall, and she can drive you and your purchases home in her own car.

complexities of the modern world than your young adult grandchild?

If you make a point of treating your grandchild as a grown-up rather than the child you remember, you may find that she gives you more than emotional support. As people age, some find it difficult to admit physical frailty, particularly to their children for whom they have always had to be strong. If you are finding some aspects of your daily life increasingly difficult, your grandchild may be the one person in the family to whom you can turn. Tell her your concerns honestly. Young adults today rarely take no for an answer, and are good at coping with bureaucracy. If you have trouble getting medical assistance or help in your home, ask your grandchild for advice. Unintimidated by the system, she may be able to pick up the phone and sort out in minutes a problem that has been bothering you for weeks. Even something as straightforward as choosing new glasses can be easier if your grandchild drives you to the appointment and back, and offers an opinion on the various styles. Don't feel guilty about this—your grandchild will accept your confidences as the final proof that you have come to terms with her growing up.

that of your own young adulthood, you have a wealth of experience upon which she can draw. She will fall in and out of love, experience rejection and failure just as generations of people before her have done, and will sometimes feel that no one else has ever been so unhappy. Be reassuring. Life has shown you that, however painful the situation seems at the time, the hurt does pass and the most appalling dilemmas can be solved.

Your relationship can be mutually supportive. Sometimes it will be her turn to offer you advice, particularly if you are baffled by technical innovations or changing social attitudes. Who better to explain the

You may feel some pangs that your grandchild's early years have passed so quickly and that their charm is lost forever. But when an assured young woman arrives for a visit, you can take pride in the part you played in helping prepare her for a fulfilling role in the adult world.

Coming-of-age celebrations
Marking your grandchild's entry into adulthood

If your son's or daughter's childhood seemed to pass in a flash, you probably feel that your grandchild has grown up even more quickly. She is now planning to celebrate her coming of age, and you are probably wondering where all the years have gone.

A person is considered a full adult when she becomes eligible to vote and therefore can participate actively in the running of her country, often at age 18 or 21. This is frequently marked in some way, especially in Western culture. However, in cultures in which religious rites of passage are considered more important than a civil acknowledgment, the legal coming of age can be quite a low-key affair.

How your grandchild celebrates her coming of age is her decision. Some young people want to mark the occasion by having a party with friends or going to a favorite restaurant. If she is away at college and being supported by her parents, she may not have enough money for anything more. Or she may simply not be a "party animal." But most young people will want to have a special celebration of some kind.

If her parents' finances are overstretched, and you are in a position to help, offer to do so. Whoever foots the bill, the party must be the one your grandchild wants to have, with her choice of guests. Most teenagers do not want their parents and their grandparents around when they are planning to have a good time with friends. Don't be offended if you are not invited. However, many grandchildren will agree to some kind of compromise which can involve everyone in the celebration in some way.

One option is to have a family gathering at home or in a restaurant and for your grandchild to have a less sedate affair with friends at another time. If you come from a culture that has retained traditional forms of entertainment in which everyone can become involved, whatever their age, a large family party may be a particularly appealing idea. Anyone from 2 to 80 can enjoy an Irish dance, for example, but for the most part, the generations do not share the same tastes in either music or dancing.

A meal in a favorite restaurant may be a good way for the family to celebrate your grandchild's coming of age, leaving her free to enjoy a less formal occasion with friends. But if this is too difficult to arrange, invite her to your home for a glass of champagne to wish her well.

ALTERNATIVE CELEBRATIONS

In some families religious rites of passage such as confirmation or a bar and bat mitzvah are more important than coming-of-age celebrations. The legal majority may be considered less important than the 15th (significant in Hispanic culture) or 16th (as in "Sweet 16") birthdays. It is then that families and friends gather at a large party to wish the young person well. Depending on the family, this may also be the birthday at which extra-special gifts are offered.

A more satisfactory alternative might be to arrange a buffet supper for everyone, followed by a disco for the young people only. If you are holding this party in your own home don't forget to warn your neighbors.

If you have been asked to provide the food for a coming-of-age party, find out if any of the guests are vegetarian and whether there are special cultural requirements or specific food allergies. If you serve traditional ethnic food that is spicy, offer a few other options, too. If you love making cakes, now is the time to put your skills to the test. A coming-of-age cake can be as original and witty as you can make it. You might want to limit the choice of drinks to soda and to beer and wine in moderation—plus champagne for the toast. Although many young people boast of their drinking prowess, most are not used to drinking and overindulgence by one guest—young or old—could spoil the entire evening for everyone.

Choosing a gift

The most traditional gift for this important occasion is jewelry, for both girls and boys—watches, rings, neck chains, bracelets, earrings, lockets, cufflinks—but you might want to choose something a little more original. If your grandchild is living away from home or travels a lot, she might like to have some good-quality luggage.

While coming-of-age gifts are usually those things which can be treasured for life,

Most 18- and 21-year-olds appreciate a high-quality watch or other piece of jewelry. This is the occasion when some parents buy—or help with the purchase of—a car. If you want to offer something more unusual, consider a beautiful photograph album with pictures of family members.

some young people prefer to have money spent on things they currently need. A young person involved in sport, for example, might appreciate a good tennis racket or some golf clubs. Depending on your grandchild's interests, you might also consider a computer, a CD player, a camera, or even a car. Check with your grandchild or her parents to make sure that you buy an appropriate brand or model. Particularly on this special occasion, you don't want to spend a lot of money on something that will not be appreciated. If you are not sure what to buy, and don't want to ask your grandchild, gifts of money—especially if she is considering a celebration trip—or shares of stocks or bonds will also be welcome.

An extra-special way to mark this important occasion is to have your grandchild professionally photographed or, if you can afford it, to have her portrait painted. This is something which will give her—and her parents—enormous pleasure now, and can also be passed on to future generations.

Weddings

Accepting your grandchild's wishes on her most special day

Your grandchild is getting married, and you are full of anticipation and perhaps longing to help out with some of the arrangements. But this is a time to wait to be asked. Although weddings are, for the most part, joyful occasions, the preparations for the event can be fraught with problems and cause many family arguments. As the day draws nearer, the bride and groom often get tense and irritable, and the parents of the bride, who usually fund and arrange the wedding, can become overstressed and weary. They may also be worried about escalating costs. It might be appropriate to offer some financial help if you are able, but don't let any member of the

A traditional ceremony, with friends and relatives throwing rice or confetti, is still the dream of many women and quite a few men. Contributions do not have to be financial—if you are able to, consider offering to make the cake or the bridesmaids' dresses.

A RELIGIOUS CEREMONY?

Your grandchild may have a strong faith and prefer to have a traditional religious wedding. If she is marrying outside the faith, however, and her partner does not wish to convert, she may face some problems.

In general, Protestant ministers may marry couples at their discretion, so that if she has her heart set on a church service, she may have one. Similarly, some rabbis are more liberal than others and will marry outsiders. The Roman Catholic Church requires regular attendance at Mass and, in common with other faiths, a period of premarital counseling. The Eastern Orthodox churches generally do not favor mixed marriages.

Some faiths are pragmatic about the marriage of divorced persons, allowing second marriages as long as the joy is tempered with a measure of "contrition" that the first marriage ended. Others are less accepting. If a religious wedding is difficult, a blessing after a civil ceremony may be an option, but many couples choose just a civil ceremony.

family pressure you into doing so.

One important part you can play at this time is to offer your grandchild and her parents—on separate occasions—an escape from the wedding-obsessed household when it all seems too much to cope with. You can act as a sounding board for all the petty irritations they may have with each other—none of which you will ever divulge, of course.

One problem with weddings is that the needs and wishes of the couple can become lost among the concerns and interference of relatives. It seems that everyone has some advice to offer and some ideas on how a wedding should be conducted, forgetting that the bride and groom want to plan things in a way that they prefer. An independent young woman may choose to marry in an emerald green dress, and be horrified if anyone suggests she has a retinue of cousins, nephews, and nieces as

Many reasons prompt the decision to marry away from home. The bride and groom are the most important people on this day—and their wishes should come first.

attendants. Listen enthusiastically to her plans—whatever your private view of them—and let her know that you are sure it will all be wonderful.

Some brides want to do things the traditional way even if their lives so far have seemed to you highly unconventional. Your granddaughter may choose to wear a white dress and veil although she and the groom have been living together.

There are many circumstances in which couples choose to have only a civil ceremony, with only a few people in attendance. You will obviously be disappointed not to be there on this special day. If you are not invited to the ceremony, show your understanding of the situation by inviting the couple for a prenuptial or postnuptial meal and take this opportunity to give them your gift and your best wishes.

Whatever kind of ceremony she chooses to have, the day can be difficult for your grandchild if her parents are divorced or separated and there are stepparents involved too. Many families believe that the estranged parents and any respective new partners should come together and smile happily for the photographer for the sake of their child. But too often the wedding becomes an occasion to reenact previous quarrels. If this is likely to happen, use all your tact and sensitivity to defuse some of the tension.

To avoid the possibility of family confrontation, some couples choose to marry in a different state without the benefit of any guests at all. Regardless of your disappointment, try to accept the positive aspects of such a decision— marrying without family members in attendance guarantees that your grandchild's special day does not degenerate into family wrangling. In such circumstances, most couples have a party for all their close relatives and friends on their return.

Although many grandparents do not play a major role in the weddings of their grandchildren, the day is still a very special one. You are able to share fully in the bride and groom's happiness without having to worry about arrangements going wrong— as you probably did when your own child got married.

Choosing a gift

Wedding presents can be a source of great anxiety. If you are living on a fixed income and there is nothing on the wedding list that you can easily afford, a gift made at home with lots of love will be just as precious to the couple. Perhaps you could make a needlepoint pillow or some other item that could easily become a treasured family heirloom. If you are not good with a crochet hook or a needle, is there a knickknack or a piece of china you know your grandchild has always loved? Now may be the time to pass it on to her. Don't feel that you have to compete with the other set of grandparents. They may be able to afford a set of stemware or flatware, but a sensitive grandchild will be aware of your financial circumstances and cherish your gift just as much.

When there isn't a wedding

Accepting your grandchild's decision to cohabit rather than marry

Once upon a time people fell in love, married, set up a home together, and had children. Most young people still do these things; the difference is that today many rearrange the order in which they do them.

It has become common for the man the bride joins at the altar to have been her partner of several years; and the flower girl or page who follows her up the aisle may be the couple's own child. Many older people, especially those who have had long and happy marriages, find it incomprehensible that so many young people appear to treat this important relationship so casually. It's true that some couples move in together after knowing each other for what may seem like a very short time, and some young men and women live with several different partners before they settle down with one. However, the majority see the decision to cohabit as a commitment and a possible prelude to a future marriage. In the light of the high divorce rate today—and if your grandchild has experienced divorce in her own family—it is not surprising that she wants to be sure that this is the person she can live with before she ties the knot.

Two things may help you understand your grandchild if she and her boyfriend decide to live together. One is that she has grown up in a different moral climate. (Perhaps the major reason that many older people find it difficult to accept cohabitation is that it is a public acknowledgment that a young couple has a sexual relationship. Her parents, probably young adults in the '60s or '70s, are likely to be more relaxed than you about premarital sex.) The other thing is that today emphasis is placed on people finding out as individuals what is right for them and seeking their own happiness and not behaving as their grandparents, parents, the church, and society think they should. You, of course, are entitled to stick

CASE HISTORY

My mom, in particular, gave me a really hard time when Bill and I moved in together. At one point we were barely on speaking terms. I'd introduced Bill to Grandma soon after I met him as I knew they'd get along, and it was Bill who suggested I talk to her to see if she could bring Mom around.

Rather to my surprise, Grandma seemed to understand why I felt Mom was being so unreasonable. She told me that, although she was engaged to Granddad at the time, while he was overseas during the war, she had gone to live with another man. She had thought maybe Granddad wouldn't come back, and this man offered her a chance of happiness. She was with him for a couple of years, then the relationship fizzled out. She told Granddad all about the relationship before they married, and he understood what had prompted her decision. She thought Bill and I were sensible to get to know each other "properly"—that was the word she used—before we made a more serious commitment.

I don't know what she said to Mom, but after that she was okay about things. I never realized Grandma had a past—perhaps Mom didn't either!

to your beliefs and maintain your own standards. But don't expect your adult grandchild to conform to them.

One way to keep a sense of proportion in this situation is to remember the attitudes that prevailed when you were growing up. Despite the insistence that no one then had sexual intercourse outside marriage, the number of illegitimate babies born then proves that they did.

Can you look more positively on the younger generation's straightforward approach? They may have a different set of values, but they do not condemn those who contravene a social code. Remember, too, that in the past a double standard often existed about sexual morality: there was an assumption that most men were sexually experienced on their wedding night, while their brides were totally innocent.

If you cannot accept the fact that your grandchild is cohabiting, you run the risk of not seeing her often, if at all. The situation is more difficult if the couple lives together in the parental home, since you may resent your child's collaboration in the whole thing. But you will not make things better by refusing to visit when you know the couple is going to be present.

Practical arrangements

No one claims that it is easy to come to terms with changes in sexual and social mores. However, your disapproval may not make any difference in the way your grandchild leads her life. You obviously do not want to lose contact with her, so perhaps both of you would be happier if she visited you alone. But

in asking this, you risk alienating her by rejecting her chosen lifestyle.

Invite them both to visit you. If the visit involves an overnight stay and you really cannot bring yourself to give them a room together, suggest that perhaps they would be more comfortable at a motel and offer to pay part or all of the cost. For many, this is preferable to insisting on separate sleeping arrangements, which only leads to embarrassment and play-acting all around. The grandchild with whom you have always had a close relationship will behave sensitively and probably make those arrangements herself.

It is a truism that people can become used to anything. However much you may dislike her lifestyle, your grandchild is showing the independence of mind and spirit that you have helped foster in her, and she remains the person you have always loved. It is also a fact that the majority of people who live together do eventually marry, and one day you may receive an invitation to her wedding.

Your grandchild may choose not to marry her partner, but their commitment to each other may be just as strong and binding. Their life together, like many marriages, is probably based on shared incomes, shared responsibilities, and a happiness in each other's company that is obvious to all.

Then and now:

Careers and relationships

Among the many rapid changes in our society in the last half-century, the role of women has evolved at breakneck speed. Now, as well as being partners and mothers, they may also have full-time jobs outside the home.

THEN

The way in which your grandchild conducts herself as both a partner and a parent probably bears little resemblance to the way you fulfilled those roles two generations ago. There has been a huge revolution in how families run their lives, and it has taken place so recently that even members of your children's generation may find it difficult to come to terms with.

Historically, the principal ambition of generations of women was to be a wife and mother. Single women often had jobs but were expected to give them up when they married; many professions were closed to women. As a result, most became financially dependent upon their husbands immediately after the wedding ceremony. Certainly as soon as children came along, most women opted to stay home and bring them up while fathers were the sole breadwinners. Now both parents are likely to work, perhaps full time, and their children are cared for in daycare centers or by caregivers.

There are several reasons why so many young mothers work outside the home. One is economic necessity—two salaries are necessary to pay a large mortgage or rent on a house. They may also have become used to a certain lifestyle and do not want to give that up because they have had a baby. But the main reason is that women no longer want to be "only" housewives and mothers. They have the opportunity to become as well-educated and as highly skilled as men, and they seek fulfillment in the workplace. They take pride in earning money for themselves and their family, and they enjoy making a contribution to society as well as to the home.

A man's place

This development has inevitably brought about changes in the way men see themselves. Not so long ago, fathers played little part in the day-to-day running of the home and the care of their children. It was rare to find a man who could change a diaper, or mix a bottle of formula. Some even felt deep embarrassment at being seen pushing a stroller.

In fact, fathers often worked such long hours that they rarely saw their children. When he did come home from work, the man of the house probably expected his supper to be on the table, the house neat, and the children tucked in bed asleep. With the exception of the war years—when women were encouraged to work

NOW

Traditionally, women were housewives and, with their children, welcomed the breadwinner home at the end of the day (far left). Today, many fathers are happy to take on this role either through genuine desire or economic expediency.

outside the home—this was the pattern of domestic life for generations. And there were doubtless many men and women who were happy with this arrangement, just as there were some who were resentful of the fact that their roles were so strictly defined on the basis of gender.

The gradual emergence of the "new man" has heralded a more flexible approach. Today's young father is likely to be present at the birth of his children, having attended prenatal classes with his partner. He will know as much about changing, bathing, and feeding the new baby as his partner and will chart each stage of development as avidly as mothers and grandmothers have always done.

But even if he has been allowed to take paternity leave, he is soon obliged to go back to work, while his partner's employer may be obliged to give her several months leave at home with the baby. According to most surveys, women—including those who have demanding careers—still take on the primary responsibility for child care and running the home.

High unemployment forces some men to remain at home as "househusbands" and main child carers, dependent on their partner's salary. Some men find this

immensely rewarding and are happy to make this contribution to their family life. Many men who stay at home with their children find that their relationship with them as they grow is enriched by this close contact. Others are proud of the new skills they acquire in these years—from teaching prereading to patiently nursing common childhood illnesses. But a man who takes on this role is still likely to have to come to terms with the fact that he is in a substantial minority when he takes his children to parent and toddler groups and other child-related activities. Some may discover that other family members and male friends find it difficult to empathize with their concerns.

Can you help?

If both partners work, the double income may allow them to pay for household help, as well as full-time care for their child. So while you may be appalled at the idea of your granddaughter, or your grandson's partner, handing over a new baby to a daycare center or caregiver and returning to work, it is not unusual to find some new mothers back behind their desks weeks, even days, after giving birth.

You may be enlisted to help out with some babysitting, but your grandchild is more likely to use professional child care. This can be a tricky area for you and your adult child—the new baby's grandparent. You may think a babysitter is far too young and inexperienced to be in charge of this precious new addition to the family. However, everyone in the family should stand back and allow the young couple and their new baby to lead their life in the way they wish— even if that lifestyle seems incomprehensible. Offer to help in any way you can.

Inheritance

Leaving your treasured possessions in loving hands

There are doubtless many things you would like to pass on to your grandchild after your death. You may have made some such provision in your will, but it can be difficult to be sure that you are giving her what she would like to receive. Of course, if you are beginning to come to terms with your own mortality (see pp. 202–205), you can ask her directly if she would like to be left the antique dresser you have treasured for years or the pearl necklace that you inherited from your own mother. But if your grandchild is less sanguine than you, she may be upset by such questions, and prefer not to think about the day you will no longer be here as her friend and supporter. She may dismiss such queries with remarks like "You're going to be around for years yet, Gran," and refuse to discuss the subject.

Throughout your grandchild's growing years, you have undoubtedly picked up leads to objects she has admired in your home, pieces of jewelry she has exclaimed over, or the patchwork quilt that has always seemed to fascinate her. Make a mental or written note when you observe her enthusiasm for some item or other. Be realistic about what you leave each grandchild. While one with a more sentimental streak will obviously appreciate possessing your collection of photographs or other bits and pieces of family memorabilia, others may attach no importance to such things. You won't want to give them to one who you suspect is going to put all those cherished family photographs in the trash once you are no longer around.

Sometimes bequests are obvious. Musicians will love an instrument you used, for example, and the grandchild who shares your passion for fishing will enjoy having your rods and tackle. Rather than waiting until you die and are denied seeing how much pleasure your gifts bring, you may decide to give away some of your possessions while you are still around to watch the recipient enjoying them. This is particularly appropriate with gifts of money. If you were planning to leave a sizable sum to your grandchild, consider giving some of it to her now, perhaps to help her through college, buy her first apartment, or set up her own business.

Some of your more valuable possessions have obvious "homes" among your children and their children, but there are many curios and mementos that one of your grandchildren will love as being part of you—irrespective of their financial value.

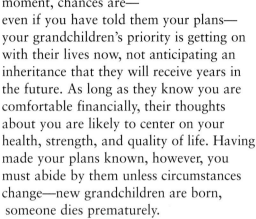

You may believe that the money you leave should be equally divided between your children and their children. On the other hand, you may feel it is illogical to treat all your grandchildren equally, as they have different needs at different times. To a single parent struggling to bring up a family on a minuscule income, any sum of money could make a huge difference. But one who is already running a successful business may have no need of financial help. She may prefer a piece of furniture or a painting.

In any case, you may choose to have an open, friendly discussion with family members about what you have decided to leave everyone and why. Otherwise, if you opt for equal shares, the less well off members of the family may resent it; in the other scenario, your more successful grandchild may be hurt at your apparent neglect. Better to explain your motives now, to avoid misplaced anticipation or an uncomfortable atmosphere.

Helping out financially when a grandchild needs assistance often makes more sense than having her wait until you die. By that time, she may be well established and no longer in need of your investment. But be sure you know how much you can afford to give and keep enough to be able to live as comfortably as you wish. Give financial gifts only if you are sure that is what you want, rather than what your relatives expect.

It is also important to remember that, although such matters may be of major concern to you at the moment, chances are—even if you have told them your plans—your grandchildren's priority is getting on with their lives now, not anticipating an inheritance that they will receive years in the future. As long as they know you are comfortable financially, their thoughts about you are likely to center on your health, strength, and quality of life. Having made your plans known, however, you must abide by them unless circumstances change—new grandchildren are born, someone dies prematurely.

If you decide to sell your house and move to a smaller place or into a residential home, you will almost surely have to reduce drastically the number of your possessions. You may, in fact, need to sell much of your furniture and other valuables to augment your income. If so, you'll have a good opportunity to invite your grandchildren to your house and ask them to choose things they would like to have. You could even hold the opposite of a housewarming party for the entire family—instead of your guests bringing presents, each of them takes away an item she has always admired.

Of course, it can be difficult to relinquish things that have been part of your life for many years. But you know they will be in good hands, and you will gain great satisfaction in years to come from seeing your favorite pieces cherished by the younger generation.

CHAPTER NINE

Your Role as Great-grandparent

In the same way that your life changed irrevocably when you became a parent, and again on becoming a grandparent, so it will change as another generation enters the world.

To help you focus positively on this new stage in your life, look back to when you became a grandparent. Perhaps you feared that you were no longer important in your child's world and that you might be excluded from his or her family life. But as your new role evolved and you achieved a blend of involvement and detachment that allowed you to take part in your grandchild's development, these misgivings were soon dispelled.

As a great-grandparent you will assume a new role, but this does not make you superfluous to the rest of the family. You have the wisdom and experience that comes only from watching generations of children grow up. Having slowed down a little and shed a few commitments, you can probably devote more time now to family matters. Until one of your children takes up the mantle, you are the keeper of your family's history, the one who lived the stories that the others enjoy. Relax and savour the continuity of family life in which you are still playing a key part.

Adjusting to change

Taking pride and pleasure in your expanding family

Attitude is an all-important part of becoming a great-grandparent. You can feel justifiably proud of your place at the top of the family tree. Or you can take change in a negative way, choosing to think that your role is slipping away and you are being pushed to one side as the generations move on.

Focus on the positive. You are in the enviable position of having seen three generations come after you. Your family is a great, lasting, growing clan, which has been and will continue to be influenced by you. If your family members see that you have a positive attitude and a commonsense approach to life, they will continue to make sure that you are a part of their social gatherings and day-to-day activities.

If you have moved into sheltered accommodations or to a nursing home and you are not as geographically close as you once were to the rest of your family, take steps to make sure that you do not feel left out of things. If writing long letters is tiring or irksome, ask a sympathetic member of the staff to help you or get hold of a tape recorder so that you can tape messages to your grandchildren and great-grandchildren.

Make the most of the visits family members pay to you. Do not use these sessions as a forum for complaints about what is happening where you live; let your family know instead that you are totally interested in their lives and in how everyone is getting along.

The family tree

It may be, with all the new arrivals over the years, that you sometimes find it difficult to remember names, ages, and such other details as jobs or schools. This happens to all of us. But you can clarify things by making a family tree when you have the time to yourself and feel like doing it. Then when visitors come, you can talk confidently about what stage the children have reached and ask relevant questions.

If your family tree is of particular interest to you, make it something special, using photographs and additional information from the past that might otherwise be forgotten. This is sure to grab the attention of younger members of your family, and they may feel inspired to support your efforts, hunting for unusual photographs or even tracing people with whom you might have lost touch. In the years to come, such a family tree will be very much treasured.

Your grandchildren and great-grandchildren will continue to enjoy your company as long as you enjoy theirs and take an interest in their concerns. Find subjects of mutual interest for conversation. Engage in activities within your capabilities that you both enjoy, such as going for a walk or to a restaurant.

Enjoy your position as matriarch. It is a great achievement to have three generations of descendants. If your grandchildren's babyhood seems a long time ago, you now have the chance to relish the pleasures of grandparenting all over again.

Coping with infirmity

If you have a serious health problem, you may feel reluctant about having the younger members of your family visit you. This is an issue that only you can settle, but it helps to remember that children see illness and infirmity in very different ways from adults.

Your great-grandchildren will love you for who you are. To them, you have always been old (children consider their parents, never mind their grandparents, as old) and perhaps even frail. As a result, what you see as greatly increased infirmity or marked lack of health or strength may hardly be noticed by much younger members of your family—and will not be feared by them, unless you are frightened yourself and let them see it.

Continue to see all your family and make your voice heard for as long as you feel well enough and strong enough to do so. Unlike cultures in which the oldest family members are considered the wisest and are cared for within the extended family unit, Western society has such a horror of old age that it sometimes tries to deny its existence. Never view yourself as an inconvenience or allow yourself to be patronized. Younger people will learn from your attitude and respect your age and experience as something to be valued rather than hidden away.

If you are very ill and too weak to receive visitors, you may want to rest alone. But don't feel that you have to be isolated. Continue sending your letters and tapes, and telephone when you can. Let your family know that you love hearing from them and that you think about them even though you can't see them at the moment. If your great-grandchildren are very young, they will appreciate a funny drawing just as much, if not more than, a letter from you, and the older children will enjoy hearing your voice.

If you choose not to see the youngest members of the family, make it clear that you still want and need to see the adults. They will understand your reasons for not having the children visit and can keep you up-to-date with photographs and snippets of information about how everyone is and what they are doing.

Although some loss of health and strength is almost inevitable at this stage in your life, it can be a marvelous consolation to witness the continuity of your family. Many people are denied this satisfaction. But you have succeeded in rearing your own children and in helping rear your grandchildren and, in turn, their children. You and your family have succeeded at the most central function in life, and you have much to be proud of.

Accepting your mortality

Coming to terms with the fact that life has an end

Whether you are fighting fit or struggling with ill health, whether you hold sustaining religious beliefs or have none, becoming a great-grandparent will inevitably cause you to consider your own mortality. Another generation has arrived, introducing new life and vitality at a time when you are bound to be slowing down a little and you have the chance to take stock of all that has happened in your lifetime.

Many people say that they get an intuitive feeling that they should start to tie up loose ends and prepare for what is to come. For many a fulfilling and happy life leaves them ready to accept death. But for others the end is unthinkable. Whatever you feel, there are ways of thinking and acting that you may find helpful. There will invariably be a rich fund of memories you can draw on to remind yourself of the positive difference your life has made to your family and friends. And whatever your spiritual beliefs, there are three generations of your flesh and blood alive because of you. Do not underestimate how much you have influenced them. People really do live on in the memories and example of others. Think of your own parents and grandparents; inevitably you have carried some of their beliefs, wisdom, funny sayings, and even looks through your life. These links go on and on.

Despite this knowledge, you may still find it difficult to accept your own mortality. All counselors and spiritual leaders agree that this is the hardest thing to accept because it is so difficult to comprehend. It may be useful to discuss this with a trained professional or member of your church first, rather than with your immediate family.

If there are matters you want to clear up or things that need saying, don't wait until you are prodded by illness or infirmity. Talk to your family now. Be prepared for the fact that younger people will try to change the subject when you speak of your mortality because it is painful for them to think of your death, and they may not understand your acceptance of the inevitable.

Funeral arrangements

One, often very calming, way of accepting your own mortality is to begin managing practical matters. Make sure your will still represents your wishes, or if you haven't made one, do so. You may find it a surprisingly affirmative thing to plan your own funeral, as much as possible. If you are a music lover, for example, choosing one or more of your favorite pieces to be played at the service is

Putting papers in order, updating a will to include the newest arrivals, and sorting family photographs are not morbid actions but positive affirmations of how much you value life and your family. By putting your affairs in good order, you can be sure that members of your family will abide by your wishes once you are gone, and you will save them unnecessary hard work at a time when they want simply to remember you.

CASE HISTORY

I was only 38 when my grandson David was born. His parents' marriage was always rocky, and David spent a lot of time with me as they tried to patch up their differences. But they were finally divorced when David was six.

David had a good relationship with both his parents, who always seemed to put him first, regardless of their problems. Then two years ago, when he was just 18, David was killed in a car crash. In the midst of all our grief, his parents started to argue about the funeral arrangements. His father wanted a religious service; his mother was adamant that David had had no faith and would have thought it inappropriate. I tried to keep out of the wrangling, but found myself dragged in to arbitrate. It was ghastly. Eventually we reached a compromise that satisfied no one but at least allowed us to bury David with some dignity.

Obviously, no one had expected David to die, and part of the problem was that we were taken by surprise. But then I started to consider what would happen if I died suddenly. I'm still relatively young and in excellent health, but you never know what's in store. I realized that no one knew what my wishes would be if anything happened to me.

My daughter thinks I'm unnecessarily morbid, but I've written a letter to her detailing my wishes for my funeral. I hope it will sit in my lawyer's safe for the next 20 years or more, but at least I know none of my family will have to go through what happened when David died.

fitting. There may be Bible or poetry readings that hold special significance for you, and they, too, could be included. By writing all this down and placing it in the hands of your lawyer or a member of the family, you are making sure that your final goodbye bears your personal stamp. You will also be saving your family some of the distress that surrounds funeral preparations.

If you do not hold any religious beliefs and feel strongly about how your funeral should be conducted, make your wishes known. Contact a humanist society for information on nonreligious funeral ceremonies; your family might be too upset to think of this and organize it otherwise.

Positive affirmations

If you feel you should do something to acknowledge your own mortality, consider writing a letter or several letters to your family. Perhaps you have not always found the right words to praise them for their achievements and the way they have related to you. If you think these things would otherwise go unsaid, try to put your thoughts on paper. Make everything positive—you will not have the chance to undo what you are going to say.

You will probably derive a great deal of satisfaction and peace of mind from writing a letter, whether you send it now or leave it with your other papers to be read after your death. Your family will take comfort in years to come from knowing you were thinking about them.

Death is the most taboo subject in our society. Even among people with strong religious faith, it is often avoided as if it were not the one certain fact of life. If you feel secure and composed enough, try to break this mold by letting your family know that because of them you are accepting and essentially unafraid. Face this last hurdle positively and frankly, and imagine how you will be remembered in the years to come by those you love and who love you.

Remaking the heritage chest

Presenting the whole story to your family

Most people rethink their position within the family when they become a great-grandparent. Now you can see your descendants stretching out in a long line before you; this is the time to savor a sense of continuity to the fullest.

On becoming parents and grandparents, many people start a heritage chest (see p. 15) containing significant family items. The collection can be added to as the years go by; it might include a lock of a child's hair, a first swimming certificate, wedding invitations, and birth announcements. This is the ideal time to update your family's memento box and check that the contents are properly stored so that they will last. You are in the unique position within your family of having lived through all the experiences that are represented in the box, and it will be helpful for future generations if you write notes giving a date—don't worry if this is only approximate if you can't recall exact details—and brief explanation where necessary.

Never underestimate the delight that such tangible family history can bring. If you do a thorough job of a heritage chest, you will be providing your family with a sense of background and roots. The younger children will be fascinated by some of the items they view as part of a bygone age, and you will make their ancestors real for them.

Practical considerations

Wrap locks of hair individually in tissue paper and place them in labeled envelopes. Remember, also, to continue the tradition by taking a snip of your new great-grandchild's hair and adding it to the collection. The adults will be fascinated by how their hair color and texture have changed.

Certificates and other documents fade with age and start to disintegrate when handled. Fingerprints can also be a problem, so use clear plastic cases to hold these items.

Many families keep children's first shoes or bootees. If you have some of these, remind your great-grandchild's parents not to throw their baby's away, but to let you have them in due course. They keep better if they are stuffed with tissue or a sachet of dried lavender.

If you have saved petals from wedding bouquets or ornaments from wedding or christening cakes, store them in small cardboard boxes, label them, and if possible, keep the flower petals pressed; otherwise, in time they will break.

Another popular keepsake is a piece of fabric from a wedding dress or christening gown. Store these between sheets of acid-free tissue, and expect them to fade with age (black paper slows down the rate of fading). Sewing the names and dates of the wedding or christening party on the back or edge of the fabric pieces will add to the enjoyment of those who want to examine the contents of the box in the future.

Younger family members will be fascinated by the odds and ends you have saved from previous generations. A stylish box adds to the charm, and if it has separate compartments it will help you file things away neatly. Don't rely on your memory— make sure everything is labeled and dated.

Invitations, birth announcements, or cards for special occasions deserve a folder of their own. Family members will be amazed at how design styles have changed over the years. Again, it is important that these are dated.

Degrees, diplomas, and other certificates keep better if they are rolled and fixed with ribbon instead of a rubber band (these decay over time). The nonchalant graduate who casually passed you his diploma years ago will appreciate the care you have taken of it when the time comes for him to show it to his own grandchildren.

Photographs generally keep better if they are stored in albums out of direct sunlight. If you have a collection of school or college photographs showing each member of your family at the same stage in their development, and you want to group them together, choose a small box or folder.

Plastic name and weight tags from the hospital or disposable paper baby gowns (unworn) can also form part of the collection, even if they may seem less appealing than other items. In years to come the children will be fascinated by how tiny their wrists must have been to wear the tag and will have difficulty imagining how they fitted into the gown.

If, like many families, yours has had its share of tragedy, don't omit the evidence from your heritage chest. If family members have died before their time, you should include a photograph, funeral card, or special poem they liked, or even a toy or game that was special to them. Everyone in your family deserves a place here and should be remembered in some way.

As new babies come into your family, you may want to include a newspaper that was published on the day they were born, or put away a coin with their birth year on it, or even some postage stamps. In the future those babies will be fascinated by how different things were when they were born.

Perhaps you have also been making a family tree; if so, you could place this, or a copy of it, in the chest. If you let your family know that you are maintaining a chest, they will be more likely to save appropriate things to go in it. Doubtless they will be eager to look at what you have collected, which will provide you with pleasure as well. But watch what the younger ones are doing to make sure that everything remains in the chest and is kept as it should be.

Survey of grandparents' legal rights

When talks fail, the law may help

Four million grandparents in the United States are raising their grandchildren, often without legal sanction, because they have taken over for parents whose problems or addictions prevent them from taking care of their children.

Grandparents who do not have legal custody of their grandchildren may get little help with the costs of support or education, although in some cases financial assistance is available from the state or Social Security. Nor—without legal guardianship—do grandparents have easy recourse if a parent wants to reclaim the child at any point. If the problem recurs, the child may need a grandparent's help again. The difficulty of grandparents in these situations has led to the formation of support organizations in some states, such as the Foundation for Grandparenting in New Mexico.

Laws vary from state to state, but in all states the courts are reluctant to terminate a parent's rights. To gain custody of a grandchild, you must present solid evidence that the parent is not acting in your grandchild's best interests and is therefore unfit as a parent. The strongest ground would be proof that the parents were inflicting physical harm or committing sexual offenses against the child. Permitting such behavior to be inflicted by others is also ground for removal of a child from his or her parent.

Parents who fail to provide a minimum level of care—food, shelter, clothing, and medical attention—or who abandon their children, failing to provide supervision or reasonable care, may be found guilty of neglect. Parents who have been convicted of a serious crime or who use drugs or excessive amounts of alcohol may sometimes be found to be unfit.

Except in life-threatening emergencies, a child cannot be removed from his or her parents without a court hearing. In most cases, hearings that relate to children are referred to a family or juvenile court. In many states the child must be placed under state supervision for a period of months before proceedings terminating parental rights may begin, and conditions justifying termination must remain unimproved for that period, demonstrating that parents have not tried to change the situation. Courts also take into account whether parents have tried to maintain their relationship with the child.

Grandparents' special role in the life of their grandchildren is acknowledged in law in many states. If a court is satisfied that your visits are in your grandchild's best interests, you should be able to maintain contact in most circumstances.

Fostering your grandchild

In the period leading up to termination proceedings, the child is placed with a temporary custodian. This may be a grandparent or other relative, a friend, or a foster parent appointed by the court. Grandparents are often the preferred custodians. If your grandchild has been living with you, you have a particularly strong case to continue the arrangement. If your grandchild is old enough, his or her wishes may be considered. Often a social services agency is legally charged with determining what care is in the child's best interests.

If you or another relative cannot care for your grandchild, or if the court feels that that is not the best choice for the child, a foster home will be found. Foster parents and foster homes must be licensed according to the standards of each state. This usually involves training to meet the special needs of foster children and examination of the health, personality, and relationships between the foster family members, as well as inspection of the health and safety standards of the home itself.

In most states you may petition the court for visitation rights while your grandchild is in foster care, although the law does not guarantee that a court will order visitation— only your right to make the petition. In determining whether to grant the request, a judge is guided by what he or she perceives to be in the child's best interests. Many factors may be considered, including your relationship with the child and with the child's parents.

Becoming a custodian or foster parent does not confer legal custody, even though the arrangement may last for years. The court usually holds out the hope that the natural parents will eventually be able to

Juvenile courts are bound by one principle: what is best for the child. It is for this reason that they are so reluctant to sever parents' rights. Maintain as close a relationship with your grandchild as you can. If the child's parents are unable to give adequate care, for whatever reason, step in and take care of your grandchild yourself if at all possible. If not, make sure the child and the courts know you are there. A close relationship is the best way to ensure that you do not lose contact, even if it is in the child's best interests to be legally adopted by others.

regain custody of their children. The children remain legally in the custody of the state until the court deems that parental rights must be terminated (see pp. 142–43). At that point, the children are officially considered by the state as orphans, and may be offered for legal adoption.

Grandparents and adoption

Grandparents may petition the court for the right to adopt, and if it is considered in the child's best interest, the adoption may be granted. Your age will be a factor in the decision. If you are in good health, and especially if the child has lived happily with you for some time or if you and the child have a very close relationship, the court is more inclined to rule in your favor.

If your grandchild is adopted by a stranger, depending on state legislation, you may be given visitation rights if the court holds that maintaining contact with you would be in the best interests of the child. You may, however, find that any existing visitation rights come to an end.

An order granting grandparents visitation rights does not necessarily prevent either natural or adoptive parents from moving out of state or out of the country, although the court may sometimes rule that grandchildren be allowed to visit their grandparents during vacations.

Sources and resources

GRANDPARENTS

Creative Grandparenting
Robert Kasey
609 Blackgates Rd.
Wilmington, DE 19803
302-656-2122

Foundation for Grandparenting
Arthur Kornhaber, MD
5 Casa del Oro Lane
Santa Fe, NM 87505
505-466-1029

Grandparent Information Center
AARP
601 E St. NW
Washington, DC 20049
202-434-2296

Grandparents Anonymous
1924 Beverly
Sylvan Lake, MI 48320
810-682-8384

Grandparents Rights
Organization
555 South Old Woodward Ave.
Suite 600
Birmingham, MI 48009
810-646-7191

PREGNANCY AND BIRTH

Be Healthy, Inc.
RR 1, Box 172
Glenville
Waitsfield, VT 05673
802-496-4944
1-800-433-5523

International Childbirth
Education Association
PO Box 20048
Minneapolis, MN 55420
612-854-8660

La Leche League International
1400 North Meacham Rd.
Schaumburg, IL 60173-4840
847-519-7730

Read Natural Childbirth
Foundation
PO Box 150956
San Rafael, CA 94915
414-456-3143

BABIES AND TODDLERS

Child Abuse and Listening and
Meditation
PO Box 90754
Santa Barbara, CA 93190
805-965-2376

National Committee for
Prevention of Child Abuse
332 South Michigan Ave.
Suite 1600
Chicago, IL 60604
312-663-3520

National Down's Syndrome
Congress
1605 Chantilly Dr., Suite 250
Atlanta, GA 20324
404-633-1555

Nursing Mothers' Council
PO Box 50063
Palo Alto, CA 94303
415-599-3669

Spina Bifida Association of
America
4590 MacArthur Blvd.
Suite 250
Washington, DC 20007
202-944-3285

Toy Library Association
2530 Crawford Ave.
Suite 111
Evanston, IL 60201
847-864-3330

SCHOOLCHILDREN

American Sports Education
Institute of America
200 Castlewood Dr.
North Palm Beach
FL 33408-5696
561-842-4100

Association for Childhood
Education of America
11501 Georgia Ave.
Suite 315
Wheaton, MD 20902
301-942-2443

Learning Disabilities Association
of America
4156 Library Rd.
Pittsburgh, PA 15234
412-341-1515

National Association for Sports
and Physical Education
1900 Association Dr.
Reston, VA 20191
703-476-3410

National Association for the Education of Young Children
1509 16th St. NW
Washington, DC 20036
202-232-8777

North American Youth Sports Institute
4985 Oak Garden Dr.
Rernersville, NC 27284
910-784-4926

ADOLESCENTS

Action on Smoking and Health
2013 H St. NW
Washington, DC 20006
202-659-4310

Alcoholics Anonymous
475 Riverside Dr.
New York, NY 10115
212-870-3400

American Anorexia/Bulimia Association
1560 Broadway
New York, NY 10036
212-501-8351

Americans for a Sound AIDS/HIV Policy
102 Elder St., Suite 11
Herndon, VA 20170
703-471-7350

The Couple to Couple League
PO Box 111184
Cincinnati, OH 45211
513-471-2000

Narcotics Anonymous
PO Box 9999
Van-Nuys, CA 91409
818-773-9999

National Association of People With AIDS
1413 K St. NW
Washington, DC 20005
202-898-0414

National Eating Disorders Organization
6655 South Yale Ave.
Tulsa, OK 74136
918-481-4044

National Family Planning and Reproductive Health Association
122 C St. NW, Suite 380
Washington, DC 20001
202-628-3535

People With AIDS Coalition
50 West 17th St., 8th Floor
New York, NY 10011
212-647-1415

Planned Parenthood
810 Seventh Ave.
New York, NY 10019
212-541-7800
1-800-230-PLAN

Sex Information and Education Council of the US
130 West 42nd St., Suite 380
New York, NY 10036
212-819-9970

FOR PARENTS

American Counseling Association
5999 Stevenson Ave.
Alexandria, VA 22304
703-823-9800

Divorce Support
5020 West School St.
Chicago, IL 60641
773-286-4541

Family Resource Coalition
200 South Michigan Ave.
Suite 1600
Chicago, IL 60604
312-341-0900

Parents Anonymous
675 West Foothills Blvd.
Suite 220
Claremont, CA 91711
909-621-6184

BOOKS

Brown, L.K. and M. *Dinosaurs Divorce* Little Brown, New York, 1996

Briggs, Raymond *Grandpa* Penguin, New York, 1992

Calderone, M. S. and Ramsey, J. *Talking with Your Child about Sex* Random House, New York, 1983

Cole, Babette *Drop Dead* Random House, New York, 1996

Fine, Anne *Madam Doubtfire* Penguin, New York, 1995

Gray, Nigel and Rogers, Gregory *Running Away from Home* Crown, New York, 1997

Hughes, Shirley *Tales of Trotter Street* Candlewick Press, Boston, 1996

Madras, L. *The What's Happening to My Body? Book for Girls: A Growing Up Guide for Parents and Daughters* New Market Press, New York, 1983

Waddell, Martin and Dale, Penny *When the Teddy Bears Came* Candlewick Press, Boston, 1994

Index

Acknowledgments

l = left; *r* = right; *b* = bottom;
t = top; *c* = center

2/3 Jay Silverman/The Image Bank;
4 Zefa; 5*l* Zefa; 5*c* Anthony A.
Boccaccio/The Image Bank, 5*r* The
Image Bank; 6/7 The Image Bank;
8 P Barton/Zefa; 9*t & b* Zefa, 9*c*
David Young Wolff/Tony Stone
Images; 10/11 Zefa; 12 L D Gordon/
The Image Bank; 13 Zefa; 14 Robert
Harding Picture Library; 15 Andrew
Sydenham; 16 Frans Rombout/
Bubbles; 17 David W Hamilton/The
Image Bank; 18/19 Zefa; 20*t* Robert
Harding Picture Library, 20*b* Silver
Cross; 21*t* Sue Ann Miller/Tony
Stone Images, 21*c* Zefa, 21*b*/25
Andrew Sydenham; 26*l* Robert
Goldman/Zefa, 26*r*/27 Andrew
Sydenham; 28 Robert Harding
Picture Library; 29 P Joseph/Bubbles;
30 J Nettis/Zefa; 31*l* Butch Martin/
The Image Bank, 31*r* Zefa; 32/33
Robert Harding Picture Library;
34 John P Kelly/The Image Bank;
35 Andrew Sydenham; 36 Zefa;
37*t* Andrew Sydenham; 37*br* Andrew
Lazell; 38/39 Zefa; 40 Andrew
Sydenham; 41*t* Robert Harding
Picture Library, 41*c & b* Andrew
Sydenham; 42*t* Early Learning Centre
42*b* Andrew Sydenham; 43*t/tc/b*
Andrew Sydenham, 43*bc* Early
Learning Centre; 44/45 Robert
Harding Picture Library; 46/47
Andrew Sydenham; 48 John Birdsall;
49*t* Zefa, 49*b* Andrew Lazell; 50*l*
The Hutchison Library, 50*r* Terje
Rakke/The Image Bank; 51 Andrew
Sydenham; 52/53 Zefa; 54 Mugshots/
Ace Photo Agency; 55 P Barton/Zefa;
56*t* Andrew Sydenham, 56*b* Zefa;
57*t* Jo Browne/Mick Smee/Tony
Stone Images, 57*b* Andrew Sydenham;
58*t* The Image Bank, 58*b* Richard
Walker/Ace Photo Agency; 59*tl/tr*
Zefa, 59*trc/cr/b* Andrew Sydenham,

59*cl* Early Learning Centre; 60 Derek
Dryland/Bubbles; 61 Richard
Pharaoh/Robert Harding Picture
Library; 62*t* Andrew Sydenham, 62*b*
Colin Thomas/Ace Photo Agency;
63*t* Dale Durjee/Tony Stone Images,
63*b* Andrew Sydenham; 64 Ian Cook/
Topham Picture Point; 65 Jennie
Woodcock/Reflections; 70/71
Andrew Sydenham; 72 Zefa; 73
Andrew Sydenham; 74/75 Zefa;
76/77 Andrew Sydenham; 78 Zefa;
79/81*t* Andrew Sydenham, 81*b*
Zefa; 82*t* Popperfoto, 82*b* Andrew
Sydenham; 83 Jeff Smith/The Image
Bank; 84 Andrew Sydenham;
85 Robert Harding Picture Library;
86 The Image Bank; 87/88 Andrew
Sydenham; 89/90 Zefa; 91/96
Andrew Sydenham; 97/99 Zefa; 100*t*
Werner Bokelberg/The Image Bank,
100*b*/101 Andrew Sydenham; 102*t*
Zefa, 102*b* Walter Hodges/Robert
Harding Picture Library; 103*tl/tr*
Early Learning Centre, 103*bl/br*
Andrew Sydenham; 104/105 Zefa;
106 Robert Harding Picture Library;
107 Zefa; 108 Steve Chenn/Robert
Harding Picture Library; 109/111
Andrew Sydenham; 112/113
Mugshots/Ace Photo Agency; 114*t*
Andrew Sydenham, 114*b* Zefa; 115*t*
Zefa, 115*b*/117 Andrew Sydenham;
118 T & D McCarthy/Zefa; 119
Zefa; 120/122*l* Andrew Sydenham;
122*r* Anne Yelland; 123 Andrew
Sydenham; 124/125 Zefa; 126 The
Image Bank; 127 David Madison/
Tony Stone Images; 128 Andrew
Sydenham, 128/129 Image Finders/
Ace Photo Agency; 129 Andrew
Sydenham; 130 Zefa; 131/132
Robert Harding Picture Library;
133*t* Chip Henderson/Tony Stone
Images, 133*b* Andrew Sydenham;
134 Alan Hicks/Tony Stone Images;
135*t* Zefa, 135*b* J Feingersh/Zefa;
136 Andrew Sydenham; 137 Zefa;

138 Robert Harding Picture Library;
139 Michael Bluestone/Ace Photo
Agency; 140 Robert Harding Picture
Library; 141 Andrew Sydenham;
142 David Young Wolff/Tony Stone
Images; 143*t* Roy Morsch/Zefa,
143*b*/144 Andrew Sydenham;
145 Jennie Woodcock/Reflections;
146*t* R Kanjman/Zefa, 146*b* Robert
Harding Picture Library; 147 Zefa;
148 Andrew Sydenham; 149 Zefa;
150*l* Nikki Gibbs/Bubbles, 150*r*
Zefa; 151 Jennie Woodcock/
Reflections; 152/153*t* Andrew
Sydenham, 153*b* Bill Bachmann/
Ace Photo Agency; 154*t* Robbie
Jack, 154*b* Laura Wickenden; 155
Andrew Sydenham; 156 Redferns;
157 Zefa; 158 Andrew Sydenham;
159 Anthony Medley/S.I.N.1;
160 Cortis; 161*t* Zefa, 161*c* David
Hoffman, 161*b* Andrew Sydenham;
162 Laura Wickenden; 163/164
Andrew Sydenham; 165 Dennis
O'Clair/Tony Stone Images; 166
Andrew Sydenham; 167 Zefa; 168
Bill Bachmann/Ace Photo Agency;
169*t* Robert Cundy/Robert Harding
Picture Library, 169*b*/172 Andrew
Sydenham; 172/173 Tim Morris
Cerullo/Rex Features; 174 Zefa; 175
The Image Bank; 176/179*b* Andrew
Sydenham, 179*t* Anthony Boccaccio/
The Image Bank; 180 Retrograph
Archive; 181/183 Andrew Sydenham;
184 Jon Henley/Zefa; 185 Zefa;
186 Chris Craymer/Tony Stone
Images; 187 National Aids Trust;
190/191 Andrew Sydenham; 192
Zefa; 192/193 Sylvain Grandadam/
Tony Stone Images; 193 Andrew
Sydenham;194 Corbis-Bettmann/UPI;
195 Laura Wickenden; 196 R
Willinger/FPG/Robert Harding
Picture Library; 197 Andrew
Sydenham; 198*t* Clive Corless,
198*b* Andrew Sydenham; 199 Clive
Corless; 200*t* Zefa, 200*b* Andy Sacks/
Tony Stone Images; 201 Zefa;
202 Mary Kate Denny/Tony Stone
Images; 203 Ron Sutherland/Tony
Stone Images; 204/210 Andrew
Sydenham; 211/212 Zefa; 213
Robert Harding Picture Library;
214/216 Andrew Sydenham.

The publishers wish to thank the
following:

Greenpeace (for poster)
Friends of the Earth (for T-shirt)
Amnesty International (for T-shirt)